Transforming Negative
Reactions to Clients

Transforming Negative Reactions to Clients

FROM FRUSTRATION TO COMPASSION

EDITED BY

Abraham W. Wolf,

Marvin R. Goldfried,

and J. Christopher Muran

AMERICAN PSYCHOLOGICAL ASSOCIATION
WASHINGTON, DC

Published by
American Psychological Association
750 First Street, NE
Washington, DC 20002
www.apa.org

To order
APA Order Department
P.O. Box 92984
Washington, DC 20090-2984
Tel: (800) 374-2721; Direct: (202) 336-5510
Fax: (202) 336-5502; TDD/TTY: (202) 336-6123
Online: www.apa.org/pubs/books
E-mail: order@apa.org

In the U.K., Europe, Africa, and the Middle East, copies may be ordered from
American Psychological Association
3 Henrietta Street
Covent Garden, London
WC2E 8LU England

Typeset in Goudy by Circle Graphics, Inc., Columbia, MD

Printer: Maple-Vail Book Manufacturing Group, York, PA
Cover Designer: Berg Design, Albany, NY

The opinions and statements published are the responsibility of the authors, and such opinions and statements do not necessarily represent the policies of the American Psychological Association.

Library of Congress Cataloging-in-Publication Data

Transforming negative reactions to clients : from frustration to compassion / edited by Abraham W. Wolf, Marvin R. Goldfried, and J. Christopher Muran. — 1st ed.
    p. cm.
Includes bibliographical references and index.
ISBN 978-1-4338-1187-6 — ISBN 1-4338-1187-1 1. Psychotherapist and patient.
2. Therapeutic alliance. I. Wolf, Abraham W., 1950- II. Goldfried, Marvin R. III. Muran, J. Christopher.
RC480.8.T73 2013
616.89'14—dc23
                                          2012005206

British Library Cataloguing-in-Publication Data

A CIP record is available from the British Library.

Printed in the United States of America
First Edition

DOI: 10.1037/13940-000

To my family.
—*Abraham W. Wolf*

To my family.
—*Marvin R. Goldfried*

To my sister.
—*J. Christopher Muran*

With deep gratitude to our clients—our most important teachers.

CONTENTS

CONTRIBUTORS

Laura S. Brown, PhD, Fremont Community Therapy Project, Seattle, WA

John F. Clarkin, PhD, Weill Cornell Medical College, New York, NY; Personality Disorders Institute, New York Presbyterian Hospital, Westchester Division, White Plains

Robert Elliott, PhD, School of Psychological Sciences and Health, University of Strathclyde, Glasgow, Scotland

Valentín Escudero, PhD, Department of Psychology, University of La Coruña, Spain

Myrna L. Friedlander, PhD, Department of Educational and Counseling Psychology, University at Albany, State University of New York

Marvin R. Goldfried, PhD, Department of Psychology, Stony Brook University, State University of New York, Stony Brook

John M. Gottman, PhD, Relationship Research Institute, Seattle, WA

Julie S. Gottman, PhD, Relationship Research Institute, Seattle, WA

Laurie Heatherington, PhD, Department of Psychology, Williams College, Williamstown, MA

Clara Hungr, MA, Derner Institute for Advanced Psychological Studies, Adelphi University, Garden City, NY; Psychotherapy Research Program, Beth Israel Medical Center, New York, NY

Phillip G. Levendusky PhD, ABPP, Department of Psychology, McLean Hospital/Harvard Medical School, Belmont, MA

Hanna Levenson, PhD, Professor, Wright Institute, Berkeley, CA

Jeffrey J. Magnavita, PhD, ABPP, Glastonbury Psychological Associates, PC, Glastonbury, CT

Shelley McMain, PhD, Centre for Addiction and Mental Health, Department of Psychiatry, University of Toronto, Toronto, Ontario, Canada

J. Christopher Muran, PhD, Derner Institute for Advanced Psychological Studies, Adelphi University, Garden City, NY; Psychotherapy Research Program, Beth Israel Medical Center, New York, NY

David H. Rosmarin, PhD, Department of Psychology, McLean Hospital/Harvard Medical School, Belmont, MA

Frederick Rotgers, PsyD, ABPP, Graduate School of Applied and Professional Psychology, Rutgers University, Piscataway, NJ; and Independent Practice

Carmen Wiebe, MD, FRCP, Centre for Addiction and Mental Health, Department of Psychiatry, University of Toronto, Toronto, Ontario, Canada

Abraham W. Wolf, PhD, Department of Psychiatry, Case Western Reserve University, Cleveland, OH

Frank Yeomans, MD, PhD, Weill Cornell Medical College, New York, NY; Personality Disorders Institute, New York Presbyterian Hospital, Westchester Division, White Plains

PREFACE

The goal of this book is to help psychotherapists better understand, manage, and transform the wide range of emotions they experience while conducting psychotherapy and to help them use these experiences to facilitate an understanding of their clients and a strengthening of the therapeutic alliance. Affective modes of communication are central to everyday discourse, yet psychotherapists have tended to marginalize their personal reactions to clients as idiosyncratic and subjective—or, worse, devalue them as intrusive, counterproductive, and unprofessional. This book is based on the premise that the affective states therapists experience when treating clients are frequently a consequence of interacting with clients who experience intense emotions and have problematic interpersonal behaviors. In addition to tracking their clients' affective states, therapists need to monitor and regulate their own affective reactions. If therapists fail to recognize such emotional reactions, or perceive them only as noise in the therapeutic process, they risk missing an important source of data that may directly or indirectly affect the therapeutic alliance and negatively influence treatment outcomes. By increasing their awareness of how clients throw them off balance, therapists are more likely to develop a more compassionate stance toward both their clients and themselves. With the exception of psychoanalytic work on countertransference, little has been written on the therapist's affective experience while conducting psychotherapy. This book adopts an integrative perspective, arguing that all therapists, regardless of orientation, are vulnerable to a wide range of problematic emotions, and all practitioners will increase their understanding of the process of psychotherapy by acknowledging how their reactions are an important source of clinical data.

The idea for this edited volume on how a psychotherapist's personal response to his or her client affects the process of psychotherapy originated from symposia organized for the 2005 and 2006 Annual Conventions of the American Psychological Association that focused on psychotherapist anger and frustration toward clients. The recordings and PowerPoint presentations of the 2005 sessions were subsequently organized into an online continuing education program through the American Psychological Association.

We, the editors of the current volume, agreed that the emphasis of this book should be not on therapist anger and frustration in the psychotherapy process but on compassion, specifically, how a therapist can transform negative reactions to clients into compassionate ones. More important is how therapists can become more compassionate not just toward their clients but also toward themselves when they experience feelings that run counter to personal and professional injunctions to be helpful. As one of us (Marvin R. Goldfried) emphasizes, therapists were people before they became therapists, and they will be influenced by all those forces to which humans are subjected. How therapists regulate these powerful experiences is every bit as challenging as helping their clients become aware of and regulate their own powerful emotions and impulses. Our goal is to present a book not about frustration but about transformation and compassion.

Therapists' personal responses to their clients are usually referred to by the term *countertransference*. The psychoanalytic literature on countertransference is extensive, and thinkers from this branch of psychotherapy should be credited as the first to recognize how a therapist's personal reactions, even the dark reactions, have overt and covert effects on the psychotherapy process. Because using the term *countertransference* would identify us with a particular school of psychotherapy, we have opted for the more general and descriptive *negative reactions*, referring to a range of responses that include frustration, irritation, boredom, and so on. Although some of the contributors to this volume make use of the concept of countertransference, others deliberately avoid the term while acknowledging the experience of these emotions in their clinical work. Our goal is inclusion, and using a term so deeply grounded in psychoanalytic thinking risks excluding other branches of psychotherapy that have their own unique take on this experience.

This book is intended for practicing clinicians, novice therapists, psychotherapy supervisors, and psychotherapy researchers. It can, we hope, help psychotherapists make sense of the range of emotions they experience while treating their clients, understand that they are not unique in experiencing such feelings, and understand that their emotional reactions are valuable sources of data about their clients that can be used to facilitate treatment.

A major goal of this book is to inform supervising psychotherapists about the importance of emphasizing the trainee's experience of a client during supervision. Novice therapists are often unaware of the range of personal reactions they experience while conducting therapy. In becoming aware, they may blame themselves or their clients for these reactions. This book can provide a framework for supervising psychologists to reframe these experiences for their students.

Finally, this book can serve as a resource for psychotherapy researchers who study the effect of therapist variables on the psychotherapy relationship and treatment outcome. Most of the literature on therapist emotional responses to clients is based on case studies. This volume provides a framework for the modeling of therapist reactions to the therapeutic alliance that will be more amenable to empirical investigation.

This volume is intended to be an integrative collection of chapters with contributions from representatives of major schools of psychotherapy and discussions of specific clinical problems. Following an introductory chapter by the editors, the first part contains six chapters, from representatives of major schools of psychotherapy. The next part contains two chapters devoted to the treatment of clients with borderline personality disorder. This diagnostic category has become iconic for provoking negative reactions among psychotherapists, and we therefore wanted to emphasize two distinct treatment models, one based on psychoanalytic theory and the other on learning theory. The next and final part has three chapters that deal with specific clinical problems. The volume concludes with a chapter that provides clinical guidelines for transforming frustration into compassion.

Transforming Negative Reactions to Clients

INTRODUCTION

ABRAHAM W. WOLF, MARVIN R. GOLDFRIED, AND
J. CHRISTOPHER MURAN

It's hard to be a psychotherapist.

In a single day, a practicing therapist encounters a range of human suffering spanning melancholic depression, major traumas and losses, character pathologies, and loneliness. From one hour to the next, therapists strive to maintain both a professional posture and a personal sensitivity to the individuals they encounter. Professional values of beneficence and nonmaleficence, and respect for the rights and dignity of others (American Psychological Association, 2010), plus training in specific modes of intervention, complement a personal commitment to being helpfully present to the individual, couple, or family in pain (Moltu, Binder, & Nielsen, 2010). In all areas of health care, but especially in psychotherapy, it is the person of the therapist and the way he or she manages the interpersonal context of treatment that are related to the process and outcome of treatment.

DOI: 10.1037/13940-012
Transforming Negative Reactions to Clients: From Frustration to Compassion, A. W. Wolf, M. R. Goldfried, and J. C. Muran (Editors)

The tension between adherence to professional values and competencies versus one's personal emotional response to people asking for help presents a challenge that has important ethical and technical implications. In addition to monitoring the client's behavior, therapists need to monitor their personal responses to the client and how, in turn, the client responds to them. Like a director who is also an actor, the therapist as participant observer seeks to engage with the client while simultaneously observing the interaction. She or he ensures that certain roles and rules are maintained while at the same time remaining sensitive to her or his own responses. As much as they seek to adhere to a professional ideal, psychotherapists were people before they became therapists, and the extent to which they continue to be people means that they will be influenced by all those forces to which humans are subjected.

The forces that pull therapists from their professional ideal are legion: frustration, boredom, fear, anger, and even hate. Even among the most skillful and experienced, resistance to these forces is at times futile. Therapists are sometimes in the position of knowing that they cannot help their client if they continue to experience such negative emotions, yet they may be unable to regain the professional and compassionate ideal that is needed to be clinically effective. Among psychotherapists in training, such moments create doubts about their suitability for this work; among more experienced therapists, such moments engender a cynicism about their work and despair about their effectiveness. They become so absorbed in their involvement as participants that their observational role is compromised.

The understanding and management of therapists' personal responses to their client has made a sea change since Freud prescribed the techniques of classical psychoanalysis. In order not to contaminate the interpersonal field, Freud insisted that analysts contain their personal reactions and maintain a posture of evenly hovering attention to the client's associations. Recent developments in intersubjective and relational psychoanalysis (Mitchell & Aron, 1999; Stern, 2010; Stolorow, Brandchaft, & Atwood, 1987) challenge this posture. They, along with theorists as divergent as radical behaviorists (Kohlenberg & Tsai, 1991), point to psychotherapists' personal reactions and the inevitability of the client's effect on them as central to the process and outcome of treatment. Rather than dismiss one's experience of irritation or boredom or anger, therapists are now challenged to understand these responses as clinical data that are as important to understanding the client as obtaining a family history or a score on a symptom checklist. Rather than despair at impasses in the at-times-difficult treatment of personality disorders, psychotherapists are enjoined to understand and acknowledge their own contributions to the interaction. They need to be fully engaged with the client and simultaneously be aware of their own personal responses and contribution to the dialogue.

Whether one understands what happens between therapist and client either as the transfer of mental contents though projective identification, modeling, or as the functional analysis and differential reinforcement of behavior, it is the interaction and responsiveness of two individuals that lie at the core of psychotherapy, and it is this premise that is the basis of this book. In bringing together representatives of diverse theoretical backgrounds, our goal is to let other therapists know that they are not alone in dealing with the wide range of personal responses they experience conducting psychotherapy, and that something can be done about these responses. Novice therapists need not despair at their frustration; neither should experienced clinicians dismiss their feelings of anger or boredom as irrelevant to what is happening in the here-and-now. The greater risk is that ignoring such responses can lead to potentially harmful effects (Castonguay, Boswell, Constantino, Goldfried, & Hill, 2010).

It is inevitable that a therapist will experience negative reactions to a client. In working with difficult clients and in experiencing difficult moments with any client, the challenge for therapists is to be compassionate toward themselves in addition to the client. The recent emphasis on self-care and caregiver fatigue is evidence of an increasing awareness of the vulnerabilities that all individuals have to this work and indicates that they should follow the same advice they give to their clients. It is not only novices who are vulnerable to self-doubt in experiencing negative reactions; when experienced professionals need to contain intense rage at a manipulative client or look at their clock every 5 minutes hoping for the end of the hour while sitting with a self-absorbed client who barely recognizes the therapist's presence, they may become self-critical, feeling inadequate and regretting joining a profession that forces them to subordinate their own needs to those of another. In spite of one's best efforts at self-care, it is impossible for therapists to inoculate themselves against the range of emotions they will inevitably experience in working with the emotional lives of others. Indeed, it is the willingness to be affected by another, to allow oneself to be impacted by another, that at times provides the most direct and immediate source of data about how a client deals with others. The challenge of the therapist is how to reflect on this experience and respond therapeutically rather than automatically.

The problem gets even more complicated. Even the most self-aware and compassionate of therapists can start to experience an alarming and unexplainable array of feelings. David Wallace (2009) opened his book, *This*

Is Water: Some Thoughts, Delivered on a Significant Occasion, About Living a Compassionate Life, with the following story:

> There are these two young fish swimming along and they happen to meet an older fish swimming the other way, who nods at them and says, "Morning boys. How's the water?" And the two young fish swim for a bit, and then eventually one of them looks over at the other and goes, "What the hell is water?" (pp. 3–4)

The feelings therapists experience are clues about the water in which we and our clients are swimming. These are the fleeting, automatic feelings that tug at therapists, reminding us that we are very much participants who at times respond on a very personal level to our clients. More alarming is the turbulence of emotions that accompany the therapeutic impasse, when the therapy activates powerful emotions in the therapist during and between sessions, and the treatment process is more like negotiating white water rapids. In such cases, not only are one's observational skills compromised, but so too can one's constraint, or lack thereof, threaten one's professionalism—and, at times, one's clinical effectiveness (Henry, Schacht, Strupp, Butler, & Binder, 1993). It is at these moments when one's accepting awareness is eclipsed and that we as therapists are challenged to be as compassionate toward ourselves as to the client to "go with the flow" of the rapids. The role of compassion is not to invalidate one's emotions in favor of a professional distance or a transcendental height but to observe and understand these feeling states in the context of the particular school or schools of psychotherapy that orient and guide the treatment process. Compassion is not just responsiveness to the suffering of the client; it is responsiveness to one's own suffering, with the goal of understanding the interaction that constitutes the psychotherapy relationship.

PREVALENCE OF THE PROBLEM

Psychotherapy has occupational hazards. Studies of practicing psychotherapists, primarily in the form of survey research, indicate high rates of depression and emotional exhaustion among members of practice divisions of the American Psychological Association (APA). Pope and Tabachnick (1994), in study of a sample of APA members drawn from the Divisions of Clinical Psychology, Counseling Psychotherapy, and Independent Practitioners who had been in therapy, reported that 61% admitted to at least one episode of what they would characterize as clinical depression, 29% reported suicidal feelings, and 4% admitted to at least one suicidal attempt. Gilroy, Carroll, and Murra (2002) found that 62% of APA Division of Counseling members indicated that they were depressed, and 42% said they had experienced suicidal ideation. In her survey of master's- and doctoral-level psychologists, Deutsch (1985) reported depression rates of 57% and suicide rates of 2%. Mahoney (1997) found, in a sample of health care professionals, that 43% reported irritability and emotional exhaustion during the previous year, 42% indicated doubts regarding therapeutic success, and 27% reported occupational disillusionment. These numbers support Freud's (1905/1933) confession that "no one who like me, conjures up the most evil of those half-tamed demons that inhabit the human breast, and seeks to wrestle with them, can expect to come through the struggle unscathed" (p. 109).

Negative experiences with difficult clients occur frequently in clinical practice and are a risk factor for professional distress and burnout, a syndrome composed of emotional exhaustion, depersonalization, and a reduction of personal accomplishment (Jenaro, Flores, & Arias, 2007). In a study of general medical practitioners, Mathers, Jones, and Hannay (1995) found that one in six outpatient visits is considered "difficult" and that difficult encounters are more likely to occur with patients who have a mental disorder. Rupert and Morgan (2005) found that greater emotional exhaustion was associated with having less control over work activities, working more hours, spending more time on administrative tasks and paperwork, seeing more managed care clients and fewer direct pay clients, and having to deal with more negative client behaviors. Sherman and Thelen (1998) found that 72% of a sample of 522 psychologists stated that work with difficult clients—for example, those with suicidal or borderline traits—along with personal relationship problems, were the most troublesome factors associated with practitioner distress and impairment. Pope and Tabachnick (1993), in their survey of 285 psychologists, found that over 80% reported experiencing fear, anger, and sexual feelings toward clients in treatment; that 90% experienced anger at a client for being uncooperative; and that over half admitted to raising their voice in anger to a client or having felt so afraid about a client that it affected their eating, sleeping, or concentration. Clients are aware of when therapists get angry at them. In a sample of 132 clients who completed long-term trauma therapy (Dalenberg, 2004), 72% reported that they had been very angry with their therapist at least once during treatment, and 64% reported that their therapist had been "illegitimately" angry at them at least once. More than half of the 64% stated that the episode had temporarily or permanently damaged the therapeutic alliance.

Personal distress, burnout, and negative experiences with clients can impair a practitioner's functioning to the point that it adversely affects the process and outcome of treatment. Pope, Tabachnick, and Keith-Spiegel (1987) reported that although 85% of APA Division of Psychotherapy members believed that it was unethical to work when too distressed, 60% admitted that they had done so in the past. In a sample of APA members of the Divisions of Clinical Psychology, Psychotherapy, and Independent Practitioners, Guy, Poelstra, and Stark (1989) reported that 74% admitted to experiencing personal distress during the previous 3 years and, of those, 36.7% indicated that it had decreased the quality of client care, with 4.6% admitting that it resulted in inadequate care. Given that the modal number of psychotherapy visits in private practice is one (Phillips, 1985), it may be that when clients perceive therapist negative responses during the first visit they do not come back to someone who does not like them.

THE INNER WORLD OF THE THERAPIST

The emphasis on the role of the therapeutic alliance (Muran & Barber, 2010; Norcross, 2002) as it relates to the process and outcome of psychotherapy has led to a greater interest in the study of how therapist negative emotions and behaviors manifest in treatment. Such negative reactions are usually discussed under the heading of *countertransference*, a concept whose history is closely tied to the history of psychotherapy. Like so many other terms that are deeply embedded in a particular theoretical context—in this case, psychoanalysis—the term has been used in so many different ways that its meaning is ambiguous.

In their study, Gelso and Hayes (2007) distinguished countertransference from the subjective experience of the therapist. They defined *countertransference* as "the therapist's internal or external reactions that are shaped by the therapist's past or present emotional conflicts and vulnerabilities" (p. 25). The therapist's subjective experience, or his or her inner, experiential world, "contains all the thoughts, images, affects, and even visceral sensations that the therapist processes at any given time" (p. 71). The therapist's subjectivity includes, but is not limited to, countertransference; countertransference is embedded in the therapist's subjective experience but rooted in the therapist's personal conflicts and vulnerabilities. The therapist's negative responses are primarily, although not necessarily, countertransferential. In reviewing the empirical literature on countertransference, Gelso and Hayes drew three conclusions: (a) countertransference originates from the therapist's unresolved psychological conflicts; (b) client factors and therapy-related events interact with therapist's unresolved conflicts to trigger countertransference; and (c) countertransference reactions exist, and probably originate, internally, in the form of private feelings and thoughts.

Gelso and Hayes (2007) plotted psychotherapists' personal experience toward their clients on four dimensions: (a) valence, (b) intensity, (c) clarity, and (d) state. *Valence* refers to the positive (caring, liking, empathic concern, attraction) and negative feelings (anger, sadness, anxiety, dislike). These experiences may be low-*intensity* reactions (boredom, low interest, low engagement) or very intense reactions in response to reports of trauma. Therapists' experience of a client may be very *clear and vivid*, whereby they are fully aware of their reactions to the client, or their experience may be dimly experienced and unclear, even if intense. Finally, experiences can vary from states of relaxation to intense *states of arousal*. Given that it is not always clear to therapists in session that their intense negative reactions to a client are based on their personal conflicts and vulnerabilities, good clinical judgment suggests that they should err on the side of restraint until they can more carefully understand the reasons for their reaction.

Even if their reactions are based on personal conflicts and vulnerabilities, however, this does not necessarily negate their reactions clinical utility to the therapeutic process. Gelso and Hayes (2007) asserted that the inner world of the therapist, including both countertransference- and noncountertransference-based reactions, is a vital element of all psychotherapies. Their metaphor of the therapist as a wounded healer emphasizes how therapists who have experienced their own share of pain are drawn to this field and how wounds that are sufficiently healed can facilitate the psychotherapy process. The therapist's subjectivity and understanding of her or his reactions to clients—countertransference or not—can be invaluable clinical data about the process of psychotherapy.

In the moment-to-moment action of a therapy session, it is not always clear whether a therapist's highly valenced, intense, confusing, and aroused personal experience is due to his or her own personal history of injuries or to other factors in the therapeutic relationship. The inner world of the psychotherapist does not always have clearly defined boundaries that identify whether such experiences are due to unresolved injuries or stem from areas that are conflict free. In the heat of the therapeutic moment, the therapist cannot always identify the source of these feelings but is in the position of needing to understand them and, ideally, use them to facilitate the therapy process. Williams's (2008) work on the therapist's self-awareness does not differentiate between countertransference and the therapist's subjective experience. It provides a framework that includes all aspects of the therapist's experience, bridging to experimental work in social psychology on self-consciousness and self-focused attention to the therapist's disruptive and distracting experiences. By focusing on the therapist's awareness and management of negative responses without attributing their source to the therapist's unresolved issues, Gelso and Hayes's (2007) cogent recommendations for managing countertransference reactions can be applied to other therapist experiences that threaten to derail the therapy process or rupture the therapeutic alliance.

Research on the psychotherapy process and outcome and the effects of countertransference indicates that a therapist's negative reactions to a client can interfere with the course of treatment. In their review of potentially harmful effects of psychological treatments, Castonguay et al. (2010) cited evidence suggesting that a therapist's inability to repair toxic relational and technical processes, those most associated in working with difficult clients, as a specific mechanism that linked impaired therapist behaviors with poor outcomes. Failure to establish and manage an effective therapeutic alliance has been found to be associated with poor outcomes. In addition to relational factors, there are complex patterns of relational and technique factors in cognitive and psychodynamic therapy that are associated with poor outcomes.

Cognitive therapists, for example, when confronted with therapeutic ruptures, increased their adherence to techniques in a rigid manner, exacerbating relationship problems that contributed to poorer outcomes (Castonguay, Goldfried, Wiser, Raue, & Hayes, 1996). High rates of transference interpretations were associated with poor outcomes, and the frequency of therapist interpretations, in particular when the therapist persisted with these interpretations, were associated with more hostile interactions in clients (Piper, Azim, Joyce, & McCallum, 1991). These findings suggest that when confronted with a resistant client, psychotherapists who react defensively (negatively) and use specific techniques in an automatic and rigid manner compromise the therapeutic process and, ultimately, the outcome of psychotherapy. When clients don't do what "they are supposed to do"—that is, what we want them to do—we as therapists are at risk of reacting negatively.

SELF-DISCLOSURE AND NEGATIVE REACTIONS

A therapist's negative reaction to clients is often discussed in connection with the topic of therapist self-disclosure. Psychotherapeutic orientations as diverse as relational psychoanalysis and radical behaviorism increasingly converge on how the therapist's subjective experience is an important source of information about the client and how judiciously expressing this experience during the session can lead to a powerful corrective experience for the client. There is an increased emphasis on relational factors among therapeutic modalities that traditionally ascribe mechanisms of change to such technical interventions as framing interpretations, engaging in Socratic dialogue, teaching and monitoring specific exercises, and even prescribing medications. In addition to "objective" sources of data, such as interviews and psychological tests, therapists acknowledge using their personal and subjective responses as a way of understanding how the client functions in the world. The articulation or disclosure of these personal reactions offers the client a unique opportunity to understand how he or she affects others and to learn new ways of responding. Rather than understanding the client's world by only listening to the client describe it, the therapist steps onto the stage of the client's world and becomes both participant and observer. Therapist self-disclosure changes the session to include both content and process and shifts from communication to metacommunication (Kiesler, 1996; Safran & Muran, 2000).

Humanistic and experiential schools of psychotherapy emphasize the therapist's authenticity and genuineness in the therapeutic relationship and value self-disclosure as evidence of the congruence of inner experience and outer expression, making the therapist transparent to the client. Person-centered psychotherapy has a strong research tradition, and the available evidence suggests that the moderate and judicious use of self-disclosure has a beneficial impact on the process and outcome of treatment (Elliot, Watson, Goldman, & Greene, 2003). In contrast, psychodynamic and cognitive behavior psychotherapy do not use therapist self-disclosure as an expression of genuiness and authenticity in the therapeutic relationship but instead describe ways of using the therapist's experience of the client in the immediacy of the therapy session as a way of providing the client feedback about how he or she affects others in subtle and not-so-subtle ways.

The intersubjective and relational schools of psychoanalysis (Mitchell & Aron, 1999; Stern, 2010; Stolorow et al., 1987) represent the most recent contribution from psychoanalysis that forge a unique perspective from interpersonal psychology, object relations theory, and self-psychology. The therapist's subjective world and personal responses are no longer contaminants to a therapeutic sterile field but rather immediate data about how clients construct their world outside of therapy. The therapist's experience of frustration, boredom, and anger are not intrusive distracters that need to be contained but emergent qualities of a uniquely constructed reality. The therapist's role is to metabolize his or her personal responses and understand how such affective "chafing" (Stern, 2010) represents an unconscious engagement in the client's enactment of past relationships. Even if such negative reactions are rooted in the therapist's unresolved issues or vulnerabilities, they are still part of the reality co-constructed by the therapist and by the client.

Although intersubjective psychoanalysis and cognitive behavior therapy are grounded in distinct philosophical and methodological assumptions, both increasingly acknowledge common ground in a constructivist perspective that emphasizes the immediacy of the therapy session. Cognitive behavior therapists understand the treatment alliance primarily as a medium through which specific techniques travel. Newer perspectives have approached the treatment relationship using functional analysis, identifying therapists' subjective reactions as responses elicited by client behaviors.

A key component of McCullough's (2006) cognitive behavioral analysis system of psychotherapy for the treatment of chronic depression is the therapist's "disciplined personal involvement." By understanding one's stimulus value to the client and self-monitoring and acknowledging one's emotional responses to a client, the therapist seeks to use the treatment session as an in vivo reinforcement condition. The therapist directly acknowledges a client's hostile response by responding, for example, "Why do you want to hurt me this way?" In making this statement, the therapist adopts an observer role, using metacommunication about the interaction between client and therapist in order demonstrate to the client how the client's statements function as potentially aversive stimuli. Kohlenberg and Tsai (1991), using a framework of radical behaviorism based on B. F. Skinner's functional analysis of verbal behavior, included the therapist's personal reactions as a sample of natural reinforcers that identify problematic clinically relevant behaviors for the client that need to decrease in frequency and those more effective behaviors that need to take their place instead. They specifically advocated for the judicious disclosure both of the therapist's negative reactions to the client's behavior that need to change and genuine expressions of caring to naturally reinforce desirable client behaviors.

Therapists' use of their personal responses to clients offers another way of understanding the client in the world. It is one thing to construct a model of clients' experience by listening to their stories and attending to subtle shadings of affect associated with those narratives; it is another to focus on how clients are displaying specific behaviors in the context of a particular therapy session and how one responds to those behaviors on a personal level. The former is more about listening to words, and the latter is more about how those words get to the therapist on a gut level. When therapists self-disclose about their own responses to a client, they are using an experiential referent for meaning that is qualitatively different from the semantic (Goldfried, 1982).

MANAGEMENT OF NEGATIVE EMOTIONAL EXPERIENCES

The self-care literature (Norcross, 2000; Smith & Moss, 2009) emphasizes preventive measures to avoid burnout and the need for self-awareness and supervision in dealing with challenging cases. These are important recommendations in preparing a therapist to reenter the daily stresses of working with difficult clients and managing the vicarious traumatization of listening to the clients' injuries. Research suggests that therapists who realize that psychotherapy is hard work are more effective. Blatt, Sanislow, Zuroff, and Pilkonis (1996) noted that more effective therapists, compared with less and moderately effective therapists, expected therapy to require more treatment sessions before clients begin to manifest therapeutic change.

Gelso and Hayes (2007) outlined a five-factor theory for the management of countertransference reactions that comprises the following: (a) self-insight, (b) conceptualizing skills, (c) empathy, (d), self-integration, and (e) anxiety management. Because our understanding of others is limited by our understanding of ourselves, and because therapy is inherently subjective, a therapist needs to be familiar with her or his internal life, and the absence of this *self-insight* could create blind spots that interfere with an accurate understanding of the client. Although there is very little research that sheds light on what therapists actually do with specific clients to manage countertransference reactions, at least two studies have suggested that effective management of countertransference feelings depends both on therapist self-insight and their *conceptualizing skills* (Latts & Gelso, 1995; Robbins & Jolkovski, 1987). The ability to articulate a theoretical understanding of the client and the dynamics of the psychotherapy relationship allows the therapist to move from a participant in the interaction to an observer position that orients the therapist and helps him or her make sense of what is transpiring. The therapist's *empathy* is an essential aspect of all psychotherapy. How a therapist accurately grasps the cognitive and affective components of the client's inner world while maintaining a distance that balances the fusion of over-identification and the alienation of underidentification is central to managing personal reactions. *Self-integration* is required to maintain a stable sense of self and personal boundaries by being able to flexibly differentiate from and identify with others. *Anxiety management* is the therapist's ability to experience aroused states with a client without responding in a defensive manner, while containing that arousal and using it as a signal, as data to understand that something is happening in the relationship.

The more pressing question for an individual psychotherapist whose self-awareness and observational skills are eclipsed either by chronic distraction or affective storms is how to make sense of these experiences and use one's own emotional responses as a means of facilitating the therapeutic process. The goal is not just to contain the behaviors that such emotional responses may precipitate (or, more likely, probably have already instigated without the therapist's full awareness) but to regain a mindful, observational stance whereby the therapist reorients, understands, and articulates what is happening in the here-and-now. Metacommunication and the judicious use of self-disclosure are powerful tools to help clients understand how they are reenacting with the therapist past relationships or to understand their stimulus value in relationships and how they influence others. Therapists who adhere to self-care recommendations is certainly more likely to use these tools to arrive at an empathic understanding of their clients. Being open to such negative emotional responses not as alien intruders that need to be suppressed but as data that provide insight into the therapeutic process requires a response that is best described as therapists being compassionate to themselves.

COMPASSION

Our concern is when we as therapists are in a predicament—the moments when our attention is redirected from the client to our own personal reactions. These reactions are usually automatic and related to cognitive–affective processes that are specific to us as persons. Whether such responses emerge from our own unresolved conflicts or are an understandable reaction to a difficult client, our subjective experience has undergone a change from a state of empathic resonance (or at least an attempt to obtain this state) to one of frustration, anger, boredom, and other negative reactions. To act on these feelings by expressing them directly, to deny that they are there, or to deal with them by the different processes that have come to be known as *defense mechanisms* all threaten to jeopardize the treatment. Our inner world as therapists is in conflict: The professional injunctions to be helpfully present are up against the emotional interference of the moment, and we are not always able to understand whether this reaction is due to our own psychological vulnerabilities or other factors. In one way or another, the client has "hooked" us. We need to respond, "But how?" If therapist self-compassion has any meaning, it is how to apply it in these situations.

Vivino, Thompson, Hill, and Ladany (2009) proposed a theory of compassion in psychotherapy based on interviews with 15 practicing psychotherapists nominated by peers as being compassionate. The theory included components of psychotherapy process and therapist variables and stated that compassion is more a way of *being with* a client than what the therapist *does with* the client. A compassionate response is elicited by being empathic to another's suffering, or to another's painful emotions or difficult behavior. Compassionate responses go beyond simple empathy, which is more connected to the moment-to-moment process of understanding. There is an engagement of the therapist with the client whereby the therapist emotionally resonates with the client's suffering through the therapist's ability to empathically connect by experiences based on her or his own suffering. This self-awareness on the therapist's part allows one to "get" the client and communicate that deep understanding in a manner that facilitates a corrective emotional experience. What is important here is that the therapist finds a way to identify with the client's pain and be present in a manner that merges the roles of person and professional and communicate that identification/ understanding in a way the client knows that one really does "get it."

The real challenges to the therapist's compassionate stance are those instances when clients communicate their suffering in ways that are not easy to understand, and when they indeed test the therapist. It is one thing for a therapist who suffered parental abuse to identify with the ambivalence of a client who describes her complicated grief at the loss of an abusive parent. Here the therapist can serve as a witness to the client's suffering. Even in the case of wounds that remain, the therapist can contain highly personal reactions and maintain a respectful distance while communicating a compassionate identification. The therapist's compassion can come through without any explicit self-disclosure. It is quite another thing when that client relates to the therapist in a provocative, hostile–dependent manner, whereby the client responds to the therapist as if he or she were an abuser. In this case, the therapist is challenged not to identify with—and even become—an abusive, rejecting figure. The challenge and potential frustration are further compounded when the client resists efforts to observe what is going on in the therapy relationship, when the client resists the therapist's invitation to step off the stage where they are participants in order to engage in discussion. The challenge is to be compassionate to the client through the storm of rage and resistance and to be compassionate toward oneself for losing patience with the process.

It's hard to be a psychotherapist. Our hope is that the contributions that follow will help make it a bit easier.

REFERENCES

American Psychological Association. (2010). *Ethical principles of psychologists and code of conduct* (2002, amended June 1, 2010). Retrieved from http://www.apa.org/ethics/code/index.aspx

Blatt, S. J., Sanislow, C. A. III, Zuroff, D. C., & Pilkonis, P. A. (1996). Characteristics of effective therapists. *Journal of Consulting and Clinical Psychology, 64,* 1276–1284. doi:10.1037/0022-006X.64.6.1276

Castonguay, L. G., Boswell, J. F., Constantino, M. J., Goldfried, M. R., & Hill, C. E. (2010). Training implications of harmful effects of psychological treatments. *American Psychologist, 65,* 34–49. doi:10.1037/a0017330

Castonguay, L. G., Goldfried, M. R., Wiser, S., Raue, P. J., & Hayes, A. M. (1996). Predicting the effect of cognitive therapy for depression. *Journal of Consulting and Clinical Psychology, 64,* 497–504. doi:10.1037/0022-006X.64.3.497

Dalenberg, C. J. (2004). Maintaining the safe and effective therapeutic relationship in the context of distrust and anger. *Psychotherapy: Theory, Research, Practice, Training, 41,* 438–447. doi:10.1037/0033-3204.41.4.438

Deutsch, C. J. (1985). A survey of therapists' personal problems and treatment. *Professional Psychology: Research and Practice, 16*, 305–315. doi:10.1037/0735-7028.16.2.305

Elliott, R., Watson, J. C., Goldman, R. N., & Greenberg, L. S. (2003). *Learning emotion-focused therapy: The process-experiential approach to change*. Washington, DC: American Psychological Association. doi:10.1037/10725-000

Freud, S. (1933). Fragment of an analysis of a case of hysteria. In J. Strachey (Ed.), *The standard edition of the complete psychological works of Sigmund Freud* (Vol. VII, pp. 7–122). London, England: Hogarth Press. (Original work published 1905)

Gelso, C. J., & Hayes, J. A. (2007). *Countertransference and the therapist's inner experience: Perils and possibilities*. Mahwah, NJ: Erlbaum.

Gilroy, P. J., Carroll, L., & Murra, J. (2002). A preliminary survey of counseling psychologists' personal experiences with depression and treatment. *Professional Psychology: Research and Practice, 33*, 402–407. doi:10.1037/0735-7028.33.4.402

Goldfried, M. R. (1982). Cognition and experience. In M. R. Goldfried (Ed.), *Converging themes in psychotherapy: Trends in psychodynamic, humanistic, and behavioral practice* (pp. 365–373). New York, NY: Springer.

Guy, J. D., Poelstra, P. L., & Stark, M. J. (1989). Personal distress and therapeutic effectiveness: National survey of psychologists practicing psychology. *Professional Psychology: Research and Practice, 20*, 48–50.

Henry, W. P., Schacht, T. E., Strupp, H. H., Butler, S. F., & Binder, J. L. (1993). Effects of training in time-limited dynamic psychotherapy: Mediators of therapists' responses to training. *Journal of Consulting and Clinical Psychology, 61*, 441–447. doi:10.1037/0022-006X.61.3.441

Jenaro, C., Flores, N., & Arias, B. (2007). Burnout and coping in human service practitioners. *Professional Psychology: Research and Practice, 38*, 80–87. doi:10.1037/0735-7028.38.1.80

Kiesler, D. J. (1996). *Contemporary interpersonal theory and research: Personality, psychopathology, and psychotherapy*. New York, NY: Wiley.

Kohlenberg, R. J., & Tsai, M. (1991). *Functional analytic psychotherapy: Creating intense and curative therapeutic relationships*. New York, NY: Plenum Press.

Latts, M. G., & Gelso, C. J. (1995). Countertransference behavior and management with survivors of sexual assault. *Psychotherapy: Theory, Research, Practice, Training, 32*, 405–415. doi:10.1037/0033-3204.32.3.405

Mahoney, M. J. (1997). Psychotherapist's personal problems and self-care patterns. *Professional Psychology: Research and Practice, 28*, 14–16. doi:10.1037/0735-7028.28.1.14

Mathers, N., Jones, N., & Hannay, D. (1995). Heartsink patients: A study of their general practitioners. *British Journal of General Practice, 45*, 293–296.

McCullough, J. P. (2006). *Treating chronic depression with disciplined personal involvement*. New York, NY: Springer.

Mitchell, S. A., & Aron, L. (1999). *Relational psychoanalysis*. Hillsdale, NJ: Analytic Press.

Moltu, C., Binder, P. E., & Nielsen, G. H. (2010). Commitment under pressure: Experienced therapists' inner work during difficult therapeutic impasses. *Psychotherapy Research, 20,* 309–320. doi:10.1080/10503300903470610

Muran, J. C., & Barber, J. P. (2010). *The therapeutic alliance: An evidence-based guide to practice.* New York, NY: Guilford Press.

Norcross, J. C. (2000). Psychotherapist self-care: Practitioner-tested, research-informed strategies. *Professional Psychology: Research and Practice, 31,* 710–713. doi:10.1037/0735-7028.31.6.710

Norcross, J. C. (2002). *Psychotherapy relationships that work: Therapist contributions and responsiveness to patients.* London, England: Oxford University Press.

Phillips, E. L. (1985). *Psychotherapy revised: New frontiers in research and practice.* Hillsdale, NJ: Erlbaum.

Piper, W. E., Azim, H. F. A., Joyce, A. S., & McCallum, M. (1991). Transference interpretations, therapeutic alliance, and outcome in short-term individual psychotherapy. *Archives of General Psychiatry, 48,* 946–953. doi:10.1001/arch psyc.1991.01810340078010

Pope, K. S., & Tabachnick, B. G. (1993). Therapists' anger, hate, fear, and sexual feelings: National survey of therapist responses, client characteristics, critical events, formal complaints, and training. *Professional Psychology: Research and Practice, 24,* 142–152. doi:10.1037/0735-7028.24.2.142

Pope, K. S., & Tabachnick, B. G. (1994). Therapists as patients: A national survey of psychologists' experiences, problems, and beliefs. *Professional Psychology: Research and Practice, 25,* 247–258. doi:10.1037/0735-7028.25.3.247

Pope, K. S., Tabachnick, B. G., & Keith-Spiegel, P. (1987). Ethics of practice: The beliefs and behaviors of psychologists as therapists. *American Psychologist, 42,* 993–1006. doi:10.1037/0003-066X.42.11.993

Robbins, S. B., & Jolkovski, M. P. (1987). Managing countertransference feelings: An interactional model using awareness of feelings and theoretical framework. *Journal of Counseling Psychology, 34,* 276–282. doi:10.1037/0022-0167.34.3.276

Rupert, P. A., & Morgan, D. J. (2005). Work setting and burnout among professional psychologists. *Professional Psychology: Research and Practice, 36,* 544–550. doi:10.1037/0735-7028.36.5.544

Safran, J. D. & Muran, J. C. (2000). *Negotiating the therapeutic alliance: A relational treatment guide.* New York, NY: Guilford Press.

Sherman, M. D., & Thelen, M. H. (1998). Distress and professional impairment among psychologists in clinical practice. *Professional Psychology: Research and Practice, 29,* 79–85. doi:10.1037/0735-7028.29.1.79

Smith, P. L., & Moss, S. B. (2009). Psychologist impairment: What is it, how can it be prevented, and what can be done to address it? *Clinical Psychology: Science and Practice, 16,* 1–15. doi:10.1111/j.1468-2850.2009.01137.x

Stern, D. B. (2010). *Partners in thought: Working with unformulated experience, dissociation, and enactment*. New York, NY: Routledge.

Stolorow, R. D., Brandchaft, B., & Atwood, G. (1987). *Psychoanalytic treatment: An intersubjective approach*. Hillsdale, NJ: Analytic Press.

Vivino, B. L., Thompson, B. J., Hill, C. E., & Ladany, N. (2009). Compassion in psychotherapy: The perspective of therapists nominated as compassionate. *Psychotherapy Research, 19*, 157–171. doi:10.1080/10503300802430681

Wallace, D. F. (2009). *This is water: Some thoughts, delivered on a significant occasion, about living a compassionate life*. New York, NY: Little, Brown.

Williams, E. N. (2008). A psychotherapy researcher's perspective on therapist self-awareness and self-focused attention after a decade of research. *Psychotherapy Research, 18*, 139–146. doi:10.1080/10503300701691656

I

NEGATIVE REACTIONS ACROSS THERAPEUTIC APPROACHES

INTRODUCTION: NEGATIVE REACTIONS ACROSS THERAPEUTIC APPROACHES

Descriptions of the field of psychotherapy typically cite the major theoretical systems of psychodynamic, experiential–humanistic, and cognitive–behavioral orientations, specific treatment modalities such as couples and family therapy, and more recently, the treatment of diverse populations. Historically, individual practitioners identified with a single community that adhered to the specific principles of behavior, psychopathology, and treatment of a theoretical system. Today, these communities are increasingly differentiated and divergent, and the boundaries that distinguish theoretical systems have become increasingly blurred. More and more, current practitioners seek to define common ground by identifying points of theoretical and technical convergence among specific theoretical systems. Results from psychotherapy outcome research support this quest for convergence. The absence of consistent differences from outcome studies that compare the effectiveness of different schools of psychotherapy has led to the claim that in addition to the specific factors that may account for the effectiveness of psychotherapy, there is also the very important impact made by the psychotherapy relationship. One development of this claim is that more emphasis has been placed on the psychotherapy relationship and identifying therapist and client factors that affect treatment outcome. A notable theme in this regard is how the therapist feels about his or her client.

In the following section, representatives of six major psychotherapy schools were asked to describe the principles of that school and respond to questions about how they acknowledge, conceptualize, and manage their negative reactions to clients. The authors were requested to consider the following questions to structure their chapters and to provide case presentations illustrating their responses.

- How does psychotherapy produce change? What are the conceptually hypothesized components of treatment?
- To what degree do practitioners adhere to specific treatment guidelines versus emphasize alliance building and relationship factors?
- What is the role of therapist self-awareness of their own negative affective states in the treatment process? Is awareness of these states "noise" that is irrelevant or even detrimental? Are these states a "signal" and a source of data regarding the treatment process?
- How does the psychotherapist contain or express negative states? Are psychotherapists encouraged to compartmentalize these states, use self-care interventions, or seek supervision and support groups?
- If the awareness of these states is recognized as part of the treatment process, then how does the psychotherapist use this awareness? What are the factors that lead a therapist to restrain expression of this awareness or to self-disclose about their internal states?
- How does phase of treatment affect management of negative states? Does anger toward a client in the early phases of treatment indicate the need to transfer to another therapist? What is the role of self-disclosure at different phases of the treatment process? How can the therapist deal with negative emotional states so as to approach the client in a more compassionate way?
- What is the role of training psychotherapists in self-awareness?
- In the supervisory process, how does the supervisor acknowledge the role of negative affective states as a source of treatment data versus the need for a trainee to seek their own psychotherapy?

1

POWER PLAYS, NEGOTIATION, AND MUTUAL RECOGNITION IN THE THERAPEUTIC ALLIANCE: "I NEVER MET A CLIENT I DIDN'T LIKE . . . EVENTUALLY"

J. CHRISTOPHER MURAN AND CLARA HUNGR

Beatrice was a 72-year-old Jewish woman who was the only daughter and the eldest in a family with three sons. Her father died in her arms of a massive heart attack when she was only 17. He ran a small bakery in New York's Lower East Side for which she assumed responsibility because her mother was not capable. Upon her father's death, her mother suffered a debilitating bout of depression, which kept her in and out of psychiatric care until her death some 30 years later. Bea ran the bakery for the next 20 years of her life, keeping her family together and supporting her brothers in their separate vocational pursuits. She ultimately sold the business and took

An earlier version of this chapter was presented as part of a panel entitled "What to Do When You Hate Your Patient" at the 113th Annual Convention of the American Psychological Association, Washington, DC, August 2005.

DOI: 10.1037/13940-001
Transforming Negative Reactions to Clients: From Frustration to Compassion, A. W. Wolf, M. R. Goldfried, and J. C. Muran (Editors)

on work in civil service. The first author of this chapter (J. Christopher Muran)—Bea's therapist—narrates his interactions with her:

When I met Bea, two of her brothers were dead, and she was estranged from the third. She never married but had a long-term relationship with a married man with whom she currently maintained minimal contact. She would often say she was "married to the bakery." She had few friends, which had been the case for as long as she could remember.

Bea came to me to address her interpersonal difficulties, her conflicts, and her isolation. She found my name in some article about brief psychotherapy that she came upon in the waiting room of some doctor's office and tracked me down through the American Psychological Association—an early indication of her resourcefulness. When she contacted me, she told me how she came upon my name but explained that she was not interested in brief psychotherapy. That was fine by me, because my practice concentrated on more open-ended work. Nevertheless, it was noteworthy that she pursued treatment with someone identified with brief psychotherapy and immediately looked to alter the parameters.

In our first meeting, which was explicitly set up as a consultation to explore the possibility of working together, she began by informing me of a problem with my voicemail system. This would be a forerunner of her knack for finding wrinkles in my practice. She then asked about my phone policy, to which I asked what she meant. "Do you return calls?" I responded, "Yes." "How about after hours?" Again, I asked what she meant. She referred to calls late at night and during the weekend. I told her about my general policy of returning calls within a reasonable time frame but added much is dictated by the nature of the specific case. She was not impressed. It seemed to her I had set up a practice primarily for my own convenience. During the course of the session, she expressed skepticism about therapy and her ability to change. She had a long history of being in therapy and had had some bad experiences. She also expressed some concern about my age and ethnicity, wondering aloud whether I could truly understand her.

When she finally asked if I would be willing to work with her, I confessed I was not sure. On the one hand, I said, I was intrigued by her situation. What I didn't say was that I was drawn in by her apparent difficultness. I thought to myself, If you really want to study negative process, this is the patient for you. On the other hand, I told her that, given her expressed concerns about me, I was wary that I may never, in a sense, be good enough. What I didn't say was that she reminded me of a very difficult patient I had been tortured by years before. I remembered how much of a toll that previous patient had taken on me and the rest of my practice. So I was wary and very measured.

Bea was taken aback by my disclosure. She seemed to soften her position when she realized that our working together was not just up to her. She went on to say she wanted to work with me. She thought I was sharp and liked my ability to smile. When I asked how she felt about my disclosure, she said she didn't like dealing with the "person" behind the "professional"—her words. She went on to describe all her difficulties dealing with and relating to others. When our time was up, I suggested that we meet again, and as she walked out of my office, she stopped with a smile and said to me, "You know, I've always thought, 'To know me is to hate me.'"

When I was first invited to give a presentation on this subject matter, I automatically thought of Bea and figured she would be a great help in any discussion of hate, anger, and hostility in a psychotherapy situation. To understand how I approached this vignette and the subject of such negative feelings, I thought I should present a few organizing conceptualizations that reflect a relational theory of person and change.

MULTIPLE SELVES AND MUTUAL REGULATION

First, therapists understand each individual as comprising multiple selves. In other words, we continually move or are moved in and out of various states of mind, or *self-states*. Self-states are the experiential products of the various processes and structures of the self, the crystallization in subjective experience of an underlying representational structure. These underlying structures refer to memory stores of multiple discrete experiences of the self in relation to significant others. These can be considered *relational schemas* (see Safran & Muran, 2000) that are abstracted on the basis of interactions with attachment figures (and others of interpersonal significance) in order to increase the likelihood of maintaining a relationship with those figures. They contain specific procedural information regarding expectancies and strategies for negotiating the dialectically opposing needs for self-definition and for relatedness.

Relational schemas are also considered emotional structures that include innate expressive-motor responses, which develop from birth into subtle and idiosyncratic variations and that serve a communicative function in that they continually orient the person to the environment and the environment to the person. They shape the person's perceptions of the world, leading to cognitive processes and interpersonal behaviors that in turn shape the environment in a way that confirms the representational content of the schemas. To the extent that they are limited in scope of internalized interpersonal experiences, they will result in redundant patterns of interactions with others, which limit the possibility of new information in the form of new interpersonal experiences. In this way, the person operates as a relatively closed system. For Bea, her persistently suspicious and antagonistic stance toward others elicited coldness from others and confirmed her belief that she existed in a cold world.

Different self-states can activate different relational schemas, resulting in a cycling through different experiential states of mind. The transition points or boundaries between these self-states vary in terms of seamlessness but are often marked by changes in vocal quality, facial expression, focus and content of verbal reports, emotional involvement, and so on. What accounts for the illusory sense of continuity and singular identity is dissociation and one's self-organizing and integral capacities. Dissociation is a cognitive process basic to optimal functioning, to feeling "like one self while being many" (Bromberg, 1998, p. 186). One's experience typically is not of multiple selves, or "mes," but instead of a single self, or "I." It is useful here to make the distinction between dissociation as a healthy process of selectively focusing attention and dissociation as an unhealthy process of severing connections between memory stores or schemas, an organization of unlinked relational schemas. The latter is a result of "traumatic overload" that leads to "breaches of communication, the demolition of bridges between the mind's islands of associated" relational schemas and that disrupts the sense of continuity and unity (Pizer, 1998, p. 74). Thus, the more conspicuous and abrupt the transitions between self-states, the more problematic the dissociative process and the more evidence of significant traumatic experience.

There is also an ongoing reciprocal relationship between the self-states of one person and those of the other in a dyadic interaction. As individuals cycle through various self-states in an interpersonal encounter, they should both influence and be influenced by the various self-states of the other. There should be subtle movements and fluctuations in intimacy and varying degrees of relatedness. Researchers who study mother–infant dyads have described this in terms of the ways in which the subjective or affective states of mother and child are interpersonally communicated and mutually regulated (e.g., Tronick, 1989). Interpersonal researchers have demonstrated this in terms of correspondence or reciprocity in the behavioral interactions of two individuals (see Kiesler, 1996). To illustrate, consider one way to understand the vignette just described: Bea's critical and skeptical opening state made me feel very cautious, which, when she became aware of this, resulted in a shift to a more anxious state in her. This was an interaction that we would repeatedly enact in our work together, especially in the early stages.

PURPOSEFUL COLLABORATION
AND EMOTIONAL CONNECTION

Another organizing concept is the therapeutic alliance. A great deal of research has demonstrated the predictive validity of the therapeutic alliance (Horvath, Del Re, Fluckiger, & Symonds, 2011). What has been most useful to us is Bordin's (1979) conceptualization of the alliance, which emphasizes the purposeful collaboration and affective bond between patient and therapist. Accordingly, to the extent the patient and therapist agree on the tasks and goals of treatment, this shapes the emotional connection between them, and vice versa. This conceptualization suggests an intrinsic relation between the technical and the relational, that no technique is without relational meaning, no intervention can be understood outside of the interpersonal context. It also suggests a view of the alliance as a mutual and dynamic process of ongoing collaboration, which stands in contrast to previous conceptualizations that emphasize therapist support or patient identification with the therapist and acceptance of therapist values of the psychotherapy process (Safran & Muran, 2000). The fact that Bea approached me requesting long-term treatment, while understanding that "to her knowledge" I was a therapist who specialized in brief therapy, as well as all her expressions of skepticism about me, my practice, and the efficacy of therapy at large, not to mention her own potential for change, did not bode well for our therapeutic alliance.

INTERSUBJECTIVE NEGOTIATION

What these expressions from Bea highlight, though, is that the struggle to establish a therapeutic alliance goes beyond an agreement on the parameters of treatment and toward the negotiation of fundamental existential dilemmas, including the struggle between the need to experience oneself as a separate subject and the need to have one's subjectivity recognized by the other in order to realize this experience. Hegel's (1807/1969) master–slave dialectic is useful in understanding this existential struggle: Hegel described the self as requiring the other in order to become aware of its consciousness or existence. He also described an unavoidable conflict between the self's wish for absolute independence and the self's need for recognition by the other. Accordingly, a precarious tension exists, one that people at least initially try to resolve by mastering the other or by submitting to the other. Either position of extremes, master or slave, involves some form of negation, some form of objectification: The former involves objectifying the other and risks isolation; the latter involves being objectified by the other and risks absolute dependency. There is an ongoing struggle to determine who defines the other and who accommodates whom. Ultimately, to recognize its subjectivity, a self must recognize another as a separate subject, and likewise the other must recognize the self as a separate subject. There must be *mutual recognition*.

Placing this notion in the context of the therapeutic relationship, J. Benjamin (1995) suggested that Winnicott's (1965) thinking on object use can be understood as a version of Hegel's (1807/1969) dialectic, whereby it is only through seeing the other survive one's destructive attempts (or attempts at negation) that one can see the other as a separate subject. Pizer (1998) developed this perspective further with his notion of *intersubjective negotia-*

tion. For him, therapists in their interventions and patients in their responses are recurrently saying to each other, "No, you can't make this of me. But you can make that of me" (p. 218). Accordingly, there are ongoing power plays between patient and therapist: accommodations and refusals to accommodate, which can convey to the patient that the world is negotiable and composed of others with separate subjectivities. With Bea, this combative dynamic was conspicuous from the start. The power plays in which we engaged were further complicated by the power assigned us from social conditions (as Foucault, 1972, described; see also Muran, 2007b): for example, by our differences in our identities as therapist–patient, as male–female, and as products from generations apart (Bea as a child of the 1930s and I of the 1960s).

RUPTURE AND RESOLUTION

Like all human relations, the psychotherapeutic process between patient and therapist is fraught with moments of conflict and hostility as the participants attempt to establish a sense of self and relatedness. We have identified these moments as *alliance ruptures*. Ruptures have received increasing attention in the research literature, with growing evidence that they are common events (e.g., they are reported by patients in as much as 50% of sessions and they are observed by third-party raters in 70% of sessions) and that they predict premature termination and negative outcome but, when resolved, predict good outcomes (e.g., Eubanks-Carter, Muran, & Safran, 2010). We have defined ruptures in three ways: (a) as breakdowns in the negotiation of treatment tasks and goals and deteriorations in the affective bond between patient and therapist; (b) as markers of tension between the respective needs or desires of the patient and therapist as they continuously press against each other; and (c) as indications of an enactment—a *relational matrix* of patient and therapist beliefs and action patterns, a vicious cycle involving the unwitting participation of both patient and therapist (Mitchell, 1988; Wachtel, 2007). This definition suggests that ruptures represent critical events and opportunities for awareness and change.

Our research program began as a study of rupture events and resolution processes with the specific aim of sensitizing clinicians to patterns that are likely to occur and facilitating their abilities to intervene (Muran, 2002; Safran, Crocker, McMain, & Murray, 1990; Safran & Muran, 1996). We have found it useful to distinguish between *confrontation* and *withdrawal* ruptures. These are defined as patient communications that mark breakdowns in collaboration or problems in negotiating needs for self-definition and relatedness. The former consist of direct expressions of hostility toward the therapist or the treatment process, and the latter involve indirect expressions by movements away from the therapist or the treatment process. It is important to note that ruptures mark the unwitting participation of both patient and therapist in an enactment, a relational matrix of cognitive–affective processes, implicit beliefs about self and others, and characteristic patterns of action from both patient and therapist.

We have proposed a typology of rupture-resolution strategies whereby ruptures can be dealt with on a surface or on a depth level. These two levels of resolution strategies can be approached either directly or indirectly (Safran & Muran, 2000). For example, a *direct surface approach* to a rupture resolution can involve simple clarification of the treatment rationale or misunderstanding between therapist and patient, and an *indirect surface approach* can involve simply changing a treatment task or goal when there is disagreement. A *direct depth approach* to a rupture resolution would involve exploring a core relational theme, and an *indirect depth approach* would involve providing a new relational experience, which can also be a consequence of any of the resolution strategy types. Our research has concentrated on the study of a direct depth strategy that explores a core relational theme, and in this regard we have developed two stage-process models for the resolution of withdrawal and confrontation ruptures. Each of the models begins with the therapist attending to the rupture marker. The critical task is for the therapist to recognize the rupture and invite an exploration of it. To progress, the therapist must facilitate a disembedding from the relational matrix or unhooking from the vicious cycle. The key to disembedding from the relational matrix is to establish communication about the communication process, or *metacommunication* (Kiesler, 1996).

Given the subject of this book and page constraints, we focus here on the resolution of confrontation ruptures. This is not meant to suggest, however, that frustration, anger, or hate is not experienced when dealing with patients who favor withdrawal ruptures. It is more a matter of intensity and likelihood. Figure 1.1 depicts the various patient states in a stage process model of confrontation resolution. Stage 1 captures the therapist's attempts to attend to the rupture marker and invite a collaborative inquiry about the rupture event. The therapist's task is to try to disembed or extricate him- or herself from the relational matrix of hostility and move toward an exploration of the rupture. Stage 2 marks this exploration and involves the unpacking of the nuances of patient and therapist perceptions and construal of the rupture event. The progression of the resolution of confrontation ruptures typically consists of moving through feelings of anger experienced in Stage 1, to feelings of disappointment and hurt at Stage 2, to contacting vulnerability and the wish to be nurtured and cared for at Stage 4. During the resolution process, there are often moments when the patient shifts away or avoids further exploration: This is Stage 3. In this regard, patients sometimes become

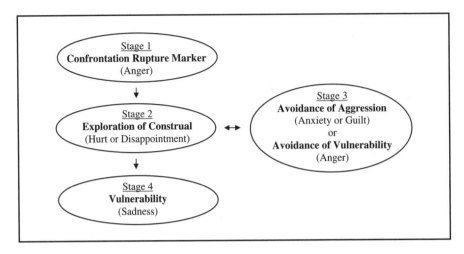

Figure 1.1. Four stages of patient states in confrontation rupture resolution.

anxious or guilty about their aggression for fear of retaliation by the therapist, or sometimes they return to their anger for fear of being exploited or taken advantage of by the therapist.

Let us return to Bea:

> As Bea was preparing to leave one of our sessions, several months into treatment, she conveyed her dismay regarding the recent criminal conviction of Martha Stewart and asked me my opinion. Bea would start her weekdays by stretching while watching Martha Stewart Living on TV and would often inform me of interesting tidbits she had learned from the program. I replied, without much reflection, that it seemed something like another Greek tragedy to me, where hubris once again resulted in the downfall of a larger-than-life figure. (I didn't say it exactly that way, but that was the gist of it. It just occurred to me that this sounds a little pedantic.)
>
> Bea started our next session by declaring her disappointment in me. (Maybe it was pedantic.) She said that I had revealed my true colors in my assessment of Martha's situation. I was taken aback because I had not given much thought to the comment, which I had made in passing. When I asked her what she meant, she said she found my judgment harsh and revealing of a surprising lack of compassion, especially given my profession. At first, I responded somewhat defensively but then also apologetically, confessing that I really didn't know Martha Stewart. She was more of a cartoon figure to me. Thus, perhaps my assessment was not fair. When I probed for more about her reaction, she replied, "It makes me wonder what you think of me." In this regard, as she explained, she thought about all the transgressions she had confessed to me: the lies, the manipulations, the various misdeeds she had committed toward others,

especially her family. She also returned to her concern about having to deal with me as a person rather than a professional.

In our next session, she started by reading something she had prepared in defense of Martha. It was two pages worth of accomplishments and the various ways Martha had served the public, including Bea. It especially highlighted Martha's strength and independence, her industriousness and fearlessness. As she read what she wrote, she became increasingly emotional and was ultimately moved to tears. When she finally put down the papers, she looked up at me and asked, "Why am I crying?" I suggested that perhaps what she had written was not just in defense of Martha but also in defense of herself. She paused and then replied, "You know, when I was running a bakery, I always thought to myself, 'I made it in a man's world.'" The bakery signified so much for Bea. It marked not only an accomplishment but also a great deal of loss.

This moment between us allowed us to discuss these meanings in a more elaborate way than we ever had before. In doing so, I also became much more aware of our differences, especially in regard to generation, gender, and ethnicity. I became more aware of what it was like for Bea as a young Jewish woman struggling to survive in New York City in the 1950s and 1960s. I became more aware of how much of a cartoon character she had been for me to this point (and maybe even how much she was colored by my previous experience with that patient I had mentioned earlier in this chapter). She took on much more dimension and became a much more sympathetic and likable figure. Bea revealed a more vulnerable self, and as a result my compassion for her markedly grew. In turn, as she was to tell me some time later, the moment marked the first time she felt I really understood her, and I became more than a young, White, male professional of a different ethnicity. I also became a person who could be sympathetic, as well as judgmental, all of which she started to consider as viable.

To illustrate the rupture-resolution model (see Figure 1.2), Stage 1 could be marked by Bea's confrontation: "I'm very disappointed in you." Stage 2 would include her disclosure, "It makes me wonder what you must think of me," and, finally, Stage 4 was reached when she started crying. (Stage 3 did not emerge in this sequence.) As is often the case, patients like Bea who are very confrontational engage in avoidance maneuvers at the same time, demonstrating *mixed markers* of confrontation and withdrawal ruptures (e.g., "You're never there for me, but maybe that's because of me!"). When negotiating these events, the first challenge for the therapist is to get such patients to stand behind or own their anger to the therapist (e.g., "Can we focus on the first part of what you just said to me?"; see Safran & Muran, 2000). There were many such challenges with Bea. Furthermore, her expressions of disappointment in me were sometimes followed by more

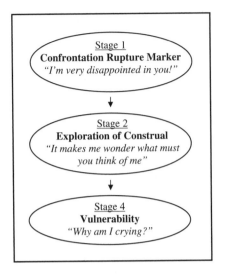

Figure 1.2. An illustration of the stages of the rupture-resolution model using Bea as an example.

avoidance and anxiety (Stage 3), which marked her fear of my rejection of her. In these instances, my task was to get Bea to recognize and explore this fear ("My sense is you're feeling uncomfortable right now. Can we focus on what that may be about?").

THERAPIST SKILLS AND TECHNIQUES

What are the critical skills necessary for a therapist to deal with or manage negative emotions? How do we train therapists to develop these skills? In collaboration with Jeremy Safran, we have developed a training model that concentrates on the development of therapist abilities to recognize ruptures and to resolve them, as well as a research program to evaluate its effect (see Muran, Safran, & Eubanks-Carter, 2010; Safran & Muran, 2000). With regard to rupture recognition, our training targets three specific skills—*self-awareness*, *affect regulation*, and *interpersonal sensitivity*—which we see as interdependent and as critical to establishing an optimal observational stance. *Self-awareness* refers to developing therapists' immediate awareness and bare attention to their internal experience. The aim here is to increase therapists' attunement to their emotions so that they may use them as a compass to understanding their interactions with their patients. *Affect regulation* refers to developing therapists' abilities to manage negative emotions and tolerate distress—their own as well as their patient's. In other words, we try to facilitate their abilities to resist the natural reaction to anxiety, to turn their attention away or to avoid dealing with it in some way, which means not attending to or exploring a rupture. *Interpersonal sensitivity* refers to increasing therapists' empathy toward their patient's experience and their awareness of the interpersonal process in which they engage with their patients.

In this regard, we try to balance therapists' attention to what they or their patients say with an increased sensitivity to how statements are communicated, the emotional impact of various expressions, and the nature of their interactions with patients. With Bea, it was initially and continually very important for me to become aware of my internal experience with her, from my wariness and anxiety to my frustration and anger. To be aware of and tolerate these negative affects allowed me to make sense of and explore what was going on between us—and, of course, to make her more mindful of her impulses and her impact on others. It was equally important to be aware of the warmth and affection I would feel increasingly across the course of treatment.

Our training model also attempts to teach the various rupture-resolution strategies from direct to indirect and from surface to depth but with special attention to the technical principle of *metacommunication,* which we have found useful for exploring core relational themes. Metacommunication consists of an attempt to step outside of or disembed from the relational matrix involving patient and therapist that is currently being enacted by treating it as the focus of collaborative inquiry. By being an observer as well as a participant, the therapist attempts to bring immediate awareness to bear on the interactive process as it unfolds. Metacommunication involves a low degree of inference and is grounded as much as possible in the therapist's immediate experience of some aspect of the therapeutic relationship. It also reflects a dialogic sensibility, which is based on the recognition not only that ruptures are the result of a collaborative effort but also that they can be understood or resolved only by a collaboration on the part of both patient and therapist (see Safran & Muran, 2000). In our model, therapists are not seen as being in a privileged position of knowing; instead, their understanding of the communication process is considered only partial. The vignettes with Bea are intended to give readers some sense of metacommunication in action.

Metacommunication can begin with questions or observations by the therapist that focus the patient's attention on three parallel dimensions of their relationship. The therapist might start by focusing the patient's attention on his or her own experience with a direct question, such as "What are you feeling right now?" or with an observation about the patient's self-state: "You seem anxious to me right now. Am I reading you right?" The therapist might also direct attention to the interpersonal field by asking, "What's going on here between us?" or observing, "It seems like we're in some kind of dance. Does that fit with your sense?" A third approach is to bring the therapist's experience into relief by asking a question that encourages the patient to be curious about the therapist's self-state: "Do you have any thoughts about what might be going on for me right now?" Alternatively, the therapist could make a self-disclosure about his internal experience such as, "I'm aware of feeling defensive right now."

We and our colleagues have previously outlined a number of general and specific principles of metacommunication (see Safran & Muran, 2000, for a comprehensive list). Some basic ones are outlined in the next several sections.

Invite a Collaborative Inquiry and Establish a Climate of Shared Dilemma

Patients can often feel alone and demoralized during a rupture, with the therapist becoming one of a string of figures who are unable to join with the patient in his or her struggle. The therapist becomes another foe instead of an ally. To counteract this expectation, the implicit message should always be one of inviting the patient to join the therapist in an attempt to understand their shared dilemma. Therapists should establish a climate that emphasizes the subjectivity of both their and the patient's perceptions. They should encourage a collaborative effort to clarify the factors influencing the emergence and maintenance of a rupture. Framing the impasse as a shared experience can transform the experience from one of isolation and demoralization for the patient to one of openness and honesty in which the patient feels safe speaking directly to the therapist about his or her feelings or overall treatment experience. This framework begins the process of transforming the struggle by defusing the patient's defensiveness against the therapist and acknowledging that the therapist and the patient are stuck together.

Focus on the Immediate Details of Experience and Behavior

The process of metacommunication is formed around an examination of the immediate experience within a session instead of a focus on events that have taken place in the past (i.e., in previous sessions or at different points in the same session). Focusing on the concrete and specific details of the here-and-now of a therapeutic interaction promotes an experiential awareness. It lays the groundwork for exploring a patient's actions and the internal experiences associated with those actions. Often, when a therapist or patient feels anxious about a particular topic, he or she tends to pull the focus away from the source of conflict by deviating from the present feelings or by falling back on abstract, intellectualized speculation. Refocusing and opening up to exploring the present moment in concrete and specific terms can avoid this defensive deviation. Explorations of the present moment can also guide patients in becoming observers of their own behavior, promoting the type of mindfulness that fosters change.

Maintaining a focus on the here-and-now also encourages a respect for the uniqueness of each encounter. Each interaction between patient and therapist is an individual moment influenced by both players. Because the therapist is a key player in the dynamic, drawing premature parallels between the therapeutic relationship and the patient's other relationships can isolate the therapist's contribution and be seen by the patient as blaming. Therefore, attempts to identify how patterns in the therapeutic relationship generalize to other relationships should always be kept as an open question and should generally be left to the patient to draw. In general, such observations and explorations should be made in a tentative fashion from a stance of genuine uncertainty.

By focusing on exploring the here-and-now of the therapeutic process, the therapeutic aim takes on the form of a contextualized exploration in the sense of a *thick description*, as described by Clifford Geertz (1973; see Muran, 2007a). In short, the thick description privileges the pursuit of particular, specific, details of the self-experience in order to clarify the individual's larger, global experience. As a corollary to this aim, therapists should try to convey the message to resist the urge to just make things different or better. They should privilege awareness over change. Change instead should be understood as a by-product of awareness, where with greater awareness comes change.

Explore One's Own Subjectivity and Contribution

Therapists' formulations should always be grounded in an awareness of their own feelings. Therapists must work toward identifying feelings and responses that the patient evokes in them. This involves a careful awareness of the nuanced changes experienced by the therapist. These shifts may sometimes be difficult to articulate, but the process of attempting to articulate, both to oneself and directly to the patient, can help clarify the experience. The process of acknowledging one's contributions to the patient can also play a critical role in beginning to clarify the nature of the cycle that is being enacted. For example, a therapist could say, "As I listen to myself talk, I hear a kind of stilted quality to what I'm saying, and I think I've probably been acting in a pretty formal and distant fashion with you. Does that fit with your experience?" If the patient is receptive, this type of disclosure can lead either in the direction of clarifying factors influencing the therapist's actions or of exploring the patient's feelings about the therapist's actions.

Encouraging a sense of "we-ness" involves being open to exploring the therapist's own contribution to and experience of the interaction. This process requires one to accept responsibility for one's own influence in the development of a rupture with the patient. When therapists disclose their own experience, they invite the patient to include the therapist as an active factor in their self-exploration. A therapist's self-disclosure may include simply asking patients whether they have any ideas about what may be going on within the therapist. The therapist may also suggest possibilities for what is occurring between them and checking with the patient. For instance, the therapist could state, "I have a sense of being defensive or critical; are you sensing this from your side?" This form of self-disclosure can help patients become aware of inchoate feelings that they are not comfortable facing, such as feeling criticized by the therapist, and can validate patients' experience of their therapist.

Monitor Relatedness and Responsiveness

Therapists should be continually tracking how the patient responds to what is being said within a session. In this regard, therapists should pay close attention to their emotional experience as an important source for understanding the quality of relatedness with patients in a given moment. An intuitive sense of the relational atmosphere can inform the therapist of whether patients are getting closer to or distancing themselves from their therapist. Specific factors to attend to may include examining whether a particular interaction is facilitating or hindering the strength of the relationship, whether the discussion of an experience is elaborative or foreclosing, or whether the patient is being expressive of his or her subjective experience or simply compliant to the therapist's view.

It is important to be aware that a patient may have difficulty acknowledging feeling hurt or criticized by the therapist or feeling angry at the therapist. Admitting such feelings may be threatening to the patient's self-esteem and may, in the patient's mind, risk offending or alienating the therapist. Therefore, if an intervention fails to deepen exploration or further inhibits it, or if the therapist senses something peculiar in the patient's response to it, it is critical to explore the way in which the patient experienced it. Over time, this type of exploration can help articulate the nature of the enactment taking place and help flesh out a relational schema being enacted by both the therapist and patient. It can also lead to a progressive refinement in therapists' understanding of their own contribution to the interaction by encouraging a retrospective awareness of their own actions.

Recognize That the Situation Is Constantly Changing

The process of metacommunication is just that, a *process*. It is important to bear in mind that the therapeutic situation is constantly changing. This again returns to the concept of appreciating each experience with a patient as a unique configuration of the current encounter, with each instance leading to a further configuration. What we are highlighting here is the need to recognize the fluidity of experience, whereby what was true about the therapeutic relationship a moment ago may not be true now. From this stance, all situations are workable provided that one fully acknowledges and accepts what the situation is. The critical idea here is the importance of the inner act of acceptance of the changing experience. This inner act facilitates a type of "letting go" and an increased attunement to the unique configuration of the moment.

Even the position of "being stuck" is a position that is workable once one accepts it and ceases to fight against it. Metacommunication emerges out of the inspiration of the moment, regardless of whether the moment is familiar or clearly understood by the therapist. Acknowledging and accepting the situation as it is can be an emotionally freeing experience that makes room for new possibilities and interpretations for what is occurring (a concept referred to by Neville Symington [1983] as an *act of freedom*). For example, therapists who say to the patient, "I feel stuck" may in the process free themselves up sufficiently to see something that had eluded them before, such as an aspect of the patient's behavior or an angle of their own bias. A disclosure of this type may contribute to a shift in the interactional dynamic, reframing the situation in a way that might uncover a new jumping-off point for exploration.

Expect Initial Attempts to Lead to More Ruptures and to Revisit Ruptures

Therapists should be aware that initial attempts to uncover relational patterns in a therapeutic rupture can lead to further ruptures and will likely need to be revisited at a later time. The overarching aim of the resolution process is to stimulate curiosity about the patient's internal experience. This process involves working toward an awareness of the feelings and behaviors associated with the style of relating, instead of trying to force things to be different. Awareness of one's self-structure is a challenging process that can take time and repetition of certain interventions. In this process there is always a risk that, in working with alliance ruptures, a moment of metacommunication with a patient can further aggravate the rupture.

Regardless of how skillful the therapist may be in framing his or her comments in a nonblaming, nonjudgmental way, metacommunication may implicitly suggest that patients should be saying or doing something other than what they are currently saying or doing. For example, the observation "I experience you as withdrawing right now" may carry with it the implication that it would be better not to withdraw. In light of this risk, it is important for the therapist to remember that facing one rupture is the beginning of a resolution process that will inevitably involve further ruptures. In other words, the experience of working through a single rupture does not stand alone as an ultimate intervention but instead should be viewed as one step in building awareness of the internal experience and consequent maladaptive relational pattern.

There is nothing magical about the process of metacommunication. It does not always follow the notion of mindfulness with nonjudgmental thinking and emotional neutrality; it can also arise defensively. Regardless of the tension from which metacommunication arises, it should be understood that it is a single moment within a string of learning experiences between the patient and therapist. One must accept the inevitability of revisiting ruptures that have not yet been fully processed or internalized while appreciating that each repetition of a parallel rupture holds a unique configuration within the ultimate process.

Along similar lines, it is also important to remember that there will be moments within the therapeutic relationship when hope will wane. During periods of a prolonged rupture or an impasse, the therapist can easily lose hope in the possibility of moving forward. Such periods of hopelessness and demoralization are part of the process, just as the process of working through impasses is the work of therapy, rather than a prerequisite.

TRAINING PRINCIPLES AND STRATEGIES

Elsewhere, we and our colleagues have outlined various fundamental principles that guide our alliance-focused approach to training (Muran et al., 2010; Safran & Muran, 2000). In the following sections, we describe a few of the most fundamental ones.

Recognizing the Relational Context

As in psychotherapy, the relational context is of utmost importance in training. It is impossible for the supervisor to convey information to the trainee that has meaning independent of the relational context in which it is conveyed. Supervision thus must be tailored to the specific needs and development of the trainee and to the context of the specific supervision situation. Supervisors need to recognize and support trainees' needs to maintain their self-esteem and calibrate the extent to which they have more of a need for support versus new information or confrontation in a given moment. It is also critical for supervisors to monitor the quality of the *supervisory alliance* in an ongoing fashion that parallels the ongoing monitoring of the quality of the alliance in therapy. When strains or tensions emerge, the exploration of the supervisory relationship should take priority over other concerns.

Establishing an Experiential Focus

For many trainees, the process of establishing an experiential focus involves a partial unlearning of things that they have already learned about conducting therapy. Often, the training of therapists emphasizes the conceptual at the expense of the experiential. Trainees study the formulations of different psychotherapy theorists and learn to apply the ideas they are learning to their clinical experience. Although this type of knowledge is essential and can be useful to organizing one's experience, it can also serve a defensive function. It can help trainees to manage the anxiety that inevitably arises as a result of confronting the inherent ambiguity and chaos of lived experience, but it can also lead to premature formulations that foreclose experience. It can result in avoiding painful and frightening, conflicting feelings that inevitably emerge for both patients and therapists. In some respects, this conceptual knowledge can be useful in navigating one's anxieties and therapeutic impasses; in others, it can serve to tighten deadlocks.

Emphasizing Self-Exploration

Although there are times when specific suggestions about ways of conceptualizing a case or intervening are useful, there is an overarching emphasis in our approach on helping therapists to find their own unique solution to their struggle with the patient. The particular therapeutic interaction that is the focus of supervision is unique to a particular therapist–patient dyad. Therapists will thus have their own unique feelings in response to a particular patient, and the particular solution they formulate to their dilemma must emerge in the context of their own unique reactions. An important aim of training, therefore, is to help therapists develop a way to dialogue with their patients about what is going on in the moment that is unique to the moment and their experience of it. Suggestions about what to say provided by supervisors or fellow trainees may look appropriate in context of a videotape being viewed but may not be appropriate to the context of the next session. The supervisor's task is thus to help trainees develop the ability to attend to their own experience and use it as a basis for intervening. In the end, the resolution of a rupture must involve the participation of the patient.

Implementing Strategies in Group Supervision

Our training program makes use of various strategies to develop therapist abilities and essential skills to recognize and resolve ruptures. The main training strategies we implement are typically done within the context of group supervision. The group setting poses many challenges for the supervisors, given the relational orientation. It can be quite daunting for the supervisor to be sensitive to the group process and the complexity of negotiating multiple supervisory alliances while trying to maintain group cohesion. This challenge is intensified when one considers the focus on rupture events and the emphasis on self-exploration. We try to establish a culture of struggle and support. We do privilege the presentation of difficult moments. Because of this, we expect that the presenting of such moments will be especially fraught with anxiety and shame in our training sessions, and so we are careful to continually track the trainee's experience and take great pains to grant control to the trainees, allowing them to feel as free as possible to rein in the process. We make it clear that although self-exploration plays a central role in the training process, it is also critical for therapists to respect their own needs for privacy and their own fluctuating assessments of what feels safe to explore in front of supervisors and fellow trainees at any point in time.

Manuals and Models

In this regard, we use the book *Negotiating the Therapeutic Alliance: A Relational Treatment Guide* (Safran & Muran, 2000) as a training manual. It provides background and justification for our relational approach to practice and training. Probably the most important benefit of this book is that it presents various clinical principles and models, including our own empirically derived rupture-resolution model, which can serve to help therapists organize their experience, regulate their affect, and manage their anxiety in the face of very difficult treatment process. A number of clinical theorists (e.g., Aron, 1999) have suggested how one's allegiance or relationship to a particular theory or model can function as another part of the process between patient and therapist that can be of particular assistance in helping the therapist manage negative experiences. As mentioned previously, this was a principal goal in our development of rupture-resolution models.

Process Coding

In our capacity as supervisors, we provide a brief orientation to various research measures of psychotherapy process, such as those that focus on vocal quality, emotional involvement, and interpersonal behavior, in order to help sensitize trainees to the psychotherapy process. This can be very important to the development of one's *clinical ear*, namely, how to observe and listen to process (and not just content). Trainees may even be asked to track one of their sessions with a particular coding scheme in mind. For example, a trainee might be asked to consider in session with a patient the Client Vocal Quality Scale (Rice & Greenberg, 1984) and its capacity to distinguish between expressions that are emotional or focused on internal experience and those that are more limited or externalized in quality. Other measures we use include the Structural Analysis of Social Behavior (L. S. Benjamin, 1974), for interpersonal process, and the Experiencing Scale (Klein, Mathieu, Gendlin, & Kiesler, 1970), for emotional involvement. The use of such measures (in addition to the rupture-resolution model) is a good example of how research can influence practice.

Videotape Analysis

We also conduct intensive analysis of videotaped psychotherapy sessions with our trainees. This provides a view of a treatment process unfiltered by the trainees' reconstructions and an opportunity to step outside their participation and to view their interactions as a third-party observer. It facilitates an orientation to interpersonal process. Videotaping has a variety of useful functions, including use as a prompt for accessing and defining a trainee's internal experience. It provides the trainee with subjective feedback about the impact of the patient on others, which can be validating when the feedback corresponds but illustrative of the uniqueness of interactions when it differs. When it comes to playing session segments, although we allow trainees to preface their presentation with some form of case history (primarily to grant the trainee a sense of control), we also encourage the playing of the session without any introduction, on the basis of the belief that all the history one needs to know is captured in the patient–therapist interactions. As for the amount of session viewed, we always err on playing more than less, and often we invite trainees to provide narration of what they remember experiencing during the session to the best of their ability as they watch it in the group setting. For the other trainees, we typically direct their attention toward their affective awareness, instead of trying to demonstrate their conceptual skills, which too often results in competition in the group and defensiveness in the presenter.

Mindfulness Training

We introduce to our trainees *mindfulness meditation*, which we consider a systematic strategy for developing an optimal observational stance toward internal experience. Often trainees have difficulty at first distinguishing between their experience and their *ideas* about their experience, and structured mindfulness exercises can help them grasp this distinction and develop openness to their experience. Such exercises also help trainees sharpen their abilities to become participant observers. We also appreciate the benefits of this training for developing affect regulation and interpersonal sensitivity. We incorporate mindfulness in supervision sessions. We typically begin each supervision session with a mindfulness-induction exercise that is led by a trainee. Having trainees lead the exercise goes a long way toward their understanding and appreciation of its value. We also encourage trainees to establish their own personal practices.

Awareness Exercises

We make extensive use of awareness-oriented exercises, including the use of role plays and two-chair techniques to practice metacommunication. The initial task upon viewing the video is defining the rupture event, but sometimes this can be defined simply from the trainee's description of the process. From either, we design an awareness exercise. For example, trainees might be asked to alternate between playing their patient and then themselves in relation to a difficult enactment observed on video, with the aim of exploring their experience (especially their fears and expectations regarding the patient) and experimenting with different ways of trying metacommunication. In addition, we might do a role play in which the presenting trainee plays the patient and the other trainees take turns trying to metacommunicate. These exercises are at the heart of the training model. They are valuable for grounding training at the experiential level and promoting self-awareness and empathy.

EPILOGUE: A GIFT OF LOVE

Early last year, Bea passed away after a yearlong battle with cancer. Ten years had passed since I had started working with her, 5 years since I first wrote about her. When we started our work, Bea was very much alone in the world—estranged from everyone in her family and having very limited contact with so-called friends. It is difficult to assess how much she benefited from our work together. She did eventually reconnect with some family members, although she struggled mightily at times with feelings of anger and mistrust toward them. In the end, she did not find much peace or satisfaction with the life she had lived, but she did not die alone. Some time during the last year of our work, she brought in an oil painting she made for me. She was an avid and quite skilled painter. The walls of her home were filled with her paintings, but in her later years she found it increasingly difficult to paint, for both physical and psychological reasons. The painting she made for me was of a Paris street scene by the impressionist Camille Pissarro—a poster of which always hung on the wall of my office. I had no idea that she had been working on this for me. She presented it to me as her "last" painting, and it was. The presenting of gifts in the context of psychotherapy deserves more consideration than I can give it in this chapter, but the most important principle is to above all understand its meaning, and so often this requires some exploration. In this case, I chose not to explore too much—its meaning was multilayered—but I ultimately understood it as a gift of love and didn't want to spoil it. It has taken the place of my long-cherished poster.

REFERENCES

Aron, L. (1999). Clinical choices and the relational matrix. *Psychoanalytic Dialogues*, 9, 1–29. doi:10.1080/10481889909539301

Benjamin, J. (1995). *Like subject, love objects: Essays on recognition and sexual difference*. New Haven, CT: Yale University Press.

Benjamin, L. S. (1974). Structural analysis of social behavior. *Psychological Review*, 81, 392–425. doi:10.1037/h0037024

Bordin, E. (1979). The generalizability of the psychoanalytic concept of the working alliance. *Psychotherapy: Theory, Research & Practice*, 16, 252–260. doi:10.1037/h0085885

Bromberg, P. M. (1998). *Standing in the spaces: Essays on clinical process, trauma, and dissociation*. Hillsdale, NJ: Analytic Press.

Eubanks-Carter, C., Muran, J. C., & Safran, J. D. (2010). Alliance ruptures and resolution. In J. C. Muran & J. P. Barber (Eds.), *The therapeutic alliance: An evidence-based guide to practice* (pp. 74–94). New York, NY: Guilford Press.

Foucault, M. (1972). *The archeology of knowledge*. London, England: Tavistock.

Geertz, C. (1973). *The interpretation of cultures*. New York, NY: Basic Books.

Hegel, G. W. F. (1969). *Phenomenology of spirit*. New York, NY: Oxford University Press. (Original work published 1807)

Horvath, A. O., Del Re, A. C., Fluckiger, C., & Symonds, D. (2011). Alliance in individual psychotherapy. *Psychotherapy*, 48, 9–16. doi:10.1037/a0022186

Kiesler, D. J. (1996). *Contemporary interpersonal theory and research: Personality, psychopathology, and psychotherapy*. New York, NY: Wiley.

Klein, M. H., Mathieu, P. L., Gendlin, T., & Kiesler, D. J. (1970). *The Experiencing Scale: A research and training manual*. Madison: Psychiatric Institute, University of Wisconsin.

Mitchell, S. A. (1988). *Relational concepts in psychoanalysis*. Cambridge, MA: Harvard University Press.

Muran, J. C. (2002). A relational approach to understanding change: Plurality and contextualism in a psychotherapy research program. *Psychotherapy Research*, 12, 113–138. doi:10.1080/713664276

Muran, J. C. (2007a). A relational turn on thick description. In J. C. Muran (Ed.), *Dialogues on difference: Studies of diversity in the therapeutic relationship* (pp. 257–274). Washington, DC: American Psychological Association. doi:10.1037/11500-029

Muran, J. C. (2007b). Reply: The power of/in language. In J. C. Muran (Ed.), *Dialogues on difference: Studies of diversity in the therapeutic relationship* (pp. 285–288). Washington, DC: American Psychological Association. doi:10.1037/11500-032

Muran, J. C., Safran, J. D., & Eubanks-Carter, C. (2010). Developing therapist abilities to negotiate the therapeutic alliance. In J. C. Muran & J. P. Barber (Eds.), *Therapeutic alliance: An evidence-based approach to practice and training* (pp. 320–340). New York, NY: Guilford Press.

Pizer, S. A. (1998). *Building bridges: The negotiation of paradox in psychoanalysis*. Hillsdale, NJ: Analytic Press.

Rice, L. N., & Greenberg, L. S. (1984). *Patterns of change*. New York, NY: Guilford Press.

Safran, J. D., Crocker, P., McMain, S., & Murray, P. (1990). Therapeutic alliance rupture as a therapy event for empirical investigation. *Psychotherapy: Theory, Research, Practice, Training, 27*, 154–165. doi:10.1037/0033-3204.27.2.154

Safran, J. D., & Muran, J. C. (1996). The resolution of ruptures in the therapeutic alliance. *Journal of Consulting and Clinical Psychology, 64*, 447–458. doi:10.1037/0022-006X.64.3.447

Safran, J. D., & Muran, J. C. (2000). *Negotiating the therapeutic alliance: A relational treatment guide*. New York, NY: Guilford Press.

Symington, N. (1983). The analyst's act of freedom as an agent of therapeutic change. *International Review of Psycho-Analysis, 10*, 783–792.

Tronick, E. Z. (1989). Emotions and emotional communications in infants. *American Psychologist, 44*, 112–119. doi:10.1037/0003-066X.44.2.112

Wachtel, P. L. (2007). Commentary: Making invisibility visible—Probing the interface between race and gender. In J. C. Muran (Ed.), *Dialogues on difference: Studies of diversity in the therapeutic relationship* (pp. 132–140). Washington, DC: American Psychological Association. doi:10.1037/11500-014

Winnicott, D. W. (1965). *The maturational process and the facilitating environment*. New York, NY: International Universities Press.

2

COGNITIVE BEHAVIOR THERAPY: A RICH BUT IMPLICIT RELATIONAL FRAMEWORK WITHIN WHICH TO DEAL WITH THERAPIST FRUSTRATIONS

PHILLIP G. LEVENDUSKY AND DAVID H. ROSMARIN

"Doc, you're incompetent and have completely wasted my time and money" were the first words out of the client's mouth at the start of a session following eight previous seemingly productive therapeutic meetings. Did this assertion engender a negative reaction in the therapist? You bet it did! The therapist was immediately engulfed by a wave of emotions, including defensiveness, anger, frustration, and surprise. Only after an extensive debriefing of a difficult situation that the client had recently encountered was the therapist able to reestablish a real-time empathic bond with the client. The bond also produced a construct that, to this day, has served as a template to help prevent or constructively resolve the therapist's negative reactions to problematic client responses or behaviors.

In this case, despite the therapist's well-intended therapeutic interventions, along with the client's highly motivated efforts to implement treatment recommendations, the wrenching emotional reaction that they shared

DOI: 10.1037/13940-002
Transforming Negative Reactions to Clients: From Frustration to Compassion, A. W. Wolf, M. R. Goldfried, and J. C. Muran (Editors)

could best be described as a profound sense of helplessness. It had long been the therapist's assumption that a common denominator of the individuals who sought his professional assistance was that they typically perceived that important aspects of their lives were out of control and causing distress. In this case example, the mutually experienced negative reactions of the client and the therapist provided a unique awareness of how such a compromised perceived sense of control could also jeopardize a productive therapeutic relationship. What follows in this chapter is an elaboration of what we consider to be the linchpin for engaging in effective cognitive behavior therapy (CBT). In particular, we believe that although CBT techniques have strong empirical support, their effectiveness in real-world clinical practice is potentiated by fully integrating them with a collaborative client–therapist therapeutic relationship.

To some readers, the inclusion of a chapter on CBT in a book on psychotherapists' emotional reactions may seem like an act of diplomacy and discretion. Of all the major schools of thought within the ever-evolving field of psychotherapy, CBT has a reputation for underemphasizing relational processes and interpersonal interactions. Instead, CBT is thought to place a primary emphasis on the practice and evaluation of therapeutic technique, to the exclusion of utilizing or even acknowledging process and relational facets of treatment. Although there have been changes in recent years, with the development of so-called Third Wave CBT (e.g., dialectical behavior therapy [DBT; Linehan, 1993]; acceptance and commitment therapy [Hayes, Strosahl, & Wilson, 2003]), the evidence-based approach that underlies CBT defines treatment outcomes in terms of symptom reduction and psychosocial functioning, and the treatment outcome literature offers little to describe the importance of the therapeutic alliance. In fact, a cursory review of the literature on empirically supported CBT treatments suggests that therapists' emotional reactions are to be controlled, or perhaps altogether discouraged, through the utilization of precisely scripted treatment protocols. The effort to rigorously standardize treatment gives the impression that there is little or perhaps no place for the contemplation or evaluation of emotional experiences in therapy. Furthermore, given its historical roots within animal models, the foundation of CBT is broadly perceived as placing an emphasis on technique and being primarily nonrelational.

In this chapter, we seek to dispel these and other misconceptions. We argue that a rich relational framework is implicitly inherent within the practice of CBT and that the pursuit of determining efficacy is not done in the service of proving the techniques work but instead is aimed at providing the therapist with proven tools to help clients more effectively manage their lives. We begin with a brief overview of CBT, in which we broadly discuss its theory of change, treatment process, and evidence base. We then describe

CBT's unspoken but nevertheless rich and omnipresent relational framework, and we provide details about how the relationships that serve as the means by which successful CBT techniques are implemented can best be navigated in clinical practice. Finally, we discuss implications for training and supervision and provide a case example from our work.

CBT: THE BASICS

CBT is predicated on the fundamental principles of behaviorism and learning theory. Human behavior, like that of all living organisms, is viewed as being chiefly determined, or shaped, by life experiences (Watson, 1930). Behaviors increase over time with positive consequences (positive reinforcement) or the avoidance of negative consequences (negative reinforcement) and decrease over time with a lack of reinforcement (extinction) or negative consequences (punishment; Pavlov, 1927; Skinner, 1969). A thorough explanation of the role of these processes in accounting for complex human behavior, such as language, has been discussed elsewhere and is beyond the scope of this chapter (Skinner, 1957). We should mention, however, that this framework underlies the majority of CBT practices regardless of the complexity of the specific therapeutic targets they are intended to address; that is, modern CBT theorists conceptualize "behavior" as a broad and inclusive category that comprises internal as well as external facets (A. T. Beck, 1975; Ellis & Harper, 1975; Meichenbaum, 1975). In this regard, human cognition and emotion, along with overt behavior, are viewed through the lens of behaviorism. Furthermore, CBT views internal and external behaviors as intrinsically interlinked, such that robust changes in both cognition and emotion can follow changes in observable actions (Barlow, 2004; Foa & Kozak, 1986) and, conversely, changes in emotion and behavior can follow alterations in thought patterns (J. S. Beck, 1995). Thus, maladaptive or dysfunctional patterns of internal behavior (e.g., depression, rumination, worry) and external behavior (e.g., anger outbursts, impulsive shopping) are conceptualized as primarily the product of previous learning and/or a failure to learn or use functional behaviors. Therefore, the goal of CBT is for the therapist and client to collectively identify maladaptive behaviors and replacement adaptive behaviors and then to extinguish the former and inculcate the latter. This is good news for clients seeking change, because it directly implies that change is highly feasible and, as suggested in this chapter, best achieved in the context of a collaborative treatment model that relies heavily on a positive and constructive therapeutic alliance.

Of course, at this juncture of history, CBT theorists recognize that human behavior (both internal and external) is influenced by multiple factors (Mineka

& Zinbarg, 2006). Evidence supporting the diathesis–stress model has emphasized that latent genetic vulnerability for certain behaviors can surface in the context of environmental and/or psychological stressors. Biopsychosocial models of mental illness have made it abundantly clear that behavior occurs at the interface of biological predispositions, environmental factors, and psychological factors (i.e., learning). Thus, modern CBT practitioners work on the basis of the premise that human behaviors, in particular, internal behaviors (e.g., cognitions and emotions), are a function of numerous factors, including human neurobiology and social processes. Nevertheless, behavioral learning that involves reinforcement, punishment, and extinction is viewed as a primary determinant, particularly in the realm of mental health. This premise is supported by recent evidence from the cognitive and clinical neuroscience literature suggesting that behavioral factors can directly affect neurobiology. For example, completion of exposure therapy (a principal technique of modern CBT that we discuss further below) has been associated with decreases in activation of the dorsolateral prefrontal cortex and the parahippocampal gyrus (Paquette et al., 2003). Similarly, changes in limbic and cortical region activity over the course of CBT with unmedicated clients with unipolar depression are similar to those observed in the course of paroxetine-facilitated recovery (Goldapple et al., 2004). Thus, although CBT practitioners are aware of the possibility that biological and social factors may be present and are possibly etiologically primary for individual clients, this would not preclude the use of behavioral methods to facilitate change. In fact, these methods can serve as a means to better address all aspects of a multidimensional treatment plan. This being the case, from the vantage point of CBT, behavior change is a primary order of business, and virtually all CBT practices are focused on this goal. That said, the savvy CBT clinician will utilize a biopsychosocial treatment conceptualization to ensure that all factors contributing to a client's distress are being addressed.

To this end, there are four primary processes involved in the clinical practice of CBT, which are largely sequential but may be iterative (in particular, the third and fourth processes). First, the CBT therapist and client conduct a *functional analysis* of the presenting problem. Treatment focuses on a collaborative assessment to identify salient contributions to the problem for which the client is seeking treatment. This invariably involves describing relationships between environmental, cognitive, and affective components and their relative impact on the client's presenting problem. Functional analyses are often drawn out on paper and can look like lots of little boxes connected by arrows. Each box represents a factor or element in a client's life across environmental (e.g., too much work to do), cognitive (e.g., concern about finances), affective (e.g., anhedonia, apprehension), and behavioral (e.g., procrastination) domains. Depending on the complexity and pervasiveness of a client's presenting problem, as well as his or her awareness and ability to articulate relevant factors, a completed functional analysis sets the stage for therapy by providing the client and the therapist with a clear understanding of issues that compromise effective control of problematic situations. Necessary revision based on continuing assessment of efficacy of the treatments offered in the context of the functional analytic assessment is an ongoing process throughout treatment.

Second, the CBT therapist and client collaboratively create a *therapeutic contract* that specifies which targets will be addressed, how this will be done, for how long, and what the roles of both parties will be. This is a critical step in the real-world application of CBT and may be underemphasized or missing in controlled treatment outcome studies. In creating the therapeutic contract with a client, the therapist works to engage the client to help him or her clearly articulate the treatment goals. Establishing "what's in it" for the client immediately provides him or her with a sense of ownership in the therapeutic process. This is clearly an exercise in fitting the treatment to the client's needs and not a modification of the client's goals to maintain the purity of the treatment model. The therapist and client then agree on prioritization of treatment goals.

The therapeutic contract (e.g., the goals toward which the client and therapist are going to work) guides the rest of the client's treatment. It consists of mutually agreed-on points at which both participants can and will intervene with the objective of learning new behaviors or unlearning old ones, thereby functionally modifying the factors that have been identified as problematic. The therapist may offer previously identified strategies that can be found in manualized treatment protocols, or the therapist can tailor strategies to the client's specific individual needs. These strategies can include behavioral interventions, such as exposure treatment (voluntarily approaching distressing situations to facilitate learning new behavior and habituation); behavioral activation (engaging in valued activities as a precursor to and catalyst of affective change); and social skills training (e.g., practicing basic social interactions with others); as well as cognitive interventions, such as identifying emotion-relevant thoughts and cognitive distortions and reframing negative perspectives on life circumstances. Identified strategies become the action component of the treatment plan, which is reviewed and agreed to by both parties before proceeding. This process provides the client with ownership of the treatment effort.

Third, the therapist and client collaborate to execute the plan in their therapeutic contract by *implementing strategies in any manner that is mutually deemed to be reasonable*. This occurs both during sessions and in therapeutic assignments between sessions. The first step in utilizing a specific strategy typically involves the therapist providing information about the treatment being recommended. This can be carried out by way of both didactic training and experiential learning, which may include behavioral modeling (i.e., a therapist showing a client in vivo how a skill is performed), observation of the client's practice of a particular strategy and provision of direct verbal feedback, or perhaps bibliotherapy, whereby the client reads assigned source material about both the causes of a problem and the treatment for it. Clients' questions and points for clarification are encouraged to facilitate training in strategy implementation.

As part of their treatment plan, clients engage in "experiments," both on their own and in the context of therapy sessions, in which they use the strategy in a specified manner for a predetermined period of time while gauging its relative therapeutic value (i.e., whether it is effective in reducing symptoms). It should be noted that there is no dictum in CBT to provide short psychotherapy. Thus, in this era of managed care, many CBT therapists encourage clients to proceed rapidly (though as thoroughly as possible) through treatment, focusing on the acquisition and practice of skills as the primary modus operandi. Ideally, however, the CBT therapist will set a pace that best suits the client's ability to achieve the objectives. In other words, the duration of this segment of treatment is entirely dependent on the mutual consideration and collaboration of the therapist and client. An excellent example of this process is seen when psychopharmacology is included in the client's treatment plan. Medical model prescriptive behaviors typically default to an attitude of "I'm the doctor, and I know best," offering a paucity of client education or potential objection. In CBT treatment plans, the objectives of the medication are well understood by clients, including the key knowledge of what's in it for them. This results in client ownership of medication compliance and greatly enhances the likelihood that treatment will be effective.

Fourth and last, the therapist conducts *functional assessment on an ongoing basis* for three purposes: (a) to determine whether the plan is proving to be effective, (b) to keep the therapist and the client accountable to the therapeutic contract, and (c) to revise the contract as necessary. As noted above, this process is often iteratively sequenced in conjunction with strategy implementation (third process); that is, as clients practice, become proficient in, and utilize skills, they are asked to provide information about both their progress (mastery and utilization of skills) and any symptom changes during their sessions. If the intervention is successful, the client and therapist may agree to continue the strategy, possibly strengthen their efforts to enhance this desired effect, or refocus their efforts on another treatment target.

If the intervention is not helpful, the therapist should offer adjustments to the implementation strategy, revision of the treatment plan, and/or troubleshooting of the functional model. This can involve situations in which negative client and/or therapist reactions may occur. For example, clients may report that the intervention brought about an *increase* in symptoms. These occurrences, when addressed by making use of the collaborative therapeutic alliance, are ironically sometimes of more value than easily mastered treatments, because they invariably provide helpful information for revising and refining the functional assessment and treatment plan. If symptoms can be exacerbated by skill use, then they can also be ameliorated by skill use. For example, if increasing one's activity level (e.g., for the purposes of alleviating depressive symptoms) results in too much stress, paring down one's responsibilities to a manageable level may be an appropriate stress-reduction intervention. In this regard, CBT therapists should reframe any reference to "treatment failures." In short, engaging in the process of CBT is, in its own right, successful treatment because it enables the therapist and client to work collaboratively, testing hypotheses and gathering information regardless of the outcomes of the particular technique. Finally, when the therapeutic objectives have been achieved, the therapist and client may choose to identify new targets or to terminate treatment. In either case, the client has learned skills that resulted in his or her ability to more effectively manage situations that at the onset of treatment were perceived to be problematic, thus enhancing the client's positive perceived sense of control.

Now that we have provided an overview of the underlying theory and essential elements of CBT psychotherapeutic process, we turn our attention toward an exploration of the rich but not commonly discussed relational framework that is inherent to the practice of CBT.

CBT: A RICH RELATIONAL FRAMEWORK

Regardless of the model on which a therapist bases his or her interventions, psychotherapy can be a challenging and sometimes difficult process. In CBT, the functional analysis and behavioral formulation of presenting problems depend on the client's motivation to disclose potentially shameful information to a therapist. Furthermore, the implementation of any plan for behavior change is inevitably fraught with complexity and ambivalence. Some behavioral interventions in particular, such as exposure, necessitate that clients remain in anxiety-provoking situations for extended periods of time, thus requiring even more motivation, as well as trust. It is therefore recognized that a strong client–therapist relationship is not only recommended but also, from our perspective, required to gain traction. It is with no hyperbole that we state the following: *The degree to which CBT therapists can navigate interpersonal interactions with clients successfully is a principal determinant for increasing client motivation that will result in positive treatment outcomes (i.e., improved functioning and symptom reduction)*. Thus, client–therapist relationships are viewed as a vital prerequisite for CBT.

The following clinical example may seem self-evident but was quite instructive for the therapist involved. A 23-year-old woman was brought to therapy by her concerned parents. On the surface, the client appeared to be an ideal treatment candidate (e.g., the proverbial "YAVIS" client: young, attractive, verbal, intelligent, and social). Coupled with the fact that the therapist was an experienced and skilled CBT practitioner, it appeared that it would be just a matter of time before a productive therapeutic alliance was achieved. Unfortunately, such an outcome never occurred. Why, you ask? In the first session, the client started by saying she would be happy to answer any of the therapist's questions but that she had absolutely no interest in engaging in psychotherapy. Undaunted, the therapist completed what she felt to be a very productive 50-minute first interview, at the end of which the client repeated, "I have no interest to engage in psychotherapy." Over two subsequent, seemingly cooperative sessions, although the therapist used every skill in her professional repertoire, each session was prefaced and postscripted with the client saying, "I have absolutely no interest to engage in psychotherapy." The therapist finally "heard" the client, and further efforts to engage her were terminated. This is an obvious example of the importance of motivation in the therapeutic process: Although all the components for a constructive therapy appeared to be in place, the client was not having any of it.

Consistent with this perspective, strategies to enhance and increase motivation are now integral to the clinical practice of CBT. For example, Miller and Rollnick's (2002) seminal work on motivational interviewing developed and advocated for the use of these client-centered approaches within CBT. These strategies include but are not limited to open-ended questions, affirmations, reflective listening, and summary reflective statements. CBT therapists should consider these strategies as comprising an integral component of all CBT interventions. Furthermore, such strategies facilitate the development of clients' self-attributed investment in the therapy. Again, CBT is a collaborative process. Clients are not merely recipients of treatment; they are expected and encouraged to take ownership of the process. Even the most motivated client will experience some level of ambivalence when coming face to face with change. Hence, the importance of addressing motivation is a key element of CBT.

From the vantage point of CBT treatment, its models of both the etiology and the amelioration (or exacerbation) of symptoms are contained within learning theory; thus, the client–therapist relationship by itself is not a sine qua non for change. It is instead viewed as a tool to enlist the necessary motivation to facilitate functional analytic assessments, negotiation of treatment contracts and plans, provision of education and training in skill acquisition, and compliance with treatment. Put differently, the therapeutic alliance within the context of CBT is not seen to be an end in and of itself; instead, it serves to assist in the information-gathering process, establish the beginnings of client ownership of the treatment that will carry the client through the challenging components of treatment, increase treatment adherence, and prevent premature termination. Whereas some other modalities view the therapeutic alliance as being reparative, in CBT it is a foundation on which to address the cognitive and behavioral factors that proximally and functionally relate to the presenting problem. Therapeutic relationships in CBT provide an important sample of the client's interpersonal functioning, which can inform case conceptualization and treatment planning (Goldfried & Davison, 1976). In this regard, the therapeutic relationship can serve as a catalyst for change inasmuch as it can help facilitate execution of treatment. Thus, CBT therapists practice and utilize relational strategies as the platform on which to build the client's ownership of treatment, therefore facilitating the therapeutic process and outcome.

In regard to the importance of the therapeutic alliance, the field of psychotherapy has historically dichotomized between psychodynamic and client-centered approaches, which focus on the process factors (e.g., transference, therapeutic alliance), and behavioral approaches, which focus on content factors (e.g., techniques). We believe that this dichotomy may be relevant when distinguishing the therapeutic process seen in controlled outcome research; however, when it comes to using CBT and most of the behavior therapy approaches with clients in real-world settings, the dichotomy is essentially nothing more than urban legend. The nature of the therapeutic method in a CBT framework—from a mutually convened assessment process to a collaborative treatment agreement—is highly relational.

It logically follows that inherent to CBT is a capacity to increase clients' self-motivated agenda to participate in a constructive process that can prevent them from having negative therapeutic reactions. That capacity provides therapists with strategies to deal with any such reactions and offers them tools to manage any negative reactions that may be engendered in their clients. Active client involvement is viewed as both essential to the treatment process and critical to treatment outcomes. Although CBT therapists do not scrutinize moment-to-moment changes in therapist and client affect, their focus on the content of treatment sessions does not mean that CBT is less relational than other forms of psychotherapy. CBT's continual focus on change in a positive, upbeat, and forward-thinking manner provides a normative and uncontrived method of navigating negative emotional experiences of both the client and the therapist.

CBT depends heavily on a mutually respectful and professional relationship in the context of psychotherapy. Perhaps the most important premises behind the therapeutic approach of CBT is that clients have the *capacity* to change and that they can be *contributing agents* of change. Cognitive–behavioral case formulations favor dimensional conceptualizations of psychopathology, which identify symptoms within specific contexts. For example, the occurrence of panic attacks or periods of depression, as well as time- and situation-specific responses that are maladaptive (i.e., ways of coping that make life harder than it needs to be), in which all human beings engage from time to time, are identified and targeted. Even self-injury, promiscuity, and substance dependence are viewed from a standpoint of maladaptive behavior patterns that clients can change.

Similarly, CBT therapists view functional impairment (i.e., the consequences of symptoms for one's life) and distress (i.e., subjective perception of symptoms) as far more clinically salient than the mere presence of symptoms, or even the severity of symptoms. CBT is thus unique in that both the definition of problems and the process of treatment are a collaborative process (Heinssen, Levendusky, & Hunter, 1995). Behavioral models of the etiology of mental illness routinely postulate that the existence or experience of distress in and of itself is part and parcel of the human condition and that client *reactions to distress* are what contribute more to the exacerbation and maintenance of psychopathology. The collaborative framework of CBT is an embodiment of these fundamental notions, which can be boiled down to the following statement: We believe that, with the therapist's collaborative assistance, clients can develop adaptive distress-reducing skills. This perspective helps defuse negative therapist reactions to frustrations that can sometimes be generated by a client's inability to make full use of the therapeutic process. No learning occurs without occasional setbacks or the need to recalibrate the treatment contract.

To this end, CBT therapists assume that clients have the unique capacity to reach beyond their comfort zone and engage in giving as well as taking, by engaging and contributing to treatment in a collaborative and professional manner. Accountability is a key, unspoken element of treatment. Furthermore, the therapeutic contract that binds both client and therapist to a predefined agreement is integral to the practice of CBT. Thus, from the onset of treatment, clients are expected to provide feedback and participate in negotiation. The contractual nature of treatment in and of itself necessitates development of expectations and provides a forum for clients to address the matter directly when therapist conduct or anticipated results are not deemed up to par.

Clients are also expected to set priorities for their treatment, and these are not, as often seen in medically modeled approaches, set by the treatment provider alone. Furthermore, given the emphasis on collaboration, CBT uniquely supports upbeat, playful, respectful, and encouraging human interactions. Clients and therapists banter in negotiating the therapeutic contract and throughout treatment. In an ideal state of affairs, setbacks (e.g., client noncompliance with the treatment plan) are met with a pleasant demeanor, possibly humor, and an agenda to get back to track. Thus, CBT provides a truly rich relational framework, which empowers clients to engage in real-life interpersonal interactions in the context of treatment. Although this collaborative problem-solving dialogue does not eliminate the possibility of negative client or therapist reactions, it sets the tone for the resolution of any such reactions.

That self-awareness is irrelevant to the practice of CBT is a misconception. In fact, the most ardent behaviorists in the field today emphasize the importance of maintaining acute awareness of client–therapist interactions. For example, functional analytic psychotherapy (Kohlenberg & Tsai, 1991), dubbed *FAP* for short, is based on the principles of radical (Skinnerian) behaviorism and emphasizes reinforcement and extinction contingencies of reward and punishment that occur in the therapeutic context during treatment sessions, more so than between-session experiences (e.g., encounters with family members) or progress (e.g., homework). FAP therapists are trained to identify and modify client–therapist interactions that constitute manifestations of both adaptive and maladaptive intra- and interpersonal processes (Kanter, Tsai, & Kohlenberg, 2010; Kohlenberg, Kanter, Bolling, Parker, & Tsai, 2002). These interactions, which are referred to as *clinically relevant behaviors* (CRBs), are classically divided into two categories: (a) CRB1s, which are instances of problem behaviors, such as negative statements about the self or failure to disclose pertinent information, and (b) CRB2s, which involve instances of alternative, adaptive behaviors (i.e., client improvement), such as realistic self-affirming statements, and appropriate disclosure and interaction with the therapist.

The mainstay of FAP involves maintaining awareness of CRBs and shaping these in-session behaviors with immediate, natural contingencies. That is, therapists seek to reinforce adaptive and functional behaviors and extinguish maladaptive ones. For example, an FAP therapist treating a histrionic young woman who displays flirtatious or overdramatic behavior in session (CRB1s) may ignore these cues or may prompt the client (verbally or otherwise) to utilize more effective ways to express herself if they persist (Busch, Dubois, & VanRullen, 2009). Conversely, an FAP therapist whose socially anxious client makes himself vulnerable to shame within the session by sharing that he feels a sense of hurt (CRB2s) may be reinforced with praise, reciprocal genuineness, or even self-disclosure, if appropriate (Busch et al., 2009). We should note that because the ultimate goal of FAP is to generalize treatment gains to clients' lives outside of sessions, reinforcement is natural and genuine and maps closely onto what may be experienced in nontherapeutic relationships. It goes without saying that this necessitates an extremely high level of awareness of both the client's and the therapist's emotional experiences during psychotherapy; that is, FAP requires the perpetual observation of every exchange of statements and nonverbal cues in session, as well as their purposeful utilization to bring about more effective patterns of communication and engagement. This is an example of self-awareness within a therapeutic modality that can directly address the therapist's negative reaction to the client.

Although FAP represents a unique approach within the CBT tradition, the prominence of self-awareness and the utilization of therapeutic interactions as a catalyst for change are found throughout the various schools of CBT philosophy. In particular, Third Wave CBT approaches, such as DBT (Linehan, 1993) and acceptance and commitment therapy (Hayes et al., 2003), explicitly emphasize client–therapist relationship factors as primary in treatment and serve as models to constructively address therapists' negative reactions to their clients. In treating clients with borderline personality disorder or other difficult-to-treat populations, DBT therapists are encouraged to maintain particular awareness of treatment-interfering behaviors, such as threatening, belittling, or bullying remarks; persistent lateness or absences from session; and failure to pay therapy fees in a timely manner. In fact, such behaviors are the first order of business in DBT (barring imminent safety concerns) and are even given priority over adherence to the treatment plan (e.g., completion of homework).

In this regard, behavioral observations in the process of treatment are an indispensable part of the assessment process. They provide real-time, in vivo examples of effective and problematic behaviors and shed immense light onto factors that may perpetuate and exacerbate the client's presenting problems. More important, DBT views shaping as occurring in the treatment context to be both integral to treatment and reparative in and of itself. Clients' behaviors are addressed (i.e., reinforced, not responded to or punished) contextually to provide natural consequences that shape behavior and directly facilitate change.

In more traditional forms of CBT, noncompliance with between-session therapeutic assignments can result in the therapist experiencing negative feelings toward the client. To address these, the therapist may utilize "mock exasperation" to bring compliance and motivation into the focus of clinical attention, by stating the following:

> I'm feeling frustrated that you haven't done your homework in three weeks. Is this a good exercise for you? If so, what can we do to help you to complete it? If not, let's revisit our treatment plan and try to figure out what might be a better set of targets at the present time,

or "Let's predict what excuses you'll be using next week for not completing your assignments." The use of relationship factors and reminders to clients about the "what's in it for them" goals of therapy can facilitate revisions to the treatment plan, including targeting successively smaller steps or targeting secondary factors that complicate compliance (e.g., stress level, lack of energy, or cognitive barriers). Relationship factors further help the therapist to impart to clients the message that the treatment process is ultimately within their own control because they have the choice of whether to participate. For example, a client comment such as "I can't do it" can be productively reframed as "You choose not to do it." Here, the therapeutic relationship is serving as a direct stimulus to observe and change behavior. Thus, the processes of self-awareness in CBT are directly parallel to interpersonal interactions outside of a therapeutic context.

An additional point worth discussing is the role of compassion in the process of CBT. Some have pointed to extreme emotional reactions of clients in the process of habituation to anxious stimuli, stating that such treatments are cruel. Such criticisms are not unique to CBT. Exposure-based therapies for symptoms of specific phobias, obsessive–compulsive disorder, and posttraumatic stress disorder all involve in vivo approaching of a feared object or situation, which commonly elicits high levels of fear in clients (and sometimes therapists as well) during a session. For example, a client who was viciously stabbed with a knife by an assailant may be encouraged to create a vivid audio recording in which he recounts in gory detail the events of the attack and then replays the recording each day for a specified period of time. Clients' affect during such exposures is often apparent and may include crying, wincing, shaking/trembling, hyperventilating, closing of the eyes, and, in rare situations, gagging (though vomiting is extremely uncommon). To the outside observer, such treatments may seem cruel and lacking in compassion. The implementation of such therapeutic techniques can often lead to negative reactions for the therapist, such as "I'm being cruel" or "I'm supposed to be helping, not harming"; however, the intention behind these evidence-based methods is to help clients achieve their therapeutic objectives.

CBT therapists recognize that the research on the efficacy and effectiveness of exposure-based strategies is unparalleled in the combined fields of mental health treatments (let alone psychotherapy), and they use such approaches as a way to help clients overcome pervasive and debilitating symptoms. CBT therapists must be ardent proponents of following through with a treatment strategy as planned and not changing on the fly in the face of emotional shifts (negative or positive). That is, therapists should encourage clients who have decided to engage in a given strategy to continue with their plan regardless of how they feel at the moment. CBT practitioners do not "let the client off" from a therapeutic exercise because the client sends cues that can elicit an emotional response in the therapist (e.g., crying, joking, reporting innocuous physical symptoms, acting seductively at the start of a preplanned exercise during a session).

Here again compassion is readily apparent: CBT therapists set aside their personal preferences for momentary peace, tranquillity, or conflict avoidance for the sake of what is best for the client. Conversely, it is possible that failing to encourage a client to engage in a painful activity that is known to be helpful could be tantamount to selfishness on the part of the therapist. This is not to suggest the therapy plan should not be altered or modified on the basis of a client's negative reaction, but such change must occur in the context of the mutually agreed-on treatment plan, not in reaction to avoiding the potential generation of a negative client or therapist reaction. Furthermore, readers must recognize that CBT therapists routinely engage in exposure exercises alongside their clients. For example, in treating a client with symptoms of obsessive–compulsive disorder, including a persistent fear of ingesting germs, a CBT therapist may consume food that has been placed on a public restroom floor together with a client. Similarly, to help a client overcome a fear of spiders, a CBT therapist may need to allow a big, hairy tarantula (perhaps even several such creatures) to crawl on his or her torso.

Such challenging acts of compassion, which often are readily apparent in CBT contexts, require CBT therapists to put aside their personal preferences for the sake of helping a client. Given the intensity of such exposure techniques, a cardinal rule that therapists must follow is to maintain a commitment to implement the preestablished treatment plan and avoid impulsive changes to it in response the their own negative reactions.

An excellent example of this was experienced by a therapist in the context of completing a client's treatment of acrophobia. Although the client was pleased with her success in mastering challenges with heights of local buildings, her ultimate goal was to go to the top of the Sears Tower in Chicago. In the spirit of assisting the achievement of this lofty goal, the therapist agreed to accompany the client even in the face of his own fear of heights. Though this was unintended, the client interpreted these efforts as role play and modeling when the therapist proved to be a very reluctant participant in taking an elevator ride to the top of one of the world's tallest buildings.

IMPLICATIONS FOR TRAINING AND SUPERVISION

Over the last 10 years, there has been an increase in opportunities for young clinicians to receive training in CBT. This presents an interesting challenge for those of us who participate in the clinical supervision of these budding CBT therapists. With the ongoing generation of robust empirical support for CBT psychotherapy techniques, there is now a tendency for graduate programs to place heavy emphasis on providing students with clinical training experiences that focus on these techniques. As one of our recent psychology interns reported, "In graduate school, my program provided me with training in a wide variety of empirically supported treatments." He went on to add, "But the problem is that here at the hospital I've never been assigned a client who fits the definition of the clients I was trained to treat. They have too many things wrong with them." He later suggested that the participants in empirically supported treatment studies bore little resemblance to the complex comorbid cases assigned to him during internship (Hufford, 2000).

There clearly is much to be gained by young clinicians who are learning the nuts and bolts of empirically supported treatments, particularly in the earlier stages of training. As they mature into sophisticated clinicians, however, their training should be supplemented with sufficient supervisory opportunities to learn how to adapt treatment models to the specific needs of the clients they are serving. This is no small task for clinical educators. Although its importance must be emphasized, consistent technical application must be accompanied by an awareness of individual client difference, not only in the realm of cultural and racial diversity but also in the client's priorities and values. In short, there is a balance between acknowledging the young clinicians' need for their own perceived sense of control and at the same time recognizing the critical importance of fostering treatment protocols that address the prioritized needs of clients to improve their capacity to better manage their problematic life circumstances. In other words, clinical educators must help young clinicians to overcome the "if you have a hammer, the world looks like a nail" dilemma and expand their therapy comfort zone.

An approach that we have found to be valuable for our trainees is to demonstrate to them the distinction between *evidence-based practice* and *practice-based evidence*. The former often places an emphasis on the pre-eminence of the techniques, whereas the latter fosters an integration of the clinician's understanding of a client's needs with any necessary modifications in clinical interventions to assure an optimal treatment outcome. This is not an altogether different challenge than that faced by today's commercial airplane pilots. Too much dependence on technology can blunt their piloting skills, which can result in tragic outcomes. In short, misuse is never an argument for disuse. CBT technical proficiency should have a high priority in training young clinicians, but at the same time educators should recognize that this skill training must be augmented with supervisory experiences that allow trainees to learn how to apply clinical interventions in a manner that emphasizes the importance of client participation and collaboration in the treatment planning and implementation processes.

The supervision and training of CBT therapists is not entirely different from the psychotherapeutic process itself. Here, too, it is assumed that burgeoning CBT psychotherapists are inherently capable of success but deficient in the necessary therapeutic skills. Admittedly, a therapist learning to implement CBT may at first seem like an automaton. It is very common for nascent CBT therapists to learn their practices from treatment manuals and to apply treatment strategies literally from the book. Similarly, learning almost any new skill—riding a bicycle, playing piano, and so on—typically involves a period of stiffness and rote replication of standard protocols. If one sets aside the "see one, do one, teach one" training model, one realizes that the nature of any complex human capability is inherently difficult to describe and implement without substantial practice. We have found that, with supervision, trainees learn to master the behavioral principles that lie behind the techniques referenced in CBT treatment manuals and then eventually learn to implement a diverse set of strategies in a natural, flowing manner in the course of psychotherapy. Most important, trainees also learn over time to recognize that there are many factors in addition to technique content that influence effectiveness of treatment and, further, that there are limitations to the extant literature on CBT, which is based primarily on the utilization of manualized treatments within specific populations of interest.

CBT training almost always involves striving toward achievement in areas of core competency. For example, in regard to assessment, trainees may be expected to conduct a functional assessment of a client's symptoms, identify realistic and appropriate targets for treatment, devise a treatment hierarchy for such targets, formulate cases in behavioral terms (i.e., discuss contingencies of reinforcement that shape the maladaptive strategies the client is using), determine the functional impairment of a client's symptoms, reformulate cases as new information arises in the course of treatment, and engage in planning for treatment termination. In regard to treatment, expectations may include the ability to provide psychoeducation to clients about the etiology of symptoms using CBT models; to gain knowledge of specific strategies, such as interoceptive exposures (desensitization to physical sensations, a technique commonly used in the context of panic disorder treatment); to chain analyses (identify contextual factors contributing to a single problematic event); to use motivation enhancement; and to appropriately use such strategies depending on symptom presentation and context.

Furthermore, and more important, therapists must be trained not simply in technical proficiency but also in the appropriate interpersonal delivery of CBT strategies that ultimately increase client participation and improve outcomes. This allows therapists to offer the highest quality care and keeps their morale high so they will be able to respond more productively to any negative reactions toward clients that occur over the course of their career.

CASE EXAMPLE

The case example we offer illustrates how an empirically supported CBT treatment plan, judged to be an ideal strategy to assist a highly motivated client achieve his primary treatment objective, proved to be ineffective. It also demonstrates that, over the course of therapy, the prioritization of treatment objectives may change as a result of the success, or lack thereof, of the CBT interventions. In addition, this case example shows how the evolution of the treatment plan depended on a productive therapeutic relationship.

Mr. T was a self-referred, 32-year-old, Caucasian male college graduate. At the time of intake, he was 75 lb (34 kg) overweight; 5 feet, 7 inches (170 cm) tall; depressed; socially isolated; and unhappy with his career as a chemical engineer. Though dressed in his typically somewhat disheveled manner, he was reasonably well groomed and good-naturedly described himself as being "kind of a dorky nerd." Mr. T sought therapeutic assistance with his almost sole goal of learning how to better control his obesity. Having done homework to determine the best option to achieve this objective, he opted to work with a therapist who was proficient in what Mr. T referred to as "behavior modification." He viewed his depression, social isolation, and vocation dissatisfaction as relatively inconsequential issues that were "just part of who I am."

During two intake sessions Mr. T was very cooperative, articulate, and single-minded, and he appeared to be motivated. The therapist was a well-trained CBT practitioner with considerable experience treating clients with the issues presented by Mr. T. There was good rapport between Mr. T and the therapist, and they agreed to implement a one-session-per-week treatment plan in which they would use empirically supported behavior therapy techniques that were judged to be an ideal strategy to help Mr. T meet his weight loss objective.

Soon after the initiation of therapy, however, it became very evident that Mr. T's depression was much more severe than he had initially reported. In fact, it was clear that his mood issues might well compromise his ability to optimally participate in the agreed-on treatment. In hindsight, the therapist would realize that the almost-total focus on weight during the intake had distracted him from completing a thorough assessment of Mr. T's depression and other related issues. In the second therapy session, Mr. T completed the Beck Depression Inventory (BDI; A. T. Beck, Ward, Mendelson, Mock, & Erbaugh, 1961) and, much to the therapist's surprise, his score was 35 (indicating severe depression). In subsequent sessions, Mr. T's BDI scores were in the 27–35 range. Mr. T did not experience his mood as dystonic, even while reporting substantial neurovegetative symptoms. He was very fond of saying "It's just who I am." In other words, Mr. T's focus on weight loss was accompanied by an almost complete denial of his depression or other problems. Even in the face of this denial, the therapist insisted that Mr. T participate in a psychopharmacology consultation. Mr. T responded to this suggestion by saying that the therapist was "giving up on him" and that therefore he must be a "real basket case."

Although initially taken aback by the intensity of Mr. T's affect, the therapist reframed the consultation recommendation by explaining that an improved mood would better allow him to achieve his weight loss goal. Unfortunately, when Mr. T was offered a prescription for an SSRI antidepressant he refused to fill it and said that needing drugs proved how "hopeless" he was. Again using restructuring, the therapist reframed the negative cognitions about medication using a biopsychosocial model; Mr. T was told that medication could best be viewed as a strategy to enhance the likelihood that an improved mood would allow him to have more success in participating in the proposed treatment plan. It also proved helpful to emphasize that the prescribing physician and the therapist had closely consulted and that both considered the medication to be a strategy that would help Mr. T achieve his treatment objectives. In short, the therapist pointed out that there was something in it for Mr. T. The therapist augmented this approach with the introduction of CBT interventions that addressed treatment compliance both for Mr. T's between-session cognitive therapy assignments and for his medication adherence.

Mr. T proved to be very adept at using the CBT techniques. Twelve weeks into treatment, his BDI score had dropped to the 8–11 range, and concurrently he was more actively participating in the recommended weight management protocol. These techniques of the protocol were tried-and-true strategies designed to help him moderate caloric intake, increase exercise, and maintain appropriate weight monitoring. In addition, the therapist imparted the message that with treatment compliance, Mr. T would surely achieve his goal; however, despite reporting a high level of such compliance, his efforts resulted in an average weight loss of only 0.25 to 0.50 lb/week (0.11–0.23 kg/week), well below the 2.0 lb/week (0.91 kg/week) target.

After 16 weeks of therapy, Mr. T and the therapist agreed to revisit the treatment contract. Mr. T reported some satisfaction with his improved mood but was very disappointed with the results of his weight loss efforts. Given that weight had essentially been the sole treatment objective, both he and the therapist experienced a significant level of frustration even in the face of the impressive success in managing the depression.

The course of this treatment was clearly having its ups and downs. The therapist's frustration was most often triggered by Mr. T's feelings of failure because the weight management techniques had such limited results, and Mr. T often trivialized the progress that was being made with his depression. To deal with this frustration, the therapist opted for using a strategy that focused on Mr. T's accomplishments instead of engaging in a shared lament over what had not yet been achieved. This is a variant on the operant conditioning premise that reinforcement is, by definition, designed to increase the frequency of targeted behaviors, which in this case would be progress made, rather than to inadvertently reinforce nonproductive "verbal behaviors" (e.g., Mr. T's increasing reports of feeling a sense of failure). The therapist determined that, for both Mr. T's and his own best interest, it would be most productive to use the essentially simple CBT technique of focusing on the half-full glass rather than the half-empty one. Expressing a continued commitment to help Mr. T achieve his weight goal, the therapist also suggested that Mr. T's improved mood was a substantial accomplishment and would serve as the foundation on which to implement treatment strategies to productively address his other issues (i.e., social isolation and career dissatisfaction).

At this critical point, Mr. T agreed to remain in therapy but with a reprioritized focus on social isolation. His decision was not a caving in to the therapist's wishes but instead was based on an increased awareness that these problems did negatively affect him. Mr. T reported feeling more in control of his mood (his BDI scores continued to remain in the 6–12 range), and with this improvement his concerns about social isolation had become more salient. Although he had earlier reported feelings of social isolation, it was only at this stage that he experienced social isolation as a problem. He reflected that, when depressed, he did not even notice there were few people in his life; neither did he care. He evidenced a very limited social repertoire, had few friends, and had never dated. The treatment used to address these deficits were behavior therapy techniques such as social and communications skills training, in vivo exposure, and anxiety management.

Mr. T's continued disappointment with his limited weight loss sometimes interfered with progress addressing the social isolation, because his weight exacerbated his low self-esteem. The therapist introduced CBT to address the esteem and self-confidence issues. Given Mr. T's strong motivation and treatment compliance, the behavior therapy was judged as having a high probability of success, with the goal of allowing him to build momentum in the wake of each small success. Mr. T learned basic communication and social skills through a combination of in-office role playing augmented with between-session assignments designed to help him practice the newly developed skills in a progression of increasingly complex social interactions. This hierarchical approach increased his ability to manage his social anxiety while practicing his evolving social competencies. This strategy worked very well and was later augmented with additional CBT techniques designed to further improve Mr. T's self-esteem along with developing internal causal attributions for his growing social success.

Over the course of the next 25 weeks, this treatment strategy helped Mr. T resolve his lifelong social isolation problem. He went from completely avoiding social situations to participating in a very active social life. Of special note is that although he had never dated, he soon was able to establish productive relationships and eventually met the woman he would ultimately marry and have a child with.

This focus on social isolation was intended to provide Mr. T with strategies to address the problem by introducing a treatment strategy that could be paced in small, incremental, and likely successful steps. This allowed him to build on a growing sense of self-confidence generated by the success he had dealing with his depression. This was far more productive than allowing the treatment to languish in the context of the limited weight loss progress. The strategy would prove to serve both Mr. T and the therapist well. At the time of this treatment refocus, both client and therapist were very frustrated. The therapist had become increasingly skeptical of the client's treatment compliance assertions, and this led to a growing concern that he was intentionally undermining the treatment and not being candid about it.

The therapist's repeated and somewhat accusatory efforts to determine why the therapy was not working resulted in a slow erosion of the positive therapeutic relationship that had developed. Finally, the therapist became frustrated with his own negative self-statements (e.g., "I've done everything I can do to help this guy lose weight—it's got to be his fault the treatment isn't working"). Acknowledging to himself that these derogatory self-statements aimed at the client had the potential to be exceptionally countertherapeutic, the therapist recognized the necessity of reevaluating the treatment plan, especially in the context of the weight loss goal. The therapist recommended a more constructive alternative to the strategy being used to address this issue: He and Mr. T would try a back-to-basics strategy in order to better understand the limited weight loss results, and they would continue to focus on the productive efforts being used to improve Mr. T's depression, self-esteem, and social skill deficits. Starting with a review of Mr. T's record, the therapist soon realized that his initial intake evaluation had been flawed. Instead of using his typical multidimensional assessment strategy, he had opted for a shortcut and focused the initial evaluation and functional analysis on Mr. T's one stated goal, weight loss. This was especially humbling because the therapist took pride in really getting to know his clients.

Such was not the case with Mr. T, because the therapist had been single-minded in responding to his intense need for an immediate remedy for his obesity. In short, the therapist really knew the symptom, but he didn't know the person. Although he acknowledged that Mr. T's insistence may have contributed to this gaffe, the therapist also recognized that his comfort with a favored treatment technique distracted him from gathering client information that might have led him in a different direction. After all, this proposed treatment had substantial empirical support, and the client was desperate for a cure. Had the therapist taken extra time during intake, he might have uncovered, among other important details, the critical fact that Mr. T's maternal and paternal sides of his family were fraught with examples of severe obesity, diabetes, and heart disease. It is not that the question was not asked—it was, but in a cursory manner that elicited Mr. T's offhand response of "Everybody's fat these days."

Sharing the shortcomings of his intake and initial treatment plan resulted in a very positive response from the client and helped revitalize the therapeutic relationship. One could argue, from a readiness-for-change perspective, that Mr. T was initially looking for a quick fix and was not interested in being more forthcoming about his family history of obesity. We will never know because the therapist, although he had the best intentions, did not really provide the client with an opportunity to participate in a comprehensive assessment but rather succumbed to his own desire to provide the quick fix.

Needless to say, once armed with this added background information the therapist was better able to work with Mr. T in reframing and reprioritizing the treatment strategies. Shifting from the "Of course you can lose weight if you just try hard enough" perspective to a more biopsychosocial model proved to be the turning point in therapy. Realizing that there likely were genetic barriers to even moderate weight loss proved helpful to Mr. T; however, of more value was the fact that this perspective allowed him to reprioritize his treatment objectives and focus on goals that he would more likely achieve. Therefore, depression, social isolation, and vocational dissatisfaction took on the highest priority, and weight loss became a secondary issue. Also, Mr. T was not interested in following the therapist's suggestion to perhaps seek other medical options for his weight loss and decided instead to pursue more modest lifestyle goals, such as eating better quality food and engaging in regular exercise. If such a biopsychosocial model had been used at the beginning of therapy, would Mr. T have been able to use it to help him reprioritize his initial treatment goal? Given the severity of his depression, our guess is probably not, but here, too, we will never know.

On the heels of successfully dealing with his depression and social isolation, Mr. T asked that his vocational situation become the focus of the revised treatment contract. Hence, career became the new priority for the therapy, while efforts to help him maintain progress towards mood stabilization, social skill development, and achieving target weight continued. The strategy used to address the vocational issue focused on CBT approaches complemented with career interest and skill assessment. Here, too, Mr. T used his treatment in a very productive fashion. He eventually made the decision to leave his engineering job to pursue longtime interests in conflict resolution and problem solving. Although it might seem like an oxymoron, he decided to pursue these interests by attending law school! After 18 months of treatment, and by invitation, the therapist attended Mr. T's wedding, and soon thereafter they mutually agreed to terminate therapy when Mr. T moved out of the area to pursue his legal education.

As readers might conclude, Mr. T was very pleased with the results of his treatment efforts and readily acknowledged that he had much pride in what he had accomplished. Although his first top-priority goal was never fully achieved, the therapy served him well. One of his most telling comments, made on the eve of termination, was what an important lesson it was for him to learn that even if efforts to control a problematic situation did not achieve expectations, they could serve as the genesis of learning to manage other problems that may have been exacerbated by the "priority" problem. Mr. T's obesity no doubt negatively influenced his mood, social life, and career, but not fully achieving the weight loss objective did not deter him from successfully resolving these important issues.

As a final note, several years after the termination of therapy, Mr. T scheduled a follow-up with his therapist. Given that they had kept in touch informally over the years, the therapist was aware of the client's marital stability and many professional successes. The really surprising feature of the in-person visit was the fact that Mr. T had lost 75 lb (34 kg). When asked how he had finally succeeded, he replied, "I took control of what I couldn't and decided to have gastrointestinal bypass surgery."

CONCLUSION

It is fair to say that the literature on empirically supported treatments offers little to suggest that the client–therapist relationship plays an important role in the actual practice of CBT. A notable exception can be found in Castonguay, Constantino, McAleavey, and Goldfried's (2010) article, in which they reviewed the research on the role of the therapeutic alliance in CBT. There is also a paucity of literature that helps inform CBT clinicians about how to integrate these validated treatments into strategies that can assist clients with comorbid diagnostic profiles (i.e., the clients typically seen in real-life practice). However, readers should not conclude that the therapeutic relationship is an inconsequential factor in CBT or that clients with complicated diagnoses cannot be effectively treated with it. Applying CBT techniques without integrating the facilitative aspects of the therapeutic relationship is like clapping with one hand. Motivation is a critical variable in the successful use of CBT, along with the clients' ownership of both the treatment goals and the techniques intended to assist them in achieving their objectives. We hope this chapter has convincingly conveyed the perspective that CBT practice efficiency is potentiated by the therapeutic relationship and that this can best be accomplished by therapists who prioritize the integration of the described relational context into their practice.

Many years ago, a mentor asserted that "if a client fails to improve, don't blame the patient; it is always the therapist's responsibility." The initial reaction to that assertion was to conclude that of course it is incumbent on the therapist to find the most effective technique. Today, after years of practice, there is recognition that this is only part of the answer and that it is equally if not more important that the therapist constructively and thoughtfully manage the therapeutic relationship to ensure that the CBT interventions achieve their potential. The full efficacy of CBT cannot be achieved otherwise.

REFERENCES

Barlow, D. H. (2004). *Anxiety and its disorders: The nature and treatment of anxiety and panic*. New York, NY: Guilford Press.

Beck, A. T. (1975). *Cognitive therapy and the emotional disorders*. New York, NY: International Universities Press.

Beck, A. T., Ward, C. H., Mendelson, M., Mock, J., & Erbaugh, J. (1961). An inventory for measuring depression. *Archives of General Psychiatry, 4*, 561–571.

Beck, J. S. (1995). *Cognitive therapy: Basics and beyond*. New York, NY: Guilford Press.

Busch, N. A., Dubois, J., & VanRullen, R. (2009). The phase of ongoing EEG oscillations predicts visual perception. *Journal of Neuroscience, 29*, 7869–7876. doi:10.1523/JNEUROSCI.0113-09.2009

Castonguay, L. G., Constantino, M. J., McAleavey, A. A., & Goldfried, M. R. (2010). The alliance in cognitive-behavioral therapy. In J. C. Muran & J. P. Barber (Eds.), *The therapeutic alliance: An evidence-based approach to practice and training* (pp. 150–171). New York, NY: Guilford Press.

Ellis, A., & Harper, R. A. (1975). *A new guide to rational living*. North Hollywood, CA: Wilshire.

Foa, E. B., & Kozak, M. J. (1986). Emotional processing of fear: Exposure to corrective information. *Psychological Bulletin, 99*, 20–35. doi:10.1037/0033-2909.99.1.20

Goldapple, K., Segal, Z., Garson, C., Lau, M., Bieling, P., Kennedy, S., & Mayberg, H. (2004). Modulation of cortical-limbic pathways in major depression. *Archives of General Psychiatry, 61*, 34–41. doi:10.1001/archpsyc.61.1.34

Goldfried, M. R., & Davison, G. C. (1976). *Clinical behavior therapy*. New York, NY: Holt, Rinehart & Winston.

Hayes, S. C., Strosahl, K., & Wilson, K. G. (2003). *Acceptance and commitment therapy*. New York, NY: Guilford Press.

Heinssen, R. K., Levendusky, P. G., & Hunter, R. H. (1995). Client as colleague: Therapeutic contracting with the seriously mentally ill. *American Psychologist, 50*, 522–532. doi:10.1037/0003-066X.50.7.522

Hufford, M. R. (2000). Empirically supported treatments and comorbid psychopathology: Spelunking Plato's cave. *Professional Psychology: Research and Practice, 31*, 96–99. doi:10.1037/0735-7028.31.1.96

Kanter, J., Tsai, M., & Kohlenberg, R. J. (Eds.). (2010). *The practice of functional analytic psychotherapy*. New York, NY: Springer. doi:10.1007/978-1-4419-5830-3

Kohlenberg, R. J., Kanter, J., Bolling, M., Parker, C., & Tsai, M. (2002). Enhancing cognitive therapy for depression with functional analytic psychotherapy: Treatment guidelines and empirical findings. *Cognitive and Behavioral Practice, 9*, 213–229. doi:10.1016/S1077-7229(02)80051-7

Kohlenberg, R. J., & Tsai, M. (1991). *Functional analytic psychotherapy: A guide for creating intense and curative therapeutic relationships*. New York, NY: Plenum Press.

Linehan, M. M. (1993). *Skills training manual for treatment of borderline personality disorder*. New York, NY: Guilford Press.

Meichenbaum, D. (1975). Self-instructional methods. In F. H. Kanfer & A. P. Goldstein (Eds.), *Helping people change* (pp. 357–391). New York, NY: Pergamon Press.

Miller, W. R., & Rollnick, S. (2002). *Motivational interviewing: Preparing people for change*. New York, NY: Guilford Press.

Mineka, S., & Zinbarg, R. (2006). A contemporary learning theory perspective on the etiology of anxiety disorders: It's not what you thought it was. *American Psychologist, 61*, 10–26. doi:10.1037/0003-066X.61.1.10

Paquette, V., Lévesque, J., Mensour, B., Leroux, J.-M., Beaudoin, G., Bourgouin, P., & Beauregard, M. (2003). Change the mind and you change the brain: Effects of cognitive-behavioral therapy on the neural correlates of spider phobia. *NeuroImage, 18*, 401–409. doi:10.1016/S1053-8119(02)00030-7

Pavlov, I. P. (1927). *Conditioned reflexes: An investigation of the physiological activity of the cerebral cortex* (G. V. Anrep, Ed. & Trans.). London, England: Oxford University Press.

Skinner, B. F. (1957). *Verbal behavior*. New York, NY: Appleton-Century-Crofts. doi:10.1037/11256-000

Skinner, B. F. (1969). *Contingencies of reinforcement: A theoretical analysis*. New York, NY: Appleton-Century-Crofts.

Watson, J. B. (1930). *Behaviorism* (Rev. ed.). Chicago, IL: University of Chicago Press.

3

THERAPIST NEGATIVE REACTIONS: A PERSON-CENTERED AND EXPERIENTIAL PSYCHOTHERAPY PERSPECTIVE

ROBERT ELLIOTT

Therapists in the humanistic–experiential therapy tradition are known for their focus on achieving and maintaining deep empathy for their clients as well as offering unconditional caring and attempting to be genuinely present to their clients. This makes them sound either saintly or hopelessly naive and idealistic. Client challenges and coping with therapist negative reactions are not generally dealt with explicitly in the literature on person-centered and experiential (PCE) therapies; nevertheless, in my experience as a therapist, therapy researcher, trainer, and supervisor, I have found, unsurprisingly, that they are common. In this chapter, I attempt to shed light on how relational difficulties, regardless of the source, are understood and handled in PCE therapies (e.g., person centered, gestalt, focusing oriented, emotion focused).

I am grateful for the support of my colleagues in the Research Clinic at the University of Strathclyde, in particular, Brian Rodgers and Michael Hough, and for that of the clients represented in the clinical examples used herein.

DOI: 10.1037/13940-003
Transforming Negative Reactions to Clients: From Frustration to Compassion, A. W. Wolf, M. R. Goldfried, and J. C. Muran (Editors)

PCE THEORY AND RELATIONAL DIFFICULTIES

The therapeutic relationship plays a central role in PCE therapies, and thus it deserves careful attention. In the sections that follow, I discuss several variables that can influence the client–therapist relationship.

Role of the Therapeutic Relationship in the Change Process

Across a range of therapeutic approaches, it is almost universally accepted that the therapeutic relationship is an important vehicle of change in therapy (e.g., Goldfried, 1982; Henry & Strupp, 1994; Horvath & Greenberg, 1994; Norcross, 2011; Orlinsky, Rønnestad, & Willutzki, 2003; Rogers, 1959; Safran & Muran, 2000). In the humanistic–experiential therapies in general, the therapeutic relationship is seen as the central change process; that is, the therapist's positive relational attitudes and behaviors are growth promoting in themselves, helping the client to understand and accept the self and thus paving the way for change in presenting problems, underlying emotion processes, and more general personality style. In addition, over time, clients come to internalize the therapist's compassionate attitude toward them, enabling them to develop self-compassion and self-acceptance. This was the original position of person-centered therapy (PCT; Rogers, 1951, 1959), and it is a view still maintained by many classical person-centered therapists today (e.g., Brodley, 1990; Freire, 2001; Grant, 1990).

The Therapeutic Relationship in Classical PCT

In Rogers's (1957, 1959) classic formulation of PCT, the relationship was viewed as comprising three interrelated therapist-offered components: (a) accurate empathy, (b) unconditional positive regard, and (c) genuineness or congruence. In addition, Rogers posited three other "necessary and sufficient conditions" for productive therapeutic change: (a) The client had to be experiencing incongruence (manifested by psychological distress), (b) the client and therapist had to be in psychological contact, and (c) the client had to *perceive* the therapist's empathy and unconditional positive regard. Over the years, a body of research built up around the three therapist-offered conditions, with recent meta-analyses showing consistent empirical support for all three conditions as predictors of outcome (Elliott, Bohart, Watson, & Greenberg, 2011; Farber & Doolin, 2011; Kolden, Klein, Wang, & Austin, 2011). Furthermore, with the current revival of the PCE therapies, there have been various attempts to reformulate these conditions, for example, as "presence" (Rogers, 1980) or "relational depth" (Mearns & Cooper, 2005); however, the tripartite core of empathy, unconditional positive regard, and genuineness, together with the ancillary conditions, continues to be almost universally accepted by PCE therapists.

The Therapeutic Relationship in the Experiential Therapies

Nevertheless, the experiential or process-guiding humanistic therapies, including emotion-focused therapy (EFT; Elliott, Watson, Goldman, & Greenberg, 2003; Greenberg, Rice, & Elliott, 1993) and focusing-oriented therapy (Gendlin, 1996; Purton, 2004), have come to offer a somewhat more complex view of the therapeutic relationship. Influenced by Bordin (1979), Rice (1983) first proposed that the therapeutic relationship serves two different functions in these approaches. First, it is a primary change process, as already described. Second, it also serves a secondary or *task* function of helping the client develop trust in therapy and the therapist, so that they can engage in the often-painful work of self-exploration, including accessing, symbolizing, and reflecting on difficult experiences. In other words, the therapeutic relationship is both an end in itself and a means to an end (i.e., helping the client engage productively in useful therapeutic activities and process). Ideally, in these approaches, the relationship fades into the background, as clients turn their attention to their own internal dialectical process; change then emerges out of this internal dialectic (e.g., between critical and experiencing aspects of the self, as in two-chair work; Elliott et al., 2003), which is supported by the therapist but in which the therapist and the therapeutic relationship play a secondary, supportive role.

Technique Versus Relationship

Originally, most PCE/humanistic therapies rejected the role of technique in favor of relationship (e.g., Rogers, 1957). For contemporary experiential therapies such as EFT, however, the whole distinction between technique and relationship is a false dichotomy, a category mistake (cf. Ryle, 1949/2009). For these practitioners, the word *technique* is just another term for the special communication skills or speech acts (cf. Searle, 1969) that the therapist uses to help the client. Some of these speech acts (e.g., empathic affirmation responses) are aimed primarily at developing, maintaining, and repairing the client–therapist relationship; these can be referred to as *relational techniques*. Other speech acts are aimed primarily at facilitating client self-exploration and the resolution of therapeutic tasks (e.g., process suggestions); these can be referred to as *task techniques*. The bulk of what the therapist does in the humanistic–experiential therapies (e.g., exploratory reflections), however, partakes simultaneously of both relationship and task functions. What all PCE therapies have in common is a set of therapeutic principles or guidelines (most commonly formulated as a version of the facilitative conditions defined by Rogers) that explicitly put relationship building, maintenance, and repair first and consider them foundational to client self-exploration or other task activities (Greenberg et al., 1993).

Therapist Self-Awareness of Negative Reactions to Clients

All therapists, but PCE/humanistic therapists in particular, must constantly strive to maintain an awareness of potential negative reaction to a client. There are many ways to address and deal with such reactions.

Relational Difficulties in PCT

It is possible to read Rogers's classical formulation as pointing to a specific set of negative therapist reactions, that is, the opposites of the main therapeutic conditions already described. In fact, one could argue that Rogers (1942, 1957) used his personal experience and research to formulate the facilitative conditions specifically to prevent the following difficulties:

- *Nonempathy.* The therapist fails to understand the client, or the therapist and client actively misunderstand (i.e., understand wrongly) each other.
- *Conditionality.* The therapist begins to act as an expert judge of the client or the client's behavior, interfering with the client's ability to do this for him- or herself.
- *Negative regard.* The therapist is unable to feel positively toward the client or even discovers that he or she has come to dislike a client or that client's behavior.
- *Incongruence.* The therapist acts in a stiff or false manner, gives mixed or contradictory messages, or attempts to cover up his or her true feelings.

The negation of the other three conditions fills out the implicit Rogerian formulation of therapeutic difficulties:

- *Client lack of distress/motivation.* The client may in fact not be in distress at all and/or may be unwilling to look at his or her distress.
- *Contact disturbance.* There may be an absence of psychological contact between client and therapist, an important issue in working with clients in psychotic, dissociated, or panicky states.
- *Client misperception.* In spite of the therapist experiencing and offering empathy, unconditional positive regard, and genuineness, the client may, for whatever reason, not perceive them or even perceive them to be absent.

Nature of Therapist Self-Awareness of Negative Reactions

So, how do person-centered therapists view negative reactions to clients when these arise? The congruence or genuineness principle is generally seen as involving two aspects: (a) therapist self-awareness and (b) transparency in relation to the client (e.g., Lietaer, 1993; see also Kolden et al., 2011). To begin, therapists are expected to be aware of their negative reactions as these arise. However, in classical PCT, negative therapist reactions are not generally seen as useful data to be worked through with the client; instead, it is considered better if they do not happen at all, because they represent a potentially harmful imposition on the client. Nevertheless, Rogers (1959) and others (e.g., Brodley, 2001) specified that persistent negative reactions should be disclosed to the client because they would be likely to be seen as incongruent, which would undermine the client's perception of the therapeutic relationship more generally.

Relational Difficulties in Experiential Therapies

In the experiential therapies, however, the nature and quality of the therapist's self-awareness of the negative reaction become critical. As Gendlin (1972) originally pointed out, a negative therapist reaction is often itself a superficial, incongruent response on the part of the therapist, that is, an unclear, surface feeling that hides another, more genuine response. More recently, emotion theory, as developed in EFT (Elliott et al., 2003; Greenberg et al., 1993), provides a more detailed theoretical understanding of the nature of therapist negative reactions, based on the distinction between secondary reactive and primary adaptive emotion responses. In brief (and slightly oversimplified), a *primary adaptive emotion* response is the immediate, direct, unlearned emotional response to a situation, whereas a *secondary reactive emotion* is a reaction to a prior emotion response.

Take, for example, therapist irritation (negative regard) with a client's behavior: If the client insists on smoking during a session after the therapist has asked the client not to, this would constitute a violation of the therapist's person and space, and the therapist would be justified in feeling irritated or annoyed. This would be, therefore, a mild, congruent form of adaptive anger; it would signal the therapist not to become aggressive but instead to take adaptive action to maintain the protective boundary represented by the no-smoking rule. On the other hand, if the therapist becomes annoyed with the client for droning on about matters that the therapist does not view as important, this is much more likely to be a form of therapist incongruence. A secondary, reactive emotion, the annoyance is not a direct reaction to the client but was instead preceded by a different, unwanted emotion, such as boredom or anxiety, of which the therapist may not have been fully aware.

Expressing annoyance at the client for talking in an external, monotone manner would be counterproductive or even harmful; however, boredom from lack of stimulation or secondary to anxiety about not being helpful might be used as a signal to try to reconnect with the client on a deeper, more lively level.

In sum, from a classical PCT point of view, persistent negative therapist reactions violate key elements of the essential therapeutic relationship and are best avoided. If necessary, they are appropriately disclosed to the client. Others, originally Gendlin (1972) and later Greenberg and Geller (2001) and Elliott et al. (2003), have argued that therapist self-awareness of the nature of such reactions provides critical information for deciding whether and how to disclose them to the client.

PCE Practice and Negative Therapist Reactions

There are various ways that PCE therapists can address and deal with negative reactions to a client. In the following sections, I address some of these.

Withholding Versus Disclosing Negative Therapist Reactions

As discussed, in PCE therapies such as EFT or focusing therapy there are times when the consensus is that negative reactions are best handled by a strategy of containing them, moderating them, or setting them aside. In these therapies, the therapist is encouraged to set aside fleeting negative reactions, which might include a momentary difficulty in empathizing, a brief judgmental reaction, a mild attempt to direct the client down a course of action the therapist favors, or a passing distracting or self-focused thought. In addition, a process of self-reflection—and preferably supervision—might be a good first option for dealing with a pattern of recurrent minor negative reactions (Brodley, 2001; Greenberg & Geller, 2001).

Strong or persistent negative reactions, however, are a different matter and should be expressed in some way to the client. This situation has long been the subject of discussion in writings on PCTs (see the review by Haugh, 2001). In general, going back to Rogers (1959), the most common position has been that, in the face of persistent negative reactions, congruence trumps empathy, unconditionality, and positive regard. In other words, in these situations it is commonly agreed that therapists should be honest and disclose their negative reaction to the client. To quote Goodman (1988), "The helper in trouble discloses on the double."

This position is of course a controversial one, for several reasons. First, framing negative reactions as a failure on the part of the therapist to maintain the required therapeutic stance can be seen as needlessly dismissing valuable interpersonal information that might be usefully worked through with the client. Second, based on research by Strupp and colleagues (e.g., Henry, Schacht, & Strupp, 1990), there is the very real danger that the disclosure of the negative reaction can harm the client, especially if it is not done carefully. For this reason, PCT therapists (see the review by Haugh, 2001) have long argued that the disclosure of a negative therapist reaction must always be in an appropriate manner, that is, in the service of and tempered by the facilitative conditions. However, as Greenberg and Geller (2001) noted, what is or is not "appropriate" has not been adequately defined. Fortunately, Gendlin (1972) began the process of laying this out in an early chapter on managing difficulties in working with clients with contact disturbances, such as psychotic or schizophrenic processes, who often present as mute, externally focused, or even hostile (see Exhibit 3.1).

The procedure, laid out originally by Gendlin (1972; an early form of which later came to be called *focusing therapy*) and, more recently, by Greenberg and Geller (2001), is a method for determining whether a negative reaction is primary adaptive or secondary reactive one. Thus, as noted earlier, experiential therapies such as focusing therapy and EFT attempt to address the congruence dilemma by differentiating critically between congruent

EXHIBIT 3.1
Gendlin (1972) on Managing Negative Therapist Reactions
to Working With Unresponsive Psychotic Clients

What I term the "inward side" of a feeling is the safest aspect to express. We tend to express the *outer* edges of our feelings. That leaves *us* protected and makes the other person unsafe. We say, "This and this (which *you* did) hurt me." We do not say, "This and this weakness of mine *made me be* hurt when you did this and this."

To find this inward edge of me in my feelings, I need only ask myself, "Why?" When I find myself bored, angry, tense, hurt, at a loss, or worried, I ask myself, "Why?" Then, instead of "You bore me" or "This makes me mad," I find the "why" *in me* which makes it so. That is always more personal and positive and much safer to express. Instead of "You bore me," I find "I want to hear more personally from you" or "You tell me what happened, but I want to hear also what it all meant to you." Instead of saying, "When you move so slowly and go back three times, it makes me mad," I say, "I get to thinking that all our time will be gone and I'll have to go without having done a thing for you, and that will bother me all day."

It is surprising how positive are the feelings in us which first come up as anger, impatience, boredom or criticism. However, it is natural, since our needs with the patient are nearly all positive ones for him. I need to be effective in helping him. I need to be successful in helping him arrive at his truth and a way to live. I need to feel therapeutic. When my feelings are for the moment constricted, tense, bad, sad or critical, it is because in terms of some of these very positive needs I have with him, we have gone off the track. No wonder then that when I ask "why" concerning my bad feelings, the emergent answer is positive feelings. I am bored because I want to hear more personal, feeling-relevant things from him. I am angry because our time is being wasted—the time on which I count to be an effective therapist. I am critical of him because I wish something better for him. (pp. 363–364) (adaptive) and incongruent (secondary reactive) therapist reactions to the client: Congruent or adaptive emotion responses are disclosed in a careful, respectful manner, whereas incongruent reactions are subjected to further self-reflection and, if necessary, supervision.

What collective guidance do PCE therapists offer for how to go about disclosing a strong or persistent negative reaction? Exhibit 3.2 contains a compendium of the collective wisdom of the PCE tradition regarding when and how to disclose negative therapist reactions (Bozarth, 1990; Brodley, 2001; Gendlin, 1972; Greenberg & Geller, 2001; Haugh, 2001; Lietaer, 1993; Mearns & Thorne, 1999; Rogers, 1959, 1961). The 14 guiding principles listed in the exhibit fall into three headings. The first five principles specify that the *negative reaction disclosure marker* is present; that is, either that the reaction is persistent and interfering or that the client has in some way picked up on the negative reaction; that it is not too far off the track of where the client wants to go in the session; and that the client is emotionally strong enough to make use of the information. Second, *therapist readiness* principles address whether the therapist is both generally mature enough and specifically prepared in the immediate situation to deal effectively with his or her negative reaction with this particular client; this requires a general stance of receptivity to and affirmation of the client, clarity of helpful intention, accurate self-awareness about the underlying nature of the reaction, and readiness to explore the client's reaction to the therapist's reaction. Finally, *therapist manner* principles point to the importance of delivering the self-disclosure in a clear but nonblaming, gentle, and genuinely caring manner that makes it clear that this is not fact but instead the therapist's own personal perspective.

Therapist Self-Awareness

Therapist readiness is clearly crucial in dealing productively with negative therapist reactions. How does the therapist make him- or herself ready to deal with these difficult reactions, in order to skillfully and gracefully deal with the relational complexities involved? Obviously, extensive self-development via life experience, prior work with clients, self-reflection, personal therapy, and supervision are all important means for developing the requisite inner resilience and awareness of one's personal sensitivities and blind spots, as are interpersonal courage and technical finesse. A key element is the therapist's response to his or her own negative reaction: It is not to be suppressed or rejected but instead should be acknowledged in a tolerant, self-accepting manner. Even when the decision is not to disclose the negative reaction, the therapist still accepts the response, which helps him or her to set it aside during the session, bookmarking it for later self-reflection and often exploration during supervision. When the negative reaction emerges, the therapist says to him- or herself, "Oh, there's a bit of [e.g., annoyance,

EXHIBIT 3.2
Person-Centered and Experiential Guiding Principles
for Disclosing Negative Therapist Reactions to Clients
in the Most Effective Manner

A. Negative Reaction Disclosure Marker
  1. The negative reaction has been interfering with empathy and unconditional positive regard (Bozarth, 1990; Haugh, 2001).
  2. The negative reaction persists over time (Brodley, 2001; Haugh, 2001; Mearns & Thorne, 1999; Rogers, 1959) or is striking (Mearns & Thorne, 1999).
  3. The client is likely to perceive the therapist as inconsistent or not genuine or has asked a direct question about how the therapist perceives him or her (Brodley, 2001).
  4. The negative reaction is relevant to the client's immediate frame of reference of concern (Mearns & Thorne, 1999).
  5. The client is in a nonfragile stage in which he or she is open to and can use and integrate the information (Greenberg & Geller, 2001; Lietaer, 1993).
B. Therapist Readiness
  6. The therapist is mature and sufficiently self-aware to be able to work from a position of nondefensive openness and receptivity to the client and is able to tolerate discomfort and to reveal vulnerability to clients as appropriate (Greenberg & Geller, 2001).
  7. The therapist's general stance is receptivity to and affirmation of the client (Greenberg & Geller, 2001).
  8. The therapist is clear that his or her intention in disclosing the negative reaction is to facilitate the client's productive use of therapy (Brodley, 2001; Greenberg & Geller, 2001; Lietaer, 1993), for example, to restore empathy and unconditional positive regard (Haugh, 2001).
  9. It is based on accurate self-awareness of the underlying nature of the negative reaction (Gendlin, 1972; Haugh, 2001; Lietaer, 1993; Mearns & Thorne, 1999), typically after careful self-reflection or supervision (Brodley, 2001; Greenberg & Geller, 2001).
  10. The therapist is prepared to explore the client's potentially complicated response to the therapist's disclosure (Brodley, 2001).
C. Therapist Manner
  11. The disclosure is stated in a clear, explicit, unambiguous manner (Haugh, 2001).
  12. It is expressed tentatively and owned as the therapist's experience, perception, or personal response to the client (Brodley, 2001; Mearns & Thorne, 1999; Rogers, 1961).
  13. It is delivered in an interpersonal manner that is both affirming/nonblaming and allowing/nondominant, even if in response to client attack or criticism (Greenberg & Geller, 2001).
  14. The disclosure is comprehensive: It communicates the central experience that is at the base of the reaction and at the same time metacommunicates the helpful intention behind the disclosure and concern about hurting or offending the client (Greenberg & Geller, 2001).

offendedness, jealousy] there in me. That's interesting!" This form of congruence can be understood as *mindful self-awareness* (Kolden et al., 2011) or *focusing* (Gendlin, 1972, 1996).

Clinical Illustration of In-Session Therapist Focusing

At times, the therapist must go further than this and carry out self-awareness work in the session in front of the client. For example, many years ago I was seeing a client with whom the therapy process was feeling difficult. She opened one session by telling me that she thought she had picked up from me that I "hated" her. I started by giving myself a moment's pause before responding. During this time, I privately acknowledged that things had been difficult between us, and I recognized a frightened, deer-in-the-headlights part of me. Realizing that she would not believe a denial and that our alliance was strong enough for us to explore what might come, I said to her, "Well, that's a really interesting question! Give me a minute to look inside and see how I really do feel about you." I then looked away from her and took probably 30 seconds of silence (which of course felt longer) to do some focusing work. I directed my attention to my bodily feeling or *felt sense* of her. As I did so, I became aware of something that was uncomfortable there. I tried applying the word *hate* to the feeling to see whether it fit, but clearly it did not. There was something uncomfortable between us, but it wasn't anger or anything like it. At that point, I felt confident enough in our shared process to be able to begin disclosing the results of my little focusing exercise to her:

> Well [I said, slowly and deliberately], "hate" really doesn't fit how I feel about you . . . but there is something uncomfortable there. Let me see if I can put it into words . . . It's some kind of anxiety, a kind of fear that you're going to want more than I can give you, and then something in me wants to back away to protect myself. [Client nodded.] This is a familiar issue for me, being afraid that people will want more from me than I can give, so I know that it's at least partly my own issue. I'm not sure exactly how this comes across to you, but I can easily imagine that you might sense me pulling back from you, and that might make you wonder if I'm angry with you. Does that fit what you are picking up? [Client agreed.] I wonder if we can look at this further?

In this example, one form of the negative reaction disclosure marker was present: The client asked me about the issue (Principle 3 in Exhibit 3.2); in addition, it was clearly in her frame of reference (Principle 4), and she appeared to be sufficiently robust psychologically to handle the process (Principle 5). It is also true that in my response I drew on extensive personal development work, including personal therapy and in particular my recent use of focusing to explore my own issues (Principle 6). As a result, my general stance with this client was one of receptivity (Principle 7), and my particular approach to her challenge was to try to repair an alliance rupture (Principle 8). Giving myself time to focus on my inner response enabled me to access it and accurately symbolize it (Principle 9), and I was certainly prepared to explore this with the client to the point of resolution (Principle 10). Finally, my response was clear (Principle 11), owned as my own experience (Principle 12), and nonblaming (Principle 13). What I failed to do, however, was to metacommunicate clearly to the client my concern about how difficult this was for her, my desire to help her, or my gratitude to her for raising the issue explicitly instead of keeping it underground (Principle 14).

Phase of Therapy and the Handling of Therapist Negative Reactions

Elliott et al. (2003) distinguished between early and later alliance difficulties. Early on, therapists are more concerned with connecting with and engaging clients in therapy, and problems with the initial formation of the alliance are likely to be more task oriented, having to do with understandings and agreements about the goals and tasks of therapy. PCE therapists expect clients to have concerns and hesitations about therapy, and they affirm clients bringing these to the therapist. Therefore, an early negative reaction by the therapist is much more likely to involve an intruding personal issue on the part of the therapist that is best dealt with outside of therapy, in particular in supervision.

On the other hand, negative reactions that persist or emerge during the working phase of therapy are much more likely to be located in the interaction of client and therapist and to derail the therapy if not dealt with directly. At this point, a sense of mutual trust and collaboration about the tasks of therapy will generally have developed and will be a resource for resolving difficulties (Horvath & Greenberg, 1994). PCE therapists are therefore more likely to disclose negative reactions to clients at this point, in particular because they provide a key indicator of an alliance rupture or difficulty that should be addressed in a dialogical manner with the client.

Relational Dialogue Task

In other words, negative therapist reactions after the early phase of therapy typically point to *alliance difficulty markers*. Furthermore, careful therapist disclosure of the processed negative reaction to the client, along the lines I have described, is one important way to introduce the relationship dialogue task (Elliott et al., 2003), which is derived in part from research on hindering therapy events (Elliott, 1985; Elliott et al., 1990) but especially builds on Agnew, Harper, Shapiro, and Barkham's (1994) research on relationship challenges and on Safran and Muran's (2000) work on alliance ruptures and the use of metacommunication for repairing them. In comparison to Safran and Muran (2000), however, Elliott et al. (2003) emphasized therapist genuineness and presence and replaced interpretive elements with empathic conjecture and experiential teaching.

Alliance difficulty markers take a variety of forms but fall under three broad headings: (a) confrontation difficulties, in which the client directly challenges the therapist in some way (Agnew et al., 1994; Safran & Muran, 2000); (b) withdrawal difficulties, whereby the client disengages from the therapy process (Agnew et al., 1994; Safran & Muran, 2000); and (c) therapist-specific difficulties, which are located primarily in the therapist (Elliott et al., 2003). The therapist may experience a negative reaction as part of any of these difficulties, but different difficulties tend to pull for different particular negative reactions. Six common alliance difficulties, along with therapist negative reactions commonly involved in each difficulty (Elliott et al., 2003), are listed in Table 3.1.

In resolving these issues, it is better to work with the client on the feelings that give rise to the difficulty than to try actively to persuade him or her out of the difficulty. This is done by using responsive reflections, self-disclosure, metacommunication, and orienting information about the nature of therapy. The important thing is to genuinely listen to the client, as part of a two-way process, with each person expressing his or her side of the difficulty and owning his or her contributions to it.

Like other therapeutic tasks, relationship dialogue work proceeds through a series of stages (see Table 3.2). First, the therapist confirms the difficulty, if it has been raised by the client, or, if it has not been raised by the client, tentatively brings the potential difficulty to the client's attention. In either case, this is done in a careful, deliberate, nondefensive manner. Second, once the client and therapist agree that there is a difficulty, the therapist proposes that they discuss this issue. If the client agrees, the client and therapist then begin by laying out their views of the problem. Third, client and therapist continue in a mutual exploration in which each person discloses his or her views of the difficulty while making sure each understands what the other is saying. The therapist models and facilitates the process by genuinely considering and disclosing his or her own possible role. Fourth, client and therapist seek to develop a shared understanding of the sources of the difficulty, especially the negative interpersonal cycle (e.g., distancer–pursuer) that might have been activated. Fifth, both parties consider the larger personal issues raised by the difficulty (van Kessel & Lietaer, 1998) and discuss possible solutions to preventing the difficulty in future. Sixth, client and therapist process the work and experience a deepened sense of connection and engagement in the work of therapy.

TABLE 3.1
Common Alliance Difficulties and Examples of Therapist Negative Reactions and Issues

Alliance difficulty	Therapist negative reaction/issue
1. *Self-consciousness and task refusal* (= withdrawal difficulty): Client refuses to do suggested therapeutic activity (e.g., exploration of painful experiences or emotion) or active task (e.g., two-chair work).	Control and competence anxieties, leading to frustration and annoyance
2. *Power/control issues:* Client sensitivity to power differences in therapy leads to task refusal (withdrawal difficulty) or complaints of being controlled, imposed on, or not duly considered (confrontation difficulty).	Competence anxieties and professional allegiances, leading to withdrawal or conversely attempts to control the client, thus confirming the client's fear
3. *Attachment/bond issues:* Client develops the feeling that the therapist does not really care for or even dislikes him or her (can be either confrontation or withdrawal difficulty).	Guilt/fear of harming others, leading to withdrawal, defensiveness, denial
4. *Covert withdrawal difficulties:* Client disengages from therapy process without saying why, either by missing sessions/coming late or by remaining on an external, superficial level.	Helplessness, leading to reactive frustration and anger, or emotional disengagement, leading to boredom or sleepiness
5. *Therapist conditionality* (therapist-specific difficulty): Strong negative reactions to the person of the client or to the client's behavior (e.g., antisocial behavior or substance abuse).	Personal issues (emotion schemes) activated, leading to anger, disgust, fear, and potential attack or abandonment of client
6. *Therapist impairment* (therapist-specific difficulty)	Exhaustion, illness, preoccupation with own difficulties, leading to disruption of empathy and competent functioning as a therapist

Helping Therapists Learn How to Work Productively With Their Negative Reactions

PCE therapists who experience a negative reaction to a client can address and resolve this issue in a number of ways, including through training and supervision.

Training

How do PCE therapy trainers help students learn to identify, process, and make effective use of their negative reactions to clients? Personal development processes are undoubtedly essential for this. Although humanistic

TABLE 3.2
Relationship Dialogue for Repair of Alliance Difficulties

Task resolution stage	Therapist activities
0. *Pre-marker identification*	Listen carefully and nondefensively for possible alliance difficulties. May need to ask directly.
1. *Confirm marker:* Nature of possible difficulty is presented to client.	*Confrontation difficulties:* Acknowledge complaint; begin by offering a solid empathic reflection of the potential difficulty, trying to capture it as accurately and thoroughly as possible. *Withdrawal difficulties:* Gently and tactfully raise the possibility of difficulty, to see if client recognizes it as a difficulty as well. Therapist manner is slow, deliberate, and open.
2. *Task negotiation/initiation:* Task is proposed, and exploration is begun.	Suggest to client that it is important to discuss the difficulty, including each person's part in it. Present difficulty as a shared responsibility to work on together. Client and therapist begin by laying out each person's view of what happened.
3. *Deepening:* Dialectical exploration of each person's perception of the difficulty	Model and facilitate the process by genuinely considering and disclosing own possible role. Help client explore what is generally at stake for him or her in the difficulty (emotion scheme).
4. *Partial resolution:* Development of shared understanding of sources of the difficulty	Summarize and confirm overall shared understanding of the nature of the difficulty.
5. *Exploration of general issues and practical solutions*	Help client explore and reflect on the more general personal issues raised by the difficulty. Encourage client exploration of possible solutions; ask what client needs. Offer possible changes in own conduct of therapy.
6. *Full resolution:* Genuine client satisfaction with outcome of dialogue; renewed enthusiasm for therapy	Encourage processing of dialogue. Reflect client reactions to the work.

Note. Reprinted from *Learning Emotion-Focused Therapy: The Process-Experiential Approach to Change* (p. 160), by R. Elliott, J. C. Watson, R. N. Goldman, and L. S. Greenberg, 2003, Washington, DC: American Psychological Association. Copyright 2003 by the American Psychological Association.

therapy trainers often do not see compulsory personal therapy as an appropriate process for teaching students how to do this, PCT trainers in particular believe that various kinds of group encounter experiences can play an invaluable role in helping students develop awareness of their blind spots and sensitivities. These groups typically combine unstructured exploration of relevant professional and personal issues, and they vary in size from eight to more than 30. (Different-sized groups create different dynamics and can focus on different issues; see Mearns, 1997.) Students are regularly confronted with differences in needs, expectations, and modes of interacting with others, which inevitably result in conflicts and relational ruptures (Mearns, 1997). If handled appropriately by trainers, these differences become occasions for students to learn how to handle such situations productively. It has been my experience that if not handled appropriately, such group experiences can be harmful.

This process starts when preexisting disparities between the needs, expectations, or actions of members of the group lead to a level of conflict that begins to generate a negative reaction on the part of one or more group members, typically a relational rupture expressed as secondary anger. This group-level alliance rupture is analogous to the relational difficulties discussed earlier. In an optimum situation, the group leaders have been monitoring the group for this and are prepared to step in actively to label what is happening and to foster a relational dialogue among the involved group members, helping them explore the triggers for the reaction and the personal issues that have been accessed. The trainer, with assistance from group members, helps the involved participants to symbolize what has happened and to clarify the negative interactional cycle that was set off. In doing this, the trainer models a calm, engaged, nonblaming stance of helping the participants access and express the underlying primary adaptive emotions, most often sadness, fear, or shame. In my experience, during a 2-year training course members of the group gradually take over this process from the trainers and help each other resolve relational ruptures.

An alternative workshop method is used in EFT training, whereby trainees take turns role playing alliance difficulties with each other. The workshop begins with a discussion of the importance of being able to handle alliance difficulties effectively. The trainer then runs through a long list of alliance difficulties, similar to those given in Table 3.1 but with more detail and examples. This is followed by a presentation of the relational dialogue task. Next, the trainer provides some examples of alliance difficulties, for example, using the stimulus vignettes developed by Tim Anderson (see Anderson, Ogles, Patterson, Lambert, & Vermeersch, 2009); these inevitably result in negative reactions on the part of several of the trainees, and trainees are encouraged to come up with appropriate responses, generally leading to lively discussions among the group. After that, trainees break up into skills practice groups of three to five people each; using the relational dialogue task, they take turns enacting clients presenting different difficulties and therapists responding.

Supervision

How do PCE therapy supervisors work with their supervisees' negative reactions to clients? Supervision is essential for helping therapists in this tradition develop greater awareness of personal issues that may be set off in work with clients or that may be imported from other areas of the therapist's life.

Such reactions constitute one of the major foci of supervision, especially in PCT, in which technique is downplayed in favor of the relational conditions. Thus, supervisees are encouraged to pay attention to any negative reactions to clients, given that these typically interfere with empathy, unconditional positive regard, and genuineness. In this context, although clearly not therapy, supervision plays an important role in personal development and enhanced self-awareness of the therapist's personal issues as these affect the conduct of therapy. Personal therapy would be recommended only if personal exploration threatened to drive out consideration of clinical work or if external stressors persistently impaired the therapist's functioning with clients.

CASE ILLUSTRATION

Claire (a pseudonym), a woman in her late 20s, came to the research clinic struggling with severe social anxiety and work conflicts. Initially, she quite liked the structure of the EFT I offered. Over the course of the first 10 sessions (out of 20 specified in the research protocol), we explored the basis of her social anxiety, identifying a sense of despondency or depression underneath it, which we in turn traced back to her mother's death when Claire was a little girl. We established that her social anxiety was organized around a core emotion scheme of herself as "rubbish" and "a lost cause" for not being able to save or support her mother and, later, her father when he too was dying; it was this that she feared others would see in her.

Nevertheless, over time Claire began to struggle with various aspects of EFT, including open-ended experiential questions, focusing, clearing a space, empty-chair work, and two-chair dialogue. At the same time, she gradually became more distressed, as frightening memories and other experiences began to emerge. It is generally the case for me that I feel energized by challenges, but after a wide range of PCE approaches (and the occasional psychodynamic interpretation as well) failed to connect with her, I began to struggle with how I might be able to help her to work productively with her painful experiences. As a result of her increasing distress and her continued rejection of my usual ways of working, I began to feel increasingly stymied and frustrated.

In Session 14, Claire reported that she had gone off her antidepressant medication because it was interfering with her ability to feel her emotions; however, she was now becoming increasingly irritable with others and critical of herself. Using focusing, she was able to locate the sense of irritability in her stomach, but she could not clarify the quality or source of the irritability or even identify whether it felt related to her going off her medication. Along the way, I did quite a bit of experiential teaching; for example, I explained that when psychotherapy works, it changes the brain; I also gave her experiential homework (to dialogue with her critic on her own). Near the end of the session, she expressed irritation with me "trying to get her to do things." I had not yet started with regular supervision, but I used my postsession self-supervision notes to become aware of and symbolize my frustration and to begin the process of figuring out what to do; thus, I wrote the following: "Too many exploratory questions? Reflect more? What? . . . Follow-up on irritability/weird feelings with me = relational rupture." As I processed my feelings during the week before our next session, I realized that I was feeling de-skilled and anxious because none of my usual ways of working were working for Claire. I also became aware of my sense of emotional attachment to these ways of working, to the part of me that was unhappy at having to let go of the comfort of working in familiar ways, and to my underlying fear that we might not be able to find a way to work together effectively. Symbolizing these feelings helped me to step back from them and to begin to open myself up to looking at alternatives with Claire.

In Session 15, Claire reported that she had been having a rough time, waking up in the middle of the night crying for her mother. She said that she was afraid that therapy wasn't working, although her social anxiety was better. Having previously explored my sense of stuckness and frustration in my self-supervision process, I felt ready to face the difficulty head on. I proposed that we explore the situation in order to see what part each of us had in it. Characteristically, she replied that the problem was her, not me: She should be able to do what I proposed, but she just couldn't. I disagreed, telling her that I believed that difficulties in therapy always involve both therapist and client. Over her objections, I confessed my sense that I had not been flexible or creative enough in helping her work around her "allergy" to chair work and told her that I also felt that I'd given her the message that she had disappointed me, which I owned as a familiar process of mine. The fact is, I went on, I was struggling with not knowing how to help her without using some form of chair work, and I was afraid that I was letting her down.

After this long speech, Claire reported that the work we had done several sessions earlier on her unfinished issues with her mother had in fact helped her but that there was more there that was still unresolved. She described several recent incidents as evidence of this, asking how she could resolve these issues without talking to chairs. I explained that the important thing was not the chair work but accessing the strong emotions and working with her unmet needs for love and support. We then moved into proxy empty-chair work, in which we imagined her mother present, but I spoke to the mother on the client's behalf. This enabled her to get to a further aspect of her core pain about her mother's death, which we worked on over the course of the remaining five sessions.

My processing of my emotions in my self-supervision and discussion with my client helped me transform my sense of stuckness into a shared challenge to our joint creativity, to find ways of working that were not just out of the book but that would work for her, with her particular sensitivities and issues. This became particularly important when, some time after the end of the scheduled 20 sessions, she relapsed and required more extensive therapy.

ANALYSIS OF CASE EXAMPLE

How does this illustration stand up to the PCE guiding principles summarized in Exhibit 3.2? The problem clearly had been interfering with my unconditional positive regard for the client and had persisted over time (Principles 1 and 2). Although Claire did not directly question my empathy or regard for her, she did express irritation with my pushing her (Session 14) and disclosed her worry that therapy wasn't helping (Session 15); these concerns indicated that the difficulty was in her immediate frame of reference and that she felt ready to address the problem (Principles 4 and 5).

For my part, I was certainly aware that I had been struggling to be helpful to the client and was feeling de-skilled by her inability to use my suggestions for working with her issues (Principle 6). At the same time, I admired Claire's personal integrity and genuinely felt compassion for what she had been through, and I was moving toward a greater receptivity to working with her processes in her way rather than mine (Principle 7). In disclosing my difficulties as her therapist, I was clear that my intention was to repair a relational rupture in order to help the therapy get back on a better track, and I was prepared to explore the problem with her, wherever it led (Principles 8 and 10). In the meantime, through self-supervision, I was able to gain some reflective distance and to identify the source of my secondary reactive frustration, which was my anxiety about feeling de-skilled and my fear of letting my client down. This enabled me to let go of my attachment to what I knew so well and had written books about; this is turn helped me access my curiosity and creativity (Principle 9).

On the other hand, the way in which I facilitated the relational dialogue could certainly have been improved: True, it was clear and unambiguous, owned as my experience, nonblaming, and fairly comprehensive (Principles 11 and 14; aspects of Principles 12 and 13); however, in retrospect I would have to say that it was not particularly dialogical, in that I did most of the talking, at times acted as an expert, and failed to empathically validate Claire's sense of blame for the difficulty (Principles 12 and 13). Furthermore, as previously noted by my friend Germain Lietaer (personal communication, November 2004), I had once again failed to help my client fully explore her side of the difficulty, including her enduring interpersonal patterns as these had played out here between us (e.g., her assuming the difficulties were her fault, a sense of nonentitlement); this is an important aspect of the relational dialogue task that I had neglected to describe in a previous book (Elliott et al., 2003). These limitations point to the value of continued self-examination and, in particular, regular supervision, which I commenced not long after the difficulty described here and which proved invaluable in my later work with this client.

CONCLUSION

Like psychotherapists of all stripes, PCE therapists do at times experience negative emotional reactions to their clients. Situations such as my experience with Claire clearly occur within PCE therapies, but they are not often discussed explicitly. In this tradition, such reactions are understood as compromising the essential therapeutic relationship conditions of therapist empathy, unconditional positive regard, and genuineness. In fact, I have hypothesized that Carl Rogers formulated these conditions precisely as an antidote to common forms of negative therapist reaction: misunderstandings, attempts to control or dominate the client, judgmental attitudes toward the client, and phoniness or offering of mixed messages in working with clients. PCE therapists monitor themselves for these negative reactions and, when these are present, important, and persistent—and when it is appropriate to do so—take action by using self-reflection and supervision to find therapeutically facilitative ways to disclose and explore these reactions with clients. In doing so, PCE therapists are aware that their negative reactions are generally secondary responses (e.g., irritation with a client for arriving late to a session) to more primary emotions (e.g., anxiety about letting the client down), which typically point to a more general relational rupture or difficulty that therefore must be identified accurately in order for the difficulty to be resolved productively with the client. Thus, a high level of ongoing, accurate self-awareness is required of therapists as they work with clients, which in turn requires personal work, self-reflection, and supervision.

REFERENCES

Agnew, R. M., Harper, H., Shapiro, D. A., & Barkham, M. (1994). Resolving a challenge to the therapeutic relationship: A single-case study. *British Journal of Medical Psychology, 67*, 155–170. doi:10.1111/j.2044-8341.1994.tb01783.x

Anderson, T., Ogles, B. M., Patterson, C. L., Lambert, M. J., & Vermeersch, D. V. (2009). Therapist effects: Facilitative interpersonal skills as a predictor of therapist success. *Journal of Clinical Psychology, 65*, 755–768. doi:10.1002/jclp.20583

Bordin, E. S. (1979). The generalizability of the psychoanalytic concept of working alliance. *Psychotherapy: Theory, Research and Practice, 16*, 252–260. doi:10.1037/h0085885

Bozarth, J. D. (1990). The essence of client-centered therapy. In G. Lietaer, J. Rombauts, & R. Van Balen (Eds.), *Client-centered and experiential psychotherapy in the nineties* (pp. 59–64). Leuven, Belgium: Leuven University Press.

Brodley, B. T. (1990). Client-centered and experiential: Two different therapies. In G. Lietaer, J. Rombauts, & R. Van Balen (Eds.), *Client-centered and experiential psychotherapy in the nineties* (pp. 87–107). Leuven, Belgium: Leuven University Press.

Brodley, B. T. (2001). Congruence and its relation to communication in client-centered therapy. In G. Wyatt (Ed.), *Rogers' therapeutic conditions: Evolution, theory and practice: Vol. 1. Congruence* (pp. 55–78). Ross-on-Wye, England: PCCS Books.

Elliott, R. (1985). Helpful and nonhelpful events in brief counseling interviews: An empirical taxonomy. *Journal of Counseling Psychology, 32*, 307–322. doi:10.1037/0022-0167.32.3.307

Elliott, R., Bohart, A. C., Watson, J. C., & Greenberg, L. S. (2011). Empathy. In J. Norcross (Ed.), *Psychotherapy relationships that work* (2nd ed., pp. 132—152). New York, NY: Oxford University Press.

Elliott, R., Clark, C., Wexler, M., Kemeny, V., Brinkerhoff, J., & Mack, C. (1990). The impact of experiential therapy of depression: Initial results. In G. Lietaer, J. Rombauts, & R. Van Balen (Eds.), *Client-centered and experiential psychotherapy in the nineties* (pp. 549–577). Leuven, Belgium: Leuven University Press.

Elliott, R., Watson, J. C., Goldman, R. N., & Greenberg, L. S. (2003). *Learning emotion-focused therapy: The process-experiential approach to change*. Washington, DC: American Psychological Association. doi:10.1037/10725-000

Farber, B. A., & Doolin, E. M. (2011). Positive regard. In J. C. Norcross (Ed.), *Psychotherapy relationships that work: Evidence-based responsiveness* (2nd ed., pp. 168–186). New York, NY: Oxford University Press.

Freire, E. S. (2001). Unconditional positive regard: The distinctive feature of client-centered therapy. In J. Bozarth & P. Wilkins (Eds.), *Rogers' therapeutic conditions: Evolution, theory and practice: Vol. 3. Unconditional positive regard* (pp. 145–155). Ross-on-Wye, England: PCCS Books.

Gendlin, E. T. (1972). Therapeutic procedures with schizophrenic patients. In M. Hammer (Ed.), *The theory and practice of psychotherapy with specific disorders* (pp. 333–375). Springfield, IL: Charles C. Thomas. Retrieved from www.focusing.org/gendlin/docs/gol_2061.html

Gendlin, E. T. (1996). *Focusing-oriented psychotherapy: A manual of the experiential method*. New York, NY: Guilford Press.

Goldfried, M. R. (Ed.). (1982). *Converging themes in psychotherapy*. New York, NY: Springer.

Goodman, G. (1988). *The talk book: The intimate science of communicating in close relationships*. New York, NY: Ballantine.

Grant, B. (1990). Principled and instrumental nondirectiveness in person-centered and client-centered therapy. *Person-Centered Review, 5*, 77–88.

Greenberg, L. S., & Geller, S. M. (2001). Congruence and therapeutic presence. In G. Wyatt (Ed.), *Rogers' therapeutic conditions: Evolution, theory and practice: Vol. 1. Congruence* (pp. 131–149). Ross-on-Wye, England: PCCS Books.

Greenberg, L. S., Rice, L. N., & Elliott, R. (1993). *Facilitating emotional change*. New York, NY: Guilford Press.

Haugh, S. (2001). A historical review of the development of the concept of congruence in person-centred therapy. In G. Wyatt (Ed.), *Rogers' therapeutic conditions: Evolution, theory and practice: Vol. 1. Congruence* (pp. 1–17). Ross-on-Wye, England: PCCS Books.

Henry, W. P., Schacht, T. E., & Strupp, H. H. (1990). Patient and therapist introject, interpersonal process, and differential psychotherapy outcome. *Journal of Consulting and Clinical Psychology, 58*, 768–774. doi:10.1037/0022-006X.58.6.768

Henry, W. P., & Strupp, H. H. (1994). The therapeutic alliance as interpersonal process. In A. O. Horvath & L. S. Greenberg (Eds.), *The working alliance: Theory, research, and practice* (pp. 51–84). New York, NY: Wiley.

Horvath, A., & Greenberg, L. (Eds.). (1994). *The working alliance: Theory, research and practice*. New York, NY: Wiley.

Kolden, G. G., Klein, M. H., Wang, C.-C., & Austin, S. B. (2011). Congruence/genuineness. In J. C. Norcross (Ed.), *Psychotherapy relationships that work* (2nd ed., pp. 187–202). New York, NY: Oxford University Press.

Lietaer, G. (1993). Authenticity, congruence and transparency. In D. Brazier (Ed.), *Beyond Carl Rogers: Towards a psychotherapy for the 21st century* (pp. 17–46). London, England: Constable.

Mearns, D. (1997). *Person-centred counselling training*. London, England: Sage.

Mearns, D., & Cooper, M. (2005). *Working at relational depth in counselling and psychotherapy*. London, England: Sage.

Mearns, D., & Thorne, B. (1999). *Person-centred counselling in action* (2nd ed.). London, England: Sage.

Norcross, J. (Ed.). (2011). *Psychotherapy relationships that work* (2nd ed.). New York, NY: Oxford University Press.

Orlinsky, D. E., Rønnestad, M. H., & Willutzki, U. (2003). Process and outcome in psychotherapy. In M. J. Lambert (Ed.), *Bergin and Garfield's handbook of psychotherapy and behavior change* (5th ed., pp. 307–389). New York, NY: Wiley.

Purton, C. (2004). *Person-centred therapy: The focusing-oriented approach*. Basingstoke, England: Palgrave.

Rice, L. N. (1983). The relationship in client-centered therapy. In M. J. Lambert (Ed.), *Psychotherapy and patient relationships* (pp. 36–60). Homewood, IL: Dow Jones-Irwin.

Rogers, C. R. (1942). *Counseling and psychotherapy: Newer concepts in practice*. Cambridge, MA: Houghton Mifflin.

Rogers, C. R. (1951). *Client-centered therapy: Its current practice, implications and theory*. Boston, MA: Houghton Mifflin.

Rogers, C. R. (1957). The necessary and sufficient conditions of therapeutic personality change. *Journal of Consulting Psychology, 21*, 95–103. doi:10.1037/h0045357

Rogers, C. R. (1959). A theory of therapy, personality, and interpersonal relationships as developed in the client-centered framework. In S. Koch (Ed.), *Psychology: The study of a science* (Vol. 3, pp. 184–256). New York, NY: McGraw-Hill.

Rogers, C. R. (1961). *On becoming a person: A therapist's view of psychotherapy*. Boston, MA: Houghton Mifflin.

Rogers, C. R. (1980). *A way of being*. Boston, MA: Houghton Mifflin.

Ryle, G. (2009). *The concept of mind*. New York, NY: Barnes & Noble. (Original work published 1949)

Safran, J. D., & Muran, J. C. (2000). *Negotiating the therapeutic alliance: A relational treatment guide*. New York, NY: Guilford Press.

Searle, J. R. (1969). *Speech acts: An essay in the philosophy of language*. Cambridge, England: Cambridge University Press.

van Kessel, W., & Lietaer, G. (1998). Interpersonal processes. In L. Greenberg, G. Lietaer, & J. Watson (Eds.), *Handbook of experiential psychotherapy* (pp. 155–177). New York, NY: Guilford Press.

4

DIFFICULTIES WITH CLIENTS IN GOTTMAN METHOD COUPLES THERAPY

JOHN M. GOTTMAN AND JULIE S. GOTTMAN

Therapists, no matter how skilled, struggle with their own negative reactions to particular clients, and we, of course, are no exception. Because we treat couples, however, we may experience frustration, aggravation, or exasperation with a particular relationship rather than with some hapless individual. Although this is true of most therapists who work with couples, we focus in this chapter primarily on our own approach to couples therapy. Before we describe the types of relationships that negatively trigger each of us in turn, it might be helpful to understand what kind of work we do in the first place and why we do it. Therefore, we begin with a brief history of how we formulated our theory about what makes relationships work and the details of that theory, which is the underpinning for the couples therapy we do. We then each present a case that exemplifies our own type of difficult relationship and what we do to manage our own negative reactions to those cases.

About 37 years ago, when Robert Levenson and coauthor John M. Gottman began conducting research about relationships, what they brought

DOI: 10.1037/13940-004
Transforming Negative Reactions to Clients: From Frustration to Compassion, A. W. Wolf, M. R. Goldfried, and J. C. Muran (Editors)

to this field was their profound ignorance. Their own relationships with women were not going very well; in truth, these relationships were often painful. Therefore, in their research, because they weren't naturally endowed with relationship wisdom, they began without any hypotheses. Like the ancient astronomers who began by simply describing the motions of the stars and planets, they thought that for a good scientific beginning they needed to start with description. They built a laboratory, created a paradigm for collecting data, and, with minor variations, stayed with it for nearly four decades.

They observed couples talking about how the day went at the end of a day, talking about their real conflicts, talking about an enjoyable topic, or spending time together hanging out for 24 hours in an apartment laboratory. They studied couples in their own homes, interviewed them, and collected physiological measures such as heart rate and blood velocity. This was in the 1970s, before the personal computer had been invented. They also showed couples their videotapes and asked them to tell them what they were thinking and feeling using their numerical rating dial, which ranged from "*very positive* (+9) to *very negative* (−9). The rating dial tapped into the couples' moment-to-moment perceptions of how they were feeling on a wide-ranging numerical scale. Thus, Levenson and John Gottman were able to study physiology, behavior, and perception, all synchronized to the video time code.

For the first 24 years of this research, Levenson and John Gottman never tried to help anyone. In fact, they asked people whether they got therapy, and they discovered that there was a reasonably high correlation between getting therapy and getting a divorce: It was more likely that couples would divorce if they got therapy than if they did not get therapy. This was especially true when one partner got individual therapy, but it was also true for couples therapy.

Levenson and Gottman simply tried to describe what was different about happy, stable couples, whom they called *the Masters* of relationships, and unhappy/stable or unstable couples, whom they called *the Disasters* of relationships. Over the years, they studied couples from every major ethnic and racial group in America, as well as committed gay and lesbian couples. In addition, John Gottman spent 10 years with the late Neil Jacobson studying couples plagued by domestic violence. They also studied couples across the life span, including through being newlyweds, becoming parents, and through old age. For every second of their videotaped interactions, they measured couples' voice tones, speech disturbances, gestures, movements, speech, emotional and facial expressions; how couples made decisions; how they used humor and affection; and other factors. They also scored and classified what the couples said in specific interviews. Finally, they designed and validated a set of questionnaires created to give a profile of strengths and weaknesses in relationships. For a review of this research, see J. M. Gottman's (1999) article and the research page of our website, http://www.gottman.com, for unpublished reports.

To their initial great surprise, they found that they could predict what would happen to a relationship with reasonably high accuracy with just the data collected in a few hours with a couple. They obtained high correlations (in the .90s), in their first 3-year follow-up study, using only physiological data in predicting relationship happiness and controlling for initial levels.

This research using science and observation enable us to "plagiarize" knowledge about how to make love work directly from the Masters and from the Disasters of relationship. For more than 20 years, Levenson and John Gottman got paid by their universities just to watch people either deteriorate or flourish. Then, 16 years ago, John Gottman and his wife, clinical psychologist Julie Schwartz Gottman, decided to work together, and we began to develop methods to prevent relationship meltdown and to help couples and the therapists working with them to convert disaster into mastery. Over the years, we have refined our theory and its attendant interventions, and we have found it successful in organizing our research on relationships and helping clinicians, in turn, to help couples; we call it the *Sound Relationship House theory* (J. M. Gottman, 1999, J. S. Gottman, 2004), and we discuss it in more detail later in this chapter.

WHAT IS "DYSFUNCTIONAL" WHEN A RELATIONSHIP IS AILING

Books have been written about what is dysfunctional in relationships. Most of these books are not based on real data, and many have turned out to be wrong. For example, in their book *The Intimate Enemy* (1968), George Bach and Peter Wyden suggested that the problem in relationships is that people suppress their resentments. On the basis of this assumption, they had partners take turns airing their resentments and hitting one another with foam-rubber bats called *batakas*. We now know from hundreds of studies that there is no cathartic effect of anger, and, in fact, doing what Bach and Wyden called therapy actually builds resentment rather than alleviates it.

What goals should be the focus for couples therapy? What needs fixing in ailing relationships? These are important questions. Let us first look at what research has uncovered about the correlates of couple unhappiness. The following are eight predictors of divorce and/or continued couple misery that are characteristic of relationships during attempts to resolve conflict that can be considered dysfunctional. These characteristics describe what is dysfunctional when a relationship is ailing.

1. *More negativity than positivity.* The ratio of positive interactions to negative interactions during conflict in stable relationships is 5:1, not 0.8:1 as it is in couples headed for divorce. Positive affect itself during conflict resolution (and in everyday interaction) is important because it reduces physiological arousal. This *balance element of the theory* also implies the unusual point of view that negativity is also necessary in relationship (i.e., negativity plays many prosocial functions). Negativity eliminates interaction patterns that do not work; it may also create a cyclical dance of emotional distance and closeness necessary for renewing courtship over time. Relationships should have at least a 5:1 ratio of positivity to negativity during conflict; that is, the ratio has to be very positive compared to negative, even when the couple is disagreeing.

2. *Escalation of negative affect: The Four Horsemen of the Apocalypse.* Some negatives are more corrosive for relationships than others. We call the factors that predict relationship demise the *Four Horsemen of the Apocalypse.* They are the following: criticism, defensiveness, contempt, and stonewalling. These contribute to a pattern of escalation of negativity, which is one dysfunctional interaction pattern.

   In the 1970s, many therapists thought that what was dysfunctional in a relationship was people being angry and hostile toward one other, but we discovered instead that in all relationships (even happy, stable relationships) it is equally likely that when one person gets angry and hostile the other person reciprocates in kind. It is the *escalation* of negativity, marked in particular by criticism, defensiveness, contempt, and stonewalling, that predicts divorce. Couples who escalate conflict divorce an average of about 5.6 years after their wedding.

3. *Turning away.* Later, we discovered that this pattern of escalation was related to a negative style in everyday interaction that we call *turning away* from bids for emotional connection. In this pattern, one partner ignores the other's attempts to connect, to get a partner's attention, interest, humor, affection, or support.

4. *Turning against: Irritability, emotional disengagement, and withdrawal.* Another negative, dysfunctional pattern emerged from our research. When we first studied them, some couples didn't escalate conflict; they just had little positivity at all during conflict (no affection, shared humor, question asking, active interest, excitement, joy, support, empathy). These couples divorced an average of 16.2 years after their wedding. Subsequent research

discovered that this pattern relates to a negative style in everyday interaction that we call *turning against* bids for emotional connection. Members of these couples responded to the other partner's bids for emotional connection in a crabby, irritable manner.

5. *The failure of repair attempts.* Our goal in therapy is not to get couples to avoid fights, even ones that are painful and alienating. Neither do we try to get couples to avoid hurting one another's feelings. Instead, our goal is to help people process their inevitable fights, moments of miscommunication, or hurt feelings and to enable them to repair the relationship. Regrettable incidents in interaction are simply par for the course. The goal is to be able to heal the emotional wounds created by regrettable incidents.

6. *Negative sentiment override.* Robert Weiss (1980) defined the concepts of positive and negative *sentiment override*. When observers viewed a message conveyed by one partner to another as neutral or even positive but the partner heard it as negative, Weiss called this *negative sentiment override*. In other words, negative sentiment overrides positive interaction. In contrast, in *positive sentiment override* even messages an outsider would see as negative are not viewed as particularly negative by the partner; at least, the message is not taken personally. In negative sentiment override, however, a negative perception is the subtext that accompanies all interactions. In negative sentiment override people also start seeing their partner as possessing negative traits, such as selfishness, insensitivity, or meanness. Robinson and Price (1980) had observers in married couples' homes observing only positive behavior; they also trained the partners to observe when positivity was being communicated by their spouse. When couples were happy, the strangers and the partners were in total agreement with one another; however, when the married couples were unhappy, they saw only 50% of their partner's positive behavior toward them (as determined by the outside observers).

Psychologist Fritz Heider (1958) described a concept known as the *fundamental attribution error*, which is a tendency in people to minimize their own errors and attribute them to temporary, fleeting circumstances but to maximize the errors of others and attribute them to lasting, negative personality traits or character flaws. It's an "I'm okay, but you're defective" pattern. That attribution error is also made by unhappy couples. We found that the negative traits people see in their partners are also related to retelling the history of their relationship in negative terms.

7. *Diffuse physiological arousal.* Physiological arousal may occur when one feels overwhelmed by the way one's partner raises an issue. When one perceives that one is being emotionally attacked during conflict, the heart rate may elevate, and the body may start to secrete adrenaline in a fight-or-flight response. When this happens, people won't process information well. They also won't have access to their sense of humor and creativity. They may tend to repeat ourselves and become verbally aggressive or want to run away. We call this state of diffuse physiological arousal—during which people want to flee, aggress, or become defensive—*flooding*. A fairly universal finding is that, during an argument, men are more likely than women to rehearse distress-maintaining thoughts, which relates to men's becoming diffusely physiologically aroused. When one is flooded, it is very important to take breaks and self-soothe in order to avoid escalating the conflict. In our practices, we use structured breaks, relaxation instructions, and biofeedback devices that help teach couples self-soothing techniques.

8. *The failure of men to accept influence from wives.* This manifests in one of two patterns of rejecting influence: (a) male emotional disengagement (this eventually becomes mutual emotional disengagement) or (b) male escalation (belligerence, contempt, defensiveness) in response to wives' low-intensity negative affect (complaining). Men who are Masters of relationships don't reject influence from their partner as often. They tend to say things like "Okay," or "Good point," or "You're making perfect sense, really," or "You're starting to convince me." This is not compliance; it is lively give-and-take. To be powerful in a relationship, one must be capable of accepting influence on some things one's partner wants.

In our research, these factors have predicted relationship demise. To understand how to help couples, however, we needed more: a theory. After subsequent analyses and careful study, we arrived at our Sound Relationship House theory of why relationships wind up as Masters or Disasters.

SOUND RELATIONSHIP HOUSE THEORY

This theory is akin to a house with seven levels. Figure 4.1 summarizes the Sound Relationship House theory. The first three levels of the Sound Relationship House theory describe friendship in relationships. As a scien-

Figure 4.1. The Sound Relationship House theory.

tist, you have to define what you mean in order to measure things reliably, and that process can also provide a recipe for success. In the first three of the following sections, we discuss what we mean by *friendship*. To be good friends, partners need to be able to do three things: (a) build love maps, (b) nurture fondness and admiration, and (c) turn toward versus away.

1. Build Love Maps

A *love map* is like a mental road map that a partner creates of his or her partner's inner psychological world. Love maps help both partners to feel known in the relationship. When partners ask each other, "What are your worries and stresses at the moment?" or "What are some of your hopes and aspirations, or some of your dreams, values, and goals in life?" people are learning more about their partners, thereby building love maps of each other's worlds. In other words, we learn who our partner is by asking questions, especially open-ended ones, and remembering the answers.

When partners ask each other a question, it's like an invitation to come closer and be seen and understood. This process deepens friendship.

2. Share Fondness and Admiration

There are two parts to nurturing affection, respect, and admiration in a relationship. First, you need a habit of mind that scans your world for qualities to admire, appreciate, and be proud of in your partner. This process is the opposite of a critical habit of mind that scans for your partner's mistakes. Second, the words of appreciation or admiration must come out of your mouth or be expressed nonverbally, not stay hidden. The idea then is to catch your partner doing something right and to say, "Thanks for doing that."

3. Turn Toward Versus Away

When people are just hanging out together, they often express their needs to one another verbally or nonverbally. We call this making *bids* for emotional connection. Partners may make bids in order to ask for attention, interest, conversation, humor, affection, warmth, empathy, help, support, and so on. When responded to well by the other partner, these tiny moments of emotional connection are like deposits made into an emotional bank account. The following is an example: "There's a pretty boat . . . " If the other partner makes no response, that's turning away from the partner's bid, so no deposit is made. If the partner responds in a crabby way, like "Will you be quiet? I am trying to read!" that's turning against the other's bid. That response may lead to a debit taken out of the emotional bank account. On the other hand, if the response is "Huh!" that's turning toward the partner's bid, and a positive deposit is made into the account. And sometimes "huh" is as good as it gets. Now, if the response is "Wow, that *is* a beautiful boat. Hey baby, let's quit our jobs and get a boat like that and sail away together; what do you say?" we call that *enthusiastic turning toward*. The size of the couple's emotional bank account contributes to the strength of their relationship.

We have discovered that love maps, fondness and admiration, and turning toward are not only the building blocks of a couple's friendship but also the basis for humor and affection during conflict, which in turn creates smoother conflict management. They are also the basis for effective repair during conflict. Best of all, a good-quality friendship is significantly related to deeper romance, more passion, and good sex in the relationship.

4. The Positive Perspective: Positive and Negative Sentiment Overrides

What happens when friendship isn't working? You go into negative sentiment override. You may hear criticism when none is intended, or you expect that your partner doesn't like you, or that he or she shouldn't be given the benefit of the doubt. On the other hand, when the friendship is working well, there will be positive sentiment override. Here, the positive sentiments about the relationship and your partner override the negative things your partner might do. You take negativity not as personal criticism but instead as evidence that your partner might be stressed.

5. Manage Conflict

We use the term *manage* conflict instead of *resolve* conflict, because relationship conflict is natural, and it has functional, positive aspects. For example, it helps people learn how to better love and understand their partners, deal with change, and renew courtship over time. Couples should try to manage, but not eliminate, conflict.

During conflict, the Masters of relationship are gentle toward one another. They soften start-up (including preemptive repair), they accept influence from one another, they self-soothe, they repair and deescalate during their conflict discussions, and they compromise.

Our research has revealed that 69% of the time when couples were asked to talk about an area of continuing disagreement, what they discussed was a perpetual issue. Perpetual problems have to do with fundamental differences between partners that stem from differences in personality or lifestyle needs. These are issues without resolution that couples often deal with for years. Master couples work to establish a calm dialogue about these problems, knowing that they will never go away or be fully resolved. The Masters of relationship seem to arrive at some acceptance of their problem. Simultaneously they also communicate acceptance of their partner, a desire to improve this problem, as well as amusement, respect, and affection. In contrast, if a couple cannot establish such a dialogue, the conflict may become gridlocked, or full of escalation or avoidance. Gridlocked conflict eventually leads to emotional disengagement.

The following are the differences between gridlock and dialogue in regard to a perpetual issue:

- *Gridlocked conflict.* Our visual image for gridlock is two fists in opposition. In gridlocked conflict, people feel fundamentally rejected by their partner. When they talk about the problem, they feel that they are just spinning their wheels and not making any headway on it. There is no possibility of compromise. Over time, they become more and more entrenched, polarized, and extreme in their positions. Conversations on this issue just lead to frustration and hurt. Over time, gridlocked partners start vilifying each other. Most commonly, people start thinking of their partner as selfish.

- *Dialogue with a perpetual issue.* In contrast, dialogue with a perpetual issue contains a lot of positive affect (amusement, laughter, affection, empathy). Couples dialoguing about a perpetual issue seem to be trying to arrive at a better understanding of the issue or some temporary compromise. They have an amused "Oh, here we go again" attitude that involves a lot of acceptance, taking responsibility, and amusement while still trying to make things better.

Why do people get gridlocked on issues in the first place? Our research has revealed that there is a very good reason most people cannot yield on their gridlocked problems. Behind each person's gridlocked position lies something deep and meaningful—something core to that person's belief system, needs, history, or personality. It might be a strongly held value or perhaps a dream not yet lived. And people can no more yield and compromise on these issues than they can give up the bones of who they are and what they value about themselves. Compromise seems like selling themselves out, which is unthinkable.

When a relationship becomes safe enough, however, and one partner clearly communicates that he or she wants to understand the underlying meaning of the partner's position, that partner can finally open up and talk about feelings, dreams, and needs. Persuasion and problem solving are postponed in favor of the goal of understanding each person's underlying dreams on the issue. We call this intervention the *dreams-within-conflict* intervention.

6. Make Life Dreams Come True

A crucial aspect of any relationship is creating an atmosphere that encourages each person to talk honestly about his or her dreams, values, convictions, and aspirations and to feel that the relationship supports those life dreams. Here, we return to love maps in a deeper way. One of our favorite films is *Don Juan DeMarco*. In that film, Johnny Depp plays a psychiatric patient who thinks he is Don Juan. He transforms the life of his psychiatrist, played by Marlon Brando. Brando is about to retire. One day, after Depp talks to him about women, Brando converses with his wife, Faye Dunaway, in their garden. He asks her what her life dreams are. After a silence, she says, "I thought you'd never ask." Making life dreams come true is about asking and remembering the answer.

7. Create Shared Meaning

A relationship is also about building a life together, a life that has a sense of shared purpose and meaning. Victor Frankl (1992) said that the pursuit of happiness is empty. He suggested that people find happiness along the way as they pursue deeper meanings in life. And so, finally, we come to "the attic" of the Sound Relationship House, where couples build a sense of shared purpose and meaning. We believe that everyone is a philosopher trying to make some sense out of this brief journey we have through life. This level of the Sound Relationship House is about creating *shared* meaning in the relationship. People do that in many ways, including creating formal and informal rituals of connection, creating shared goals and life missions, supporting one another's basic roles in life, and agreeing on the meaning of central values and symbols (e.g., "What is a home?"). So here we return once again to build love maps but at a deeper level; thus, the seventh level of the Sound Relationship House loops back to the first level.

DIFFICULT CLIENTS WITHIN GOTTMAN METHOD COUPLES THERAPY

Individual therapy requires that only an individual and therapist be present in the consulting room; in relationship therapy, however, it is assumed that the two people appearing in the consulting room not only know one another but also have some sort of a relationship. But what is a "relationship"? Relationship therapy assumes that there is some sort of contract of mutual nurturance between the partners present in the consulting room. It is generally assumed that, for a married couple, the wedding has created a contract of mutual trust, commitment, investment in the relationship, mutual dependence, nurturance, and fidelity that forms the basis of the vows the individuals made to one another in the wedding ceremony.

The establishment of mutual trust has been the focus of our recent quantitative research (e.g., J. M. Gottman, 2011). Establishing mutual trust means that each person can count on the fact that his or her partner is working to ensure their best interests, instead of pursuing purely selfish interests. This means that the partner is "there for them." In other words, trust is built in a relationship by often putting one's self-interests second, after the partner's interests or the relationship's interests.

Hence, in couples therapy the working alliance is unique because it must be created and nurtured with both partners. At times, this can be difficult for the therapist because the therapist may have less empathy with one partner than the other. Furthermore, in the interest of building mutual trust, the therapist may at times be the lone advocate for the relationship itself and find him- or herself at odds with a self-centered versus a relationship-centered way of thinking of one or both partners. The couples therapist needs to establish working alliances with both individuals so that both will cooperate in taking care of one another's needs and the needs of the relationship. In our laboratory, this is assessed as a struggle between *me-ness* and *we-ness*.

Therapists' negative affect at times may stem from their own criticism of one member who is resistant to abandoning me-ness in favor of we-ness. The therapist, through countertransference, may then also fall victim to the Four Horsemen, judging instead of understanding the client. The therapist then needs to do internal work to express genuine empathy and help the resistant person have compassion for the partner's pain. That internal work involves transforming judgment to understanding and acceptance. In our work we have benefited from the thinking of Dan Wile (1999) in helping the therapist speak for the client who—at the moment—is least likely to recruit the therapist's empathy. Wile's method of speaking for this client aims to transform an attack–defend mode into collaborative self-disclosure, often through the intermediate mode of accepting responsibility for miscommunications. Wile does this by dramatizing the client's message and including positive feelings and mixed feelings to soften the attack quality and transform it into self-disclosure, always checking with the client for whom he is speaking.

The Sound Relationship House therefore makes specific assumptions of what a relationship is. It assumes, on the basis of research, that these people (i.e., the members of the couple) have agreed to a certain set of mutually held beliefs (J. M. Gottman, 1999). It assumes that they have agreed to try to become one another's friends, meaning that they agree to the goals of knowing one another well and to being known, respecting and loving one another, and turning toward one another's needs. In dealing with the inevitable conflict that emerges in any relationship, the theory also assumes that the partners will attempt to fairly resolve solvable conflicts and work toward compromise. Furthermore, it assumes that, in the relationship, the partners have agreed to accept one another and mutually respect each other's existential values, which form the basis for dialogue when they face perpetual conflicts. Finally, the theory assumes that the partners have agreed to try to honor one another's dreams and to create a sense of shared meaning and purpose in building their lives together.

The theory therefore clearly defines which kinds of clients will be generically difficult. These difficult couples will be the ones who do not want to meet the above conditions. In other words, the couples will struggle with one or more of the following attributes:

- There will be a broken contract of commitment, investment in the relationship, mutual nurturance, and fidelity that once formed the basis of their vows to each other;
- one partner (or both) does not wish to know the other well;
- one (or both) does not wish to be known;

- one (or both) does not wish to show respect for the other partner;
- one (or both) does not wish to show love for the partner;
- one (or both) does not wish to turn toward and meet the other's needs;
- one (or both) does not wish to attempt to fairly resolve solvable conflicts;
- one (or both) does not wish to compromise on any conflict;
- one (or both) of them does not wish to accept the other;
- one (or both) does not wish to convey a mutual respect for existential meanings of the other's position;
- one (or both) does not wish to dialogue about perpetual conflicts;
- one (or both) does not wish to honor the other's dreams; or
- one (or both) does not wish to create a sense of shared meaning and purpose in building their lives together.

Therefore, the theory defines the *minimal conditions necessary* for there to be a "relationship" to work on in the clinical consulting room.

CASE EXAMPLES OF DIFFICULT CLIENTS IN COUPLES THERAPY

What follows are descriptions of three difficult cases—all examples of partners' refusal to agree to one or more of the conditions necessary for a relationship to exist—and our reactions to them.

A Joint Difficult Case: The Wife Did Not Match Up to His Mistress

This couple was seen by both of us working together. They completed only the three assessment sessions and decided not to continue with therapy. The couple was married and had a preschool-age child. The wife lived in Seattle, Washington. For his work, the husband commuted between Seattle and another major city. The presenting problem was that in the other major city the husband had a mistress, and he could not decide between his wife and his mistress. He claimed that he loved his wife and child and valued their joint parenting. He said he cared about the history he and his wife had together.

However, in some very fundamental ways he preferred his mistress to his wife because he claimed that his wife was a very negative person, while the mistress was a very positive person. By "negative" he meant that in Seattle when he came home from work his wife often had a set of complaints that she voiced to him about her difficulties during the day parenting a young child and scaling back her own career to be a mother. He reported that he didn't think he should have to listen to this negativity when he had worked hard all day. He reported that his mistress didn't complain but instead nurtured and comforted him at the end of a day.

His wife claimed that she was primarily negative because she felt betrayed and insecure by his having a mistress in another city. She cried in the first session; then he reported being annoyed by her tears. The husband disagreed that his mistress caused his wife's negativity. He said that his wife was constantly negative even before he had a mistress, and, in fact, it was precisely her negativity that "drove him" to seek solace with another woman who was more pleasing to him. The husband said that he was irritated by his wife's pain about the infidelity and felt no need to deal with her pain.

Fundamentally, this husband did not think he should have to turn toward his wife's needs. In his view, a relationship was about the wife turning toward his needs and not reciprocity in turning toward each other's needs. The mistress offered him precisely the contract he wanted. Therefore, his solution was to divorce the wife, arrange shared custody with his child, and then marry the mistress. At the base of the difficulty was his belief that he should have to turn toward his wife's bids for connection only if they contained no negative affect. He could not tolerate negative affect because he was stressed by it, and his own, more important needs were then ignored.

In this husband's mind his marriage did not require fidelity or a responsibility to meet his wife's needs. In actuality, then, this couple did not have a relationship.

When we told the couple that relationship therapy was contraindicated when an ongoing affair existed and that the affair would have to be ended before therapy could start, the husband hostilely refused to meet that condition and stomped out of the office, never to return.

Julie's initial response to this moment was sympathy for the wife, negative judgment of the husband, and the urge to say to the wife, "Good riddance." Undoubtedly there was also some underlying hurt pride and a sense of defensiveness: What was wrong with this husband that we couldn't turn him around?

After reflection, however, Julie fell back on a fundamental belief that comes in very handy at moments like those of the last session: The couple therapist's primary job is to witness each partner's truth and the dynamics of the relationship and to give the partners tools and insight if they want them. Ultimately, however, it is each partner's choice as to whether or not to proceed toward a deeper relationship. The therapist cannot and should not make that decision for the couple, regardless of how hopeful the therapist may be for the resurrection of a failed relationship. Thus, in this example, Julie retreated to her overall philosophy about treatment, shrugged her shoulders, and reasoned that the husband in this case, for whatever reasons he held within, did not want this relationship; therefore no work could be done. The challenge was to refrain from judging the husband's resistance to choosing one relationship, preferably the one with his wife over the other with his mistress, and the husband's refusal to commit to a marital rebuilding process. Phrases such as "narcissistic," and "wants to have his cake and eat it, too," jumped to mind. But who was she to judge? Perhaps at this time, his decision was an impossible one, a perfect 50/50 cost–benefit analysis compounded by terrible anxiety about loss, rendering a choice infinitely difficult to make. The resultant frustration was aided by the hope that this wife, once divorced, would happily stumble on a wonderful new partner who could appreciate her for everything she was worth and that the husband would eventually land in individual therapy where he could figure out his commitment issues and get it together (literally).

John's Difficult Case: The Wife Did Not Respect Her Husband and Did Not Wish to Meet His Needs

This couple was in their mid 30s. Marty was the CEO of a successful business, jointly owned with his wife, Diane. She did not work in the company but was a stay-at-home mother of three children and an avid golfer. Marty was a very active and committed father. Diane had always been very athletic. Marty was also somewhat athletic, but he disliked the game of golf. He had initially been a commando and then a career military officer in the army's special forces. He had risen to the rank of colonel and had been a Pentagon adviser to the President on counterterrorism. A great deal of their current social life centered around the golf country club, although Marty wasn't as involved there as Diane was.

Marty had come from a physically abusive and highly critical home, and he had learned to stay under his parents' radar to avoid punishment. He had felt invisible during his childhood, even though he was very successful academically and in sports. His parents never came to any of his games or gave him any praise for his academic success. Diane had also had a difficult childhood with a very controlling and critical mother and passive father. She coped with her childhood stresses by building her friendship network and becoming very popular in both high school and college. Later, she had spent some time working as a model and was now very fashion conscious.

Diane initially presented a number of issues that made her unhappy in the marriage. One of her chief issues was that she had suffered a serious illness several years ago prior to coming for therapy, and she didn't feel that Marty was there for her when she was ill. A second issue she presented was that she wasn't sure she was still in love with Marty. That grieved Marty, and he spoke about being deeply remorseful about having chosen work over being as involved with Diane during her illness, as she had wanted him to be. A third issue Diane presented was that Marty wasn't very much fun anymore, and all of her fun centered on her friends at country club activities that Marty didn't usually attend.

When I asked Marty about his issues, he said that he wanted to do whatever he could so that Diane would be happily married again. He also wished that Diane could be less angry and that they could argue less, but he thought that would happen once Diane was happier.

What made this couple difficult clients for John emerged when they began working on the couple's needs. First we had worked successfully on the attachment injury from Marty's not being there for Diane during her illness. Next, Diane listed a number of other, very specific needs she had related to Marty's being more supportive at home with housework and chores, participating more in the country club, and being more romantically attentive to her. Marty initially had said he had very few needs in life and that his only real need was for Diane to be happy. To meet Diane's needs, they attended more country club events, went on more romantic dates, and went on a vacation to Hawaii that Marty had planned, but Diane didn't find the time together very satisfying.

In the course of working on conflict, John encouraged Marty to talk about what he needed from Diane. Diane objected to these questions and said that she had not come to therapy to meet Marty's needs and didn't think that was her role. She announced that she had come to therapy to have Marty court her, not for her to court Marty. John disagreed with her and explained that for a relationship to work well both people had to be willing to meet one another's needs.

At the beginning of the next session, Diane said that she had become very angry with John and decided that John was destroying their marriage. John's annoyance with Diane began. John then began seeing a psychiatrist weekly who supervised him whenever he experienced frustration with Diane. The issues John had with Diane stemmed from his own relationship with his own sister. In that relationship John was at times competitive with his sister for their parents' attention. His sister's assertiveness and his own passivity in John's primary family left John with unresolved resentments. These resentments surfaced as Diane's anger toward Marty left John identifying with Marty against Diane. To deal with the difficulty John then had in being compassionate toward Diane, John decided to work harder to "do a Dan Wile" for Diane during their sessions when he felt critical of Diane.

Diane kept coming to the sessions, but she was now very angry with both John and Marty. John validated her anger at him, because Diane had started with the assumption that only Marty needed to change to make this marriage better but, as the therapy proceeded, John had stated that both partners needed to change. That felt like a betrayal to Diane. John spoke for Diane to Marty, expressing her desire for changes to begin on Marty's side as a prerequisite for her own desire to change.

John also began speaking for Diane about Marty's unavailability to her. He started working on Marty's turning toward Diane more, on a day-to-day basis and on the Gottman–Rapoport blueprint for constructive conflict (see http://www.gottman.com). However, because the conflict blueprint required Marty to state his own needs, John elicited Diane's cooperation with that assumption of the blueprint.

The blueprint encouraged Marty to start thinking of what he needed from Diane. Marty began thinking of these needs and asking for individual sessions in which he talked about how lonely he was in the marriage. Diane also wanted equal time with John in individual sessions, which were then scheduled. Diane was sullen and angry during her individual sessions and said that the relationship wasn't getting any better for her. John worked hard on himself to empathize with Diane's frustration with Marty and the therapeutic process.

The amount of conflict between Marty and Diane declined dramatically in the next few sessions of therapy. Diane felt heard and became somewhat happier. However, that happiness was short lived as Marty began talking more about what he needed from Diane and talking about how lonely he felt in the marriage. He announced that he was particularly disturbed about the amount of time and attention she was giving to Henry, a married physician in the country club. Diane had planned and organized a birthday party for Henry that was supposed to take place in their home, in which Marty was to play the role of bartender.

Marty went further. Diane became very defensive when Marty said that he was jealous and that he suspected that her relationship to Henry was at least an emotional affair and perhaps a sexual affair. Diane denied this allegation. However, Marty announced that he had followed them during one of their days together, and they had seemed like lovers to him. Diane was furious that Marty had followed them, but she then admitted to having strong feelings for Henry. Marty said that whatever was going on, he needed Diane to end her relationship with Henry. Diane refused. The birthday party took place in their home, and Marty was a sullen bartender.

Over the course of several subsequent sessions, Marty talked more about his needs. He said that he had suppressed his own needs, first as a boy at home because he was afraid of his parents and then again as required of a soldier in the army. He felt that it was important for him to talk about how Diane had recently stopped being romantically and sexually responsive to him. He also raised an issue about the way she dealt with conflict with their children. He said that he hated her hitting the children, and he talked more about his own childhood abuse. Diane said that she believed that hitting children was effective and that was how she had been raised. Marty told her that in his private time with the children, they had complained about the hitting and asked him to get their mother to stop. Diane refused to discuss this issue with him.

In one subsequent session Diane admitted that the problems she was having with Marty stemmed from the fact that she didn't respect him anymore. He said that that explained a lot and then sarcastically asked her what it would take for her to respect him other than his being a good provider and a good father. She replied that because she was only attracted to and only respected athletic men, she might respect him more if he did something really athletic and challenging, like climbing Mount Ranier, which is known in the Northwest as a challenging climb. Surprisingly, Marty agreed, and he began to train for the adventure. Diane felt validated.

After Marty climbed Mount Rainier, there was a major turning point in the therapy. He had stated his need for Diane and the children to be there and greet him when he came down the mountain, and he was shocked that she wasn't there. He later discovered that she had decided instead to go to a country club function with Henry. At that point Marty stated his huge disappointment with Diane not meeting him with the children after his climb. He also repeated his demand that Diane end her relationship with Henry, but this time he stated his need as an ultimatum. He said that if she didn't end her relationship with Henry, whatever its nature, Marty was moving out and filing for divorce.

When Diane again refused to end her relationship with Henry, Marty moved out of their house and hired a lawyer. Diane hired another. There were no further sessions of couples therapy after that point, although John urged them to continue therapy to work out how to buffer their children in the divorce.

The couple divorced. Marty bought a house a few blocks from his former home. He got joint custody of the children, and his relationships with his children became closer. He eventually began dating a woman he had initially met on the Ranier climb.

Julie's Difficult Case

James and Sheila entered couples therapy as a last-ditch attempt to save a dying marriage. The marriage was James's third and Sheila's first. Both had been raised in the Mormon faith in Utah, but there the similarities ended. James had grown up with a terribly abusive father and, after his parents divorced when James was 10, a desperately poor mother. Throughout his preadolescence and teen years, his mother worked long hours, leaving him straggling in the desert that surrounded their trailer. Sheila, meanwhile, grew up in a hardworking farm family that was stable but emotionally silent. She had no idea how to build intimate relationships, especially sexual ones.

James educated himself through his neighbor's porn magazines. Later, his first two marriages, to women 19 and 21 years old, respectively, fulfilled him sexually but lacked responsible partnership. In short, both women bled him dry with debt. Sheila was much more mature, a hard worker, and the perfect candidate for partnership and parenthood. To Sheila, James represented an equally hard worker and a bright and promising star in both his profession and faith.

Their courtship was deeply respectful, romantic, and very physically limited according to the precepts of their faith. Only kisses on the cheek were shared. Both partners looked forward to their marriage night.

Come the night, all hell broke loose. James wanted wild and crazy sex, as he put it, after waiting so long, and virgin Sheila wanted tender, gentle, and patient initiation. Neither got what they wanted. Sheila was trauma- tized by James's insistence on fellatio, cunnilingus, and intercourse in vary- ing positions during their first bedroom hour. She tried to be a dutiful wife, but as their honeymoon later churned into months of home life—savings account- and résumé-building, plus having three children in 5 years—they found themselves shipwrecked with conflicting needs. They both believed in what they called the "traditional marriage" model, in which the husband's word should be final and the wife's duty should be to run the home and be a total support to her husband. This amounted to details like James leaving his wife every day with a list of things to get done, then asking her for a report in the evening about their accomplishment. It also meant that she would lay out his toothbrush and toothpaste and pajamas each night and his clothes for work before sunrise the next day. Finally, James demanded that they have sex on a schedule—Monday, Thursday, and Saturday nights—and that he be the determiner of its type. He mostly preferred giving Sheila scripts to fol- low in which she had to role play a characterized woman of some type, and he would criticize her if she didn't get the tone of the words right. Many of the words involved terms that she considered lewd and disgusting and self- deprecating; nonetheless, he admonished her to use them. She followed his orders; however, by the time Julie met with them 14 years later in her therapy office, Sheila did so while being totally split off from herself in a dissociative posttraumatic state. James hadn't noticed.

After the first three sessions with this couple in their assessment phase, Julie had her first negative reactions. Thinking of herself as a femi- nist from way back and believing herself to be a social activist, she found it exceedingly difficult to have compassion for this husband. He represented everything she had fought against in the late 1960s and 1970s (prepare yourselves for the judgment): a tyrant lording himself over "his" woman, a sexual abuser—perhaps even a rapist, and a narcissist. Yes, James was warm, smart, and funny; he even looked like Alan Alda. But what a piece of work he was as a husband. Meanwhile, Sheila was sweet, smart, too, and deeply oppressed, *and* she wanted nothing more than to better please her husband sexually.

The hardest thing Julie had to manage was her overwhelming desire to change this marriage into what Julie thought was best: a nice, feminist and egalitarian marriage in which household duties were split, parenting responsibilities were shared, and needs for both were equally honored. Instead, Julie had to listen to what these partners wanted, first and foremost. This was hard.

To overcome her own negative feelings toward the husband, Julie also used the Dan Wile method of speaking for him compassionately. She built a strong therapeutic alliance with James. James wanted a more sexually adventurous wife. Sheila wanted to understand what was wrong with her sexually and to fix it. Using her re-formed alliance with James, Julie introduced the partners to the notion of posttraumatic stress disorder and how Sheila suffered from it, not because of anyone's fault (specifically, James's) but because of bona fide ignorance on both their parts about what a healthy sexual relationship should be—one that was responsive to both their needs.

James was subsequently able to own that his sexual education rose almost entirely from the pornographic pages of his childhood. There he had formulated his images of the perfect sexual partner. His fascination with pornographic sex had continued up to now through daily use of Internet porn sites for masturbation. Sheila knew about this but wasn't bothered by it because it took some pressure off of her to do even more for him. On further evaluation, it was clear that James was addicted. He could no more refrain from visiting sites than from drinking water daily. Julie referred him to a good sex addiction specialist, and he began individual work immediately.

Much to James's chagrin, Julie also recommended that they put a moratorium on all sexual activity until Sheila had a chance to do some recovery from the sex-related trauma from their marriage and to figure out what she actually liked sexually. This was no small order for James, because his other avenue for sexual release, masturbating to Internet porn, had now also been cut off. Yet James, without hesitation, agreed. This surprised Julie, who had become more compassionate toward him. It turned out that James, beneath the bluster, was sweet, kind, bewildered, very much in love with his wife, and confused, himself, about what a healthy marriage should be. He was, in many ways, a babe in the woods where marriage and sexuality were concerned, just like his wife. He had no idea what role emotional intimacy played in the bedroom, but he knew that indeed, he had felt something missing from the start, something he desperately wanted, and it wasn't better role plays.

Over the months, Sheila read Lonnie Barbach's (2000) book, *For Yourself: The Fulfillment of Female Sexuality*, and did all the exercises. James, of course, wanted to know all the details of what she was learning and what she was doing, but with Julie's encouragement, Sheila created boundaries to protect her own private world.

Sheila was also encouraged to write out descriptions of whatever past traumatic sexual episodes with James she needed to heal from and to share her writings with James in session. Again, James surprised Julie, nearly crying in every session with guilt at how he'd affected his wife. In short order, Julie's feelings toward James dramatically changed. No longer the egotistical, self-centered bully, he now appeared to be an essentially fine human being who had definitely gotten the wrong idea about sex from a culture that perpetuated the myth of woman as sex slave. He had married a woman who had no idea that she had a right to her own needs, sexual and otherwise, and in doing her "duty" had underscored the validity of his myth.

Over time, they resumed their bedroom life in a very different way—slow, tender, and rather conventional, by James's standards. But despite the "creative" constriction, James was buoyed by the actual presence of his wife in the act, both physically and emotionally, which enabled James to expand his own sexuality into one that was more heartfelt and tender.

They left therapy 18 months later. Sheila still laid out James's toothbrush and toothpaste every night and reported on her activity lists at dinner. James still wrote the lists, scheduled sex, and ruled the roost. Julie still bristled at the sounds of obedience. But for all that, their marriage was now one of mutual respect, adoration, love, and healing—and maybe a tiny bit more egalitarianism.

CONCLUSION

Couples therapy is no easy road. The therapist must stay objective yet compassionate with both partners and, above all, stay true to the needs of the relationship as well as the needs of each partner. With twice the clients in the room plus a relationship, there's lots of room for the therapist's negative reactions to arise. So as a couples therapist, one has to be adept at jumping from client chair to chair, empathizing with the partners as they slump in distress, and squarely supporting the connection between them, while managing all the internal reactions triggered at every turn. These are not easy tasks, and they are ones on which we both will be working far into the future.

REFERENCES

Bach, G. R., & Wyden, P. (1968). *The intimate enemy: How to fight fair in love and marriage*. New York, NY: Avon Books.

Barbach, L. (2000). *For yourself: The fulfillment of female sexuality*. New York, NY: Signet.

Frankl, V. (1992). *Man's search for meaning* (4th ed.). Boston, MA: Beacon Press.

Gottman, J. M. (1999). *The marriage clinic: A scientifically based marital therapy*. New York, NY: Norton.

Gottman, J. M. (2011). *The science of trust: Emotional attunement for couples*. New York, NY: Norton.

Gottman, J. S. (Ed.). (2004). *The marriage clinic casebook*. New York, NY: Norton.

Heider, F. (1958). *The psychology of interpersonal relations*. New York, NY: Wiley. doi:10.1037/10628-000

Robinson, E. A., & Price, M. G. (1980). Pleasurable behavior in marital interaction: An observational study. *Journal of Consulting and Clinical Psychology, 48*, 117–118. doi:10.1037/0022-006X.48.1.117

Weiss, R. L. (1980). Strategic behavioral marital therapy: Toward a model for assessment and intervention. In J. P. Vincent (Ed.), *Advances in family intervention assessment and theory* (Vol. 1, pp. 229–271). Greenwich, CT: JAI Press.

Wile, D. (1999). *After the fight*. New York, NY: Guilford Press.

5

MANAGING NEGATIVE REACTIONS TO CLIENTS IN CONJOINT THERAPY: IT'S NOT ALL IN THE FAMILY

LAURIE HEATHERINGTON, MYRNA L. FRIEDLANDER, AND VALENTÍN ESCUDERO

Family therapy may be the one modality that can arouse negative emotional reactions from the therapist even before treatment begins. Especially for novice therapists but also for experienced clinicians who treat only individuals, the thought of working simultaneously with multiple individuals, especially people who tend to be unhappy with each other, can be daunting. One envisions needing to figure out how to be a conversational "traffic cop," how to contain angry adolescents in front of their parents or warring spouses in front of their children—all the while trying to avoid becoming enmeshed in the family's dynamics. Such scenarios can make the relative peace of sitting with a single client seem considerably more appealing.

To be sure, there are times in family therapy when these visualizations are quite realistic. There tends to be a lot going in family therapy sessions, and clients' behaviors have complex and reverberating effects on everyone in the room and on the system as a whole, as do strategic interventions. Also,

DOI: 10.1037/13940-005

Transforming Negative Reactions to Clients: From Frustration to Compassion, A. W. Wolf, M. R. Goldfried, and J. C. Muran (editors)

unlike clients in group therapy, family members go home together, and this additional element must be considered at all times.

Family therapy *is* different. Despite the complexity, therein also lies a special kind of excitement, because this treatment modality affords a unique opportunity for momentous change to happen right in the consulting room. Moreover, the flip side of needing to think systemically about the complex problems of families is thinking systemically about possible therapeutic solutions, which makes this work immensely interesting and gratifying when it works out for the best.

In this chapter, we discuss, analyze, and propose solutions for managing various kinds of negative emotional reactions that therapists tend to experience when working conjointly with families. First we address problematic reactions that arise from the family's dynamics; those that originate within the therapist; and those that are related to working with wider systems, such as social services and other providers who are involved with the family. We then present a systemic schema for understanding negative reactions, followed by some general guidelines for managing them and for addressing this issue in training and supervision. Throughout the chapter, a variety of approaches to working with families is represented, but the overriding theoretical orientation is integrative and systemic.

NEGATIVE REACTIONS RESULTING FROM THE FAMILY'S DYNAMICS

In couple and family therapy, the presence of multiple family people, often in conflict, typically at different life stages, sometimes with secrets, and usually with varying fears, needs, and desires, means that sometimes negative reactions in the therapist are responses to the challenging family dynamic itself, as discussed below.

Families That Make Poor Choices

As therapists, we are trained to be open, accepting, and nonjudgmental. We are aware of the many diverse lifestyles, choices, and circumstances in which families function and thrive, and we are taught that our personal values must not slide, unexamined, into the therapeutic agenda. Nonetheless, we often find ourselves having problematic responses to our clients' bad choices.

One such example is the Johnston family,[1] who sought help for a young child with behavior problems. The first session revealed a serious drinking

---

[1] All names throughout this chapter are pseudonyms.

problem on the husband's part; in the second session, the wife's loneliness emerged. Several nights a week found the couple in the local bar, while their two children (a young teen and a 9-year-old) remained home alone. In another case, Darlene Rosin, a preteen girl, was referred for several "individual" issues, including having minor motor tics and entertaining her friends at school with off-color stories and drawings. The treatment began with conjoint sessions as well as sessions alone with Darlene; the Rosin parents were exceptionally hard to engage and could not seem to focus on or agree on goals for therapy. There was no change in behavior despite the best efforts of the therapist. Nonetheless, the family came reliably and seemingly wanted to keep coming. Sensing that there was some piece missing, the therapist asked Darlene during an individual session, "What am I missing here? Something is not adding up." This question opened a floodgate, as the girl revealed that her mother was having an affair with a family friend, a "secret" that was known to everyone but that had never been acknowledged in the family.

In a different case, Nadine Alois, a young single mother, struggled with the aggressive and defiant behavior of her three young children, including the 6-year-old's habit of using matches to light small fires. Initial work on behavior management involved instructing Nadine to remove all matches from the home. She did not, however, and before the next session, the boy set a fire that spread and resulted in an evacuation of the entire apartment complex. Fortunately, no one was injured, but the therapist had strong feelings toward the family that he found difficult to contain. In particular, he was angry with Nadine for not complying with his directive as well as upset about his own feelings of perceived incompetence.

In each of these cases, the therapist considered the choices made by the clients with reactions ranging from rue (all these families) to anger at the parents, fear for the children, resentment at being kept in the dark about a family secret (the Rosin family), and a nagging feeling of guilt for not having been able to prevent the fire setting (the Alois family). These negative feelings were unwelcome and were a hindrance to the empathy needed to work effectively with the families. In cases such as these, where does one even begin?

One starting place is with matter-of-fact acknowledgment, first on the part of the therapist and then in conversation with the clients, that all of these events involved choices. Like any choices, they had consequences, some short term and some longer term. The choices had consequences for individuals in the family, for the various subsystems (spousal, parental), and for the family as a whole. It may help therapists to ask themselves how, from the clients' perspective, those choices may have seemed reasonable at the time, especially in the short term (e.g., staying connected with one's husband or protecting the family from a nasty scene). Therapists who can approach problems such as these with empathy—or at least some understanding—are in a good position to help family members consider how the choices they made were not consistent with their long-term goals. In an optimal situation, family members will begin to collaborate to find alternative ways to meet their needs.

This strategy is especially difficult to carry out, however, when the poor choices are made by the parents, with detrimental effects on the children's health and well-being. A sense of urgency in all these cases, but especially in the case of Nadine Alois, complicated the therapist's emotional response to the family, engendering a felt need to "make everything right, *right now.*" Although novice therapists who work with individuals can also fall prey to rescue fantasies, this trap is even greater for beginning family therapists. Certainly, family therapists need to be prepared for and take swift action when a child's welfare is endangered, but therapists also need to accept the impossibility of "making everything right, right now."

In the Alois case, for example, an immediate referral to child protective services resulted in the children being moved to foster care. During the ensuing year, Nadine continued to learn parenting skills, which were critically necessary for her own and her children's well-being. The work was not smooth or linear, and Nadine's individual issues were soon revealed. Because of her resistance to the parenting training, Nadine's personal problems had to be addressed, and the work on parenting skills was temporarily set aside. The therapy was ultimately successful, and the children were returned to their mother's care.

Therapists should anticipate that problematic families such as these do not have neat and orderly solutions; however, they should be encouraged by research evidence that making some early progress in reducing negativity—in even just one problem area—can enhance retention in family therapy (Sexton & Alexander, 2003) and by the fact that in a family system, progress in one area can have positive, reverberating effects in other areas. For instance, when a family secret is revealed and dealt with in a safe, constructive manner, the process of doing so illustrates for the family the value of facing difficult issues head on rather than avoiding them. These lessons can be applied later to other difficult issues as they arise for the family.

Families That Do Not Improve

Some families and some family dynamics in therapy are simply harder than others. Difficult cases are those in which progress is slow or sometimes nonexistent; these cases can cause therapists to feel immensely frustrated and ineffectual. In extreme circumstances, therapists' negative feelings are expressed, directly or indirectly, as anger or even as rejection of the family.

There are at least two types of stagnant therapy. One type occurs with *multiproblem families*. Consider a family in which the parents and teenage son are in serious conflict, with externalizing behavior by the son, unemployment of and depression in the father, terminal illness in a grandparent, and associated feelings of loss and grief. Perhaps the car has just broken down as well and the family dog has a medical crisis. These circumstances feel overwhelming to the family, and they can be overwhelming for the therapist as well. In cases like these, nothing in the single-protocol toolbox—cognitive behavior therapy for depression, functional family therapy for externalizing disorders, career counseling for employment, emotion-focused two-chair work for dealing with loss—will be effective on its own.

First, the therapist needs to help the family articulate and agree on treatment goals, prioritizing the most pressing needs while acknowledging the importance (for future work) of the less pressing ones. Establishing a shared sense of purpose for the conjoint therapy—to honor each person's needs and to promote emotional commitment within the family—is critical (see Friedlander, Escudero, & Heatherington, 2006, for an extended discussion of this process). The family may decide, for example, that the shared priorities are to help the son stay in school and out of trouble with the law and to prevent the father from sinking further into depression. It may be that one family member, typically the mother, is taking on most of the burden, which leaves her and the family vulnerable to even more severe crises if her mental or physical health fails. To forestall such occurrences, the source of a family's strength and resilience should be an early component of the assessment process.

Next, the therapist and therapy team (note that working with a team is extremely helpful in cases like these) need to conceptualize the family's problems in systemic terms (Friedlander et al., 2006). What, if any, systemic patterns are maintaining the family's problems? Are there systemic impediments to change? What underlying issues should be addressed so the clients can make progress? Are there issues of attachment that should be explored (Diamond, Siqueland, & Diamond, 2003), or is this a family whose strong emotional bonds can be used to therapeutic benefit? Indeed, what are the family's strengths? Nearly all families have some strengths, but it is all too easy to overlook them when little progress is being made. In any case, therapists (and supervisors) need to acknowledge and accept that multiproblem families are indeed highly difficult. For clients with chaotic home lives, it may seem that systematically pursuing a therapeutic agenda is repeatedly thwarted by crises, that just when one problem is fixed and the treatment gets back on track, another crisis ensues.

Other families that do not improve regardless of the therapist's best effort are *mystery families*. In the Allen family, a middle-class family that seemed to be functioning fine in both work and school domains, the mother and teenage daughter presented with conflict between them, mostly around the daughter's extreme anger, which palpably colored every interaction between them but which the daughter minimized. The mother claimed to be baffled about the source of her daughter's anger. The mother had been divorced and remarried about 5 years earlier; the daughter saw her father occasionally and indicated that she was satisfied with the arrangement. The stepfather declined to attend the therapy sessions, because he saw the issues as being solely between his wife and stepdaughter; the daughter indicated that the stepfather was "OK" and not the source of any trouble in the family.

After several sessions held conjointly and with the daughter alone, the therapist remained baffled about the problems and the treatment goals. The daughter behaved like a "therapy hostage" (Friedlander et al., 2006) and was minimally cooperative. Concerned about whether there was some kind of abuse going on or another important secret, the therapist asked the family directly, "What am I missing?" The response was "Nothing," according to both daughter and mother, who also was losing interest in therapy. The family wound up drifting away, a highly frustrating outcome for the therapist as well as, doubtless, for the clients. Roughly 3 years later, the therapist had a chance encounter with the mother, who reported that her daughter had finished high school and was happy and successful in college and that their relationship was difficult and still not fully satisfactory. Unfortunately, the public circumstances of this chance encounter did not lend itself to a discussion about what the mother thought, 3 years after therapy, about the seemingly failed treatment.

To be sure, there are cases in which a poorly chosen or poorly timed intervention or the lack of an appropriate intervention is the source of failure. There are other cases, however, including that of the Allens, in which the discomforting sense that nothing is happening occurs because one or more clients are simply not in a state of readiness for change. Family members can find themselves in treatment but, for whatever reason, are at a Precontemplation or Contemplation stage of change (Prochaska & DiClemente, 1983, 2005). Just as with individuals, families can be distressed but not ready, either collectively or individually, to move forward. Stages of change and motivational interviewing techniques are only now beginning to be discussed in regard to family therapy (cf. Kelch & Demmitt, 2010; Madsen, 2009), and creative use of these approaches may be of help when therapists are confronted with mystery families.

Families That Cannot Collaborate

Some families do not improve or improve very slowly, simply because they do not or cannot focus together on the task at hand. The therapist may assign a specific in-session task, for example, "Discuss the issue of your daughter's curfew" or "Can you please talk with your mom about your wanting her to stay out of your personal life . . . that you want more independence?" (Friedlander, Heatherington, Johnson, & Skowron, 1994). Instead of engaging in the task, the clients do everything else: complain about the therapy process, clam up, change the topic, joke around, bring up an unrelated complaint, and so on. The possibilities for avoiding engagement, especially in conjoint sessions, are endless, and every family therapist has seen a host of stalling maneuvers. After repeated and failed efforts to help family members commit to and sustain engagement with each other, a therapist may sense that he or she is working harder than the family. It is not long before feelings of exasperation set in.

This realization can actually be helpful in that it is a marker of the family's disengagement, which is the first step toward resolving it. Family members resist engagement for all sorts of reasons, including a lack of felt safety in the therapeutic session (Friedlander et al., 2006), motivated avoidance of certain topics, competing goals, and differences in maturity and developmental levels.

More important than why family members resist engagement, however, is how to handle the resistance. Resistance may be due to overt conflict that is readily observable in the session, the typical reluctance of adolescents to self-reveal to adults (Higham, Friedlander, Escudero, & Diamond, 2012), or a secret or other hidden dynamic within the family. To overcome resistance, therapists need to encourage family members to engage directly with one another. Sustaining engagement on therapeutic tasks has been studied empirically, and on the basis of intensive case analyses, Friedlander et al. (1994) developed an evidence-based conceptual model consisting of five iterative steps. First, clients must be helped to recognize their own contributions to the impasse. Second, they must communicate with one another about the engagement impasse. Third, they must genuinely listen to and acknowledge each other's thoughts and feelings, both expressing their own and hearing others. Fourth, this exchange helps them come to new constructions of or understandings about the impasse. Fifth, somewhere during this process the therapist must help family members recognize or uncover some motivation for engaging— typically, to strengthen the emotional affective bonds between them. At each step along the way, therapist interventions can facilitate progress toward engagement (Friedlander et al., 1994). In short, successful, sustained engagement involves both interpersonal and intrapersonal work "through which the dynamics of the family impasse are explored and motivations for engagement are made salient. Once engagement is achieved, the possibility of solving real-life family problems is enhanced" (Friedlander et al., 1994, p. 446).

Of course, not all engagement impasses and not all negative emotional reactions on the therapist's part are due to dynamics originating within the family. In the next section, we discuss how the person of the therapist can be a factor in negative reactions and how these reactions can be managed effectively.

NEGATIVE REACTIONS ORIGINATING WITHIN THE THERAPIST

After several years of pleading with her husband, Jim, to bring her stepchildren to family therapy, Marianne Hartwick finally succeeded. She convinced Jim to use the therapist's help to tell his 14- and 16-year-old daughters that their mother had committed suicide, that she had not died of a heart attack, as he had led them to believe for the past 13 years. Unaware of the family secret and Jim's crippling feelings of guilt, the therapist saw this taciturn man as morose, distant, uncaring, and withholding—in short, a carbon copy of the therapist's own father. In fact, Jim was nothing like this. Instead, the momentousness of what he was prepared to do paralyzed him with fear. Feeling unsafe with this therapist and unable to articulate the basis for his distrust, he refused to return after the initial session.

According to Haley (1987), therapists are responsible for all treatment failures. Although this may be an extreme view, there is increasing awareness in the field—based on empirical evidence—of the role therapists play in unsuccessful therapy, in particular the harmful attitudes and behaviors that contribute to treatment failure (Castonguay, Boswell, Constantino, Goldfried, & Hill, 2010). Harm can occur without the therapist's knowledge, for example, from unintentional acts or from acts of omission. As we have discussed, the complexity of working with multiple clients simultaneously, especially when the clients are having serious conflicts with each other, and the topics themselves (e.g., sexual intimacy, family power dynamics) render this treatment modality ripe for iatrogenic therapist reactions. In this section, we discuss problematic responses that have their origins in a therapist's lack of knowledge or experience, values, or personal background.

Lack of Knowledge or Experience

Empathic responding is as essential in family therapy as it is in individual treatment (Flaskas & Perlesz, 1998; Friedlander et al., 2006). The ability to respond with empathy demands not only affective attunement but also cognitive perspective taking, which Kohut (1984) called *vicarious introspection*, or the ability to put oneself in the shoes of another.

Therapists who are not parents themselves, as well as those who have never experienced a long-term romantic relationship or the death of a close family member, can find it difficult to fully understand clients who find them-selves in these circumstances. Therapists of any age who are not parents can only draw on their memories of childhood and not on a personal experience of having been totally responsible for the care of a child. For example, one novice therapist was unable to fathom the complex feelings of self-blame, anger, and helplessness felt by parents who came to therapy with their teenager, who was spiraling out of control. The therapist faulted the parents and applauded the adolescent's independence, even though it was bordering on self-destructive. At the suggestion of his supervisor, the therapist read some parenting books and then spoke with his own parents about their experience of his rebellious adolescence. Shocked to discover his own naïveté in this area, the therapist found several other means, including close supervision, to ensure that his work with parents and adolescents was evenhanded. Naturally, it is not pos-sible for any therapist to have had all of the life experiences of the families who seek help, but working with diverse families over time provides thera-pists with greater understanding of and empathy for issues that are personally foreign to them.

At times, therapists can be hindered by their own strong feelings during major developmental life stages, even—or especially—when their personal experiences are objectively similar but psychologically quite different than those of their clients. One therapist, having just experienced the thrill of a first baby, was confused when her efforts to join with a woman client, Kylie, who had also just given birth, failed. Kylie's circumstances were quite differ-ent from the therapist's, however, because this baby was her third, and the recent death of her own father, to whom she had been very close, was far more compelling for her at the time. What had failed, in fact, was the intro-spection needed for the therapist to recognize the differences between her own psychological circumstances and those of her client.

Nowhere is this issue more salient than in conjoint therapy when the therapist is experiencing his or her own marital distress or dissolution. A supervisor was taken aback to realize that in every one of her supervisee's cases with divorcing parents, the children's misbehavior—even when extreme—was not addressed, and the therapist consistently sided with the mother in coparenting arguments. Gentle probing in supervision revealed that the ther-apist was so disillusioned with marriage and so mistrustful of other people in general that she was subtly communicating to the clients hopelessness about mending broken attachments.

Lack of theoretical knowledge and/or technical skill also can prompt a therapist's negative reactions. When therapists lack understanding about how systems function, they can easily get caught up in power struggles, for example, by not appreciating the nature and complexity of circular causality. Invariably seeing one individual as right and the other as wrong can blind a therapist to the polarization that naturally takes place when a system is in acute distress. The result can be a seriously split working alliance (Heatherington & Friedlander, 1990; Muñiz de la Peña, Friedlander, & Escudero, 2009; Pinsof & Catherall, 1986).

Take the case of the Hendersons, for example. In sessions with their teenage children, Jenna Henderson blamed her husband, Art, for his gambling, his "moodiness," his "paranoia," and his isolation from the rest of the family. In session, Jenna spoke convincingly in a calm, measured fashion, whereas Art was loud and defensive. Not surprisingly, the therapist had trouble seeing the family's struggle from Art's perspective. The therapist insisted that Art seek individual help for his "long-standing personality problems," and her frustration mounted as Art became increasingly belligerent. Finally, when Art blew up and stomped angrily out of the room, the therapist's misguided recommendation seemed wholly justified. What she had failed to understand, however, was the overfunctioning–underfunctioning dynamic in this couple that led Jenna to appear far more emotionally mature than she actually was. Because of the therapist's ignorance of systems dynamics, Jenna took the prize in therapy, but the family lost.

Another case helps illustrate how a little knowledge, poorly applied, can be risky. In this case, a young novice therapist fresh from a powerful workshop demonstration of structural family therapy (Minuchin, 1974) saw a family consisting of a mother, her two young children, and the grandmother. The grandmother lived upstairs from the mother and children. She and her daughter had frequent disagreements, and she was critical of her daughter's parenting. The grandmother had also taken over the task of waking the children in the morning and getting them ready for school; she set her alarm clock every morning and left her apartment to go downstairs to her daughter's. The therapist's initial case formulation was that mother and grandmother were enmeshed. The therapist was critical of this situation and began intervening to build clearer boundaries between the two and to strengthen the mother–children subsystem. When this strategy failed and the therapist became visibly annoyed, the grandmother disclosed in a between-session phone call to the therapist that her daughter had a cocaine habit, was often up late into the night, and was therefore consistently unavailable to the children; thus, if the grandmother did not take over, the children would not have gotten to school or had any semblance of a normal upbringing. In other words, what the therapist perceived as dysfunctional was in fact functional for this family, which was accustomed to close extended family relationships and fluid boundaries between generations. Here, the therapist's lack of knowledge and his own stage-of-life separation issues (he was seeking more independence from his own family of origin) combined to create the negative reactions and misguided interventions.

Clash of Values

By its very nature, most family therapy is problem focused rather than symptom resolution focused. Although there are several effective approaches for helping families deal with major mental illness, substance abuse, and anorexia, among others (Friedlander & Diamond, 2012), most people seek professional help when their within-family conflicts seem overwhelming or irreconcilable. Many family conflicts involve a clash of values related to lifestyle ("Mothers shouldn't work outside the home"), parenting ("Teenagers today have much too much freedom"), elder care ("Why does your father have to live with us?"), religion ("I won't give up my faith just to be with you"), loyalty ("Why do you tell your sister everything about our private life?"), gender equity ("Why do you leave all the housework to me?"), sexual preference ("How can you just accept that our son is gay?"), and so forth.

Values are a reflection of worldview, and therapists are as prone as everyone else to believing that their own perspective is the correct one. When family members' struggles over core values strike a chord with the therapist, it is often difficult to maintain neutrality or see the issue systemically. In one treatment that was initiated because of the children's acting-out behavior, the preteen son revealed that his mother, Connie, was having an affair with the next-door neighbor. Although Connie's husband, Steve, told the therapist (in a session without the children) that he was hurt, he wanted Connie to feel fulfilled. If the neighbor were better able to do that, then he (Steve) would be content to sit back and tolerate the affair, as long as Connie did not leave him and the children. The therapist found it extremely difficult to help this family because of her own sense of moral outrage at Connie, whom she saw as narcissistic and unfeeling. What the therapist failed to see, however, was that Connie's blatant affair was the only way she knew to get Steve to pay attention to her, that she desperately wanted her marriage to improve so as to keep the family together, and that Steve's passivity was fueling the impasse. By siding with Steve, the therapist was unable to help this couple through a highly difficult point in their marriage. The family terminated treatment—without divorcing but also without hope.

Values in regard to extramarital affairs are naturally challenging for therapists. Another common clash of values, less obvious perhaps, has to do with the precedence of the spousal or the parental relationship. Benita divorced Alan in order to find a "soul mate," because she no longer felt passionately toward Alan. Benita saw their marriage as more like one of siblings than lovers, although she praised Alan for being "an excellent father, a good person, and a good provider." Their three children were suffering tremendously after their mother's departure, as was Alan. When he brought the children to therapy, with the goal of adjusting to their new single-parent situation, the therapist told the children that their mother had "made a self-centered decision." This remark not only hindered the family's healing process but also seriously damaged the children's relationship with their mother.

Personal Background

Like the families they serve, therapists have a personal history that can be either a source of understanding or a hindrance. The degree to which the identity of the therapist figures in the therapy is largely a matter of choice; however, the therapist's personal identity can also exert a covert influence on what takes place in treatment.

Therapists who have limited personal experience with cultural diversity, broadly defined (i.e., religion, socioeconomic status, race/ethnicity, disability, adoption, gender, and sexual orientation), need to make significant efforts to develop multicultural competencies. Naturally, developing these competencies (and being aware of one's biases) is essential regardless of the modality of therapy, but it is particularly important in couple and family therapy, for two reasons (Friedlander et al., 2006).

First, the presence of differing cultural identities (e.g., an interracial or interfaith marriage) within a couple or family requires a high level of sensitivity on the therapist's part. The therapist needs to explore how the clients construe their differing identities in order to help the family find some middle ground. It goes without saying that siding with one family member in a cultural conflict can be particularly harmful for the family's well-being.

Second, a family's cultural values and presenting concerns are often inextricably linked. Consider, for example, first-generation Mexican parents who are struggling with their highly United States–acculturated adolescents, who are rejecting nearly all of their parents' advice and house rules. Consider as another example a Chinese family who came for help because, now that the parents had both completed advanced degrees in the United States, the father was determined to return the family to China so that his wife could care for his elderly parents full time. The children adamantly wanted to remain in the United States. The therapist was outraged by the father's insistence and what she saw as his sexism and selfishness. Not understanding Chinese culture or values, the therapist took the mother's side immediately and forcefully. The man quit treatment abruptly, and the family gave up on therapy as a method for resolving their (primarily) cultural dilemma.

Countertransferential feelings were likely operating for this therapist, who—as a married professional—valued her career equally with her marriage. In this case, the therapist was easily able to detect the basis for the family's dropout after the fact. In many situations, however, therapists remain unaware of how their personal reactions, stemming from their own family histories, interfere with effective treatment (Friedlander et al., 2006). Allison, a novice therapist who had entered the field without fully understanding how her father's alcohol abuse had affected her development, routinely failed to assess clients for substance dependence or domestic violence. Jason, a more seasoned family therapist, came from a highly functional and happy, traditional family, in which his mother had little voice or relational power. Until he was directly accused of sexism by a particularly assertive female client, Jason was unaware of the subtle ways in which he silenced the women with whom he worked. Shaken by this client's accusation, Jason took a hard look at himself and, through peer consultation and reviewing audiotapes of his work, was able to provide a more gender-neutral experience for his clients.

NEGATIVE REACTIONS FROM THE WIDER SYSTEM

Working with families therapeutically implies working with systems, not only direct systems (the family, couple subsystem, sibling subsystems) but also indirect systems (e.g., those that involve individuals not physically present in therapy sessions; Pinsof, 1994). On the client side, the indirect system consists of members of the nuclear or extended family who do not participate in the therapy sessions but are nonetheless influential, as well as unrelated people in the neighborhood who are closely connected with the family. The indirect therapist system consists of the individuals in the professional network connected with the case or the therapist's work, such as the therapeutic team, supervisor, the agency in which the therapy is taking place, and the payer sources (e.g., managed care, insurance, state government financial assistance agencies).

In family therapy it is not uncommon that therapists' negative reactions, although focused on the clients, are generated in part by the wider indirect system. These problematic responses can contaminate the direct therapeutic system, at times even without the awareness of the therapy participants, as the examples given in the following several sections illustrate.

"He Is Not Coming, but He Is Controlling My Therapy!"

Sixteen-year-old Manuel and his sister, Rosa, 14, came to therapy with their mother, who was unhappy about the high level of conflict between the siblings and worried that their aggressive behavior was spilling over into the school context. In contrast to their mother's description, Manuel and Rosa appeared to be quite agreeable and highly complementary with each other. They explained that their mother had been exceptionally anxious in the last several months and was overly sensitive to any expression of disagreement between them, exaggerating their occasional "typical" sibling arguments. In the course of therapy, the mother considered various perceptions and interpretations of Manuel and Rosa's behavior and, with the help of the therapist, was able to modify some of her reactivity to her children, becoming more effective in disciplining them. At that point in therapy, the mother requested individual sessions to focus on her general lack of satisfaction in her personal life.

Manual and Rosa's father was invited by the therapist, through the other family members, to attend the therapy from the outset, but he never complied; instead, he offered (again, through the other family members) the excuse that he was too busy with professional commitments. Nonetheless, the therapist was content with the situation mostly because the three other family members were engaged and perceived some positive changes. At a crucial point in the treatment, however, the mother began complaining about her children's behavior, re-creating the pattern she had displayed at the beginning of therapy (i.e., focusing on and magnifying small disputes between the children). When Manuel and Rosa explained to the therapist that their mother was merely repeating their father's opinions about the problem and about the futility of therapy, the therapist's first reaction was to insist on inviting the father to discuss his point of view. The emotional tone of this invitation was clearly negative, however, and it resulted in the mother strongly defending the father. The adolescents lost trust in the therapist, feeling that they were now in the midst of a rivalry between the therapist and their father. The clients subsequently terminated therapy, perhaps in an effort to avoid the looming conflict at home over this matter.

Negative therapist reactions to the behaviors of nonparticipant family members who block the therapy's progress or who influence continuation in treatment are both common and understandable. Even when the family remains in therapy, therapists may come to understand that an influential nonparticipant is criticizing or disqualifying the work; there is a risk that negative reactions by the therapist may be projected onto the family members who are attending, threatening the working alliance. The best strategy in such cases is to try to solicit the participation of the reticent or critical family member by contacting him or her directly in a positive, constructive manner. In our experience, this can be done by inviting the family member to participate for a small number of sessions (or even in simply a part of one session) in order to understand his or her opinion and perspective on the family situation. Various strategies for engaging reluctant family members in treatment are informed by the systematic research on this topic by Szapoznik and colleagues (Szapocznik et al., 1988; Szapocznik & Williams, 2000).

"They Send the Family to Psychotherapy but Want Me to Control the Family"

When clients who are referred from social or child protective services agencies are seen conjointly, the therapeutic work often starts with a coercive agency intervention, for example, temporary separation of the children or restrictive conditions for some members of the family as the only alternative to mandated therapy. The first difficulty for a therapist in such cases is how to change the initial attitudes of mandated clients, which may include reticence, open or hidden anger, or even defiance (Friedlander et al., 2006). Negative reactions in the therapist may be aroused by the clients' implicit or explicit message that "We do not have a problem." An even more challenging situation is presented when the family's attitude is confrontational: "We do not have a problem, YOU are our problem." Attitudes like these indicate that family members see the therapist as a representative of coercive governmental interventions from which they are suffering (Escudero, 2009).

This difficult situation, which is to some extent endemic to mandated therapy, can be managed by therapists who have had specific training on creating therapeutic alliances with mandated clients. Yet another important relevant issue is the coordination of the wider professional systems with the family therapy itself. When coordination is not done, the therapist may feel the full burden of controlling the risks for child maltreatment, resulting in negative feelings toward the family as well as the referring system. Obviously, such reactions can contaminate the relationship with the family and impede the course of therapy. Indeed, many novice therapists who work with families referred from child protective services think, "I am a *therapist*—I am not here to control this family!"

There are three basic strategies for preventing and managing these kinds of negative reactions. First, it is necessary to understand that in such cases there is a dialectic of control versus therapy that is unavoidable when family intervention is undertaken in the context of a child protective services referral. Second, the therapist should pursue the objective of making the two components of the intervention—control and therapy—complementary, rather than reject the element of control as an opposition to therapeutic work. Complementarity can be approached by coordinating the therapy with the controlling functions of the protective services agencies. For example, therapy can be presented as in the service of the parents' goal to provide the best care possible for their children and to recover privileges that were taken away (e.g., custody, visitation). Finally, therapists should strive to avoid contaminating the roles of control agent (social worker of protective services) and mental health provider. The referral source should help the family therapist by clearly distinguishing for family members the nature and context of the therapy from other controlling interventions; that is, the social service workers should optimally assume the role of social control while making clear to the family that the therapy is offered to them, independently, with the therapist acting as their consultant.

"They Send Them to Family Therapy, but They Do Not Do Their Part"

Family therapists are sometimes asked to treat families that are receiving other services; the referral sources anticipate that therapy will complement their own interventions. Providers of drug addiction services, specialized psychiatric services, physical rehabilitation services, and infertility treatments, for example, may make such referrals. In some cases, especially with multiproblem families, a number of treatment professionals may be working simultaneously with the family, creating a complex professional web. Negative reactions related to the sharing of responsibility may arise in this context.

In one case, family therapy was requested for Jim, age 19, and his parents, by a drug addiction treatment center. The parents had requested help from this center when they realized that Jim's rude and antisocial behavior was related to his use of large amounts of marijuana and other substances. Jim and his parents initially had a positive attitude toward family therapy, and some improvements in their communication were achieved in 4 or 5 weeks. Family members began to talk openly about Jim's addiction as well. Their initial optimism evaporated, however, when it became clear that Jim's use of substances had not changed. The therapist felt highly critical of the drug treatment center for Jim's lack of progress. These feelings were amplified by the feelings of hopelessness and pessimism in the family, and the therapeutic alliance changed from positive to highly problematic. In this case, the therapist's response to the other treating professionals created a negative situation that ultimately damaged his own alliance with the family.

Therapists (and supervisors) need to be cognizant when they find themselves being critical of a family member who mentions a suggestion, opinion, or recommendation of another professional involved in the family's treatment. The consequences of this criticism are potentially double barreled and have to do with safety in the therapeutic relationship: First, the clients may begin to believe that the therapist does not trust his or her colleagues; second, the clients may begin to worry that they will become the target of the therapist's negative reactions.

The key to avoiding or resolving these kinds of negative reactions is early and ongoing attention to establishing a good alliance between professional helpers (Friedlander et al., 2006). Establishing a working relationship early in treatment, clarifying expectations, and sharing concerns and information will be well worth the effort. Where possible, a joint meeting with the professionals in which the clients are present and involved can be helpful in setting the stage for a strong three-way working relationship that avoids negative triangulation.

"How Am I Going to Help This Family With the Conditions Imposed by the Payer?"

Restrictions on the length and nature of therapy that is financed by a public institution (as is common in Europe) or an insurance/managed care company (common in the United States) can be external stressors to the therapeutic system and the origin of negative reactions within the therapist. Although all therapists are likely to feel pressured and frustrated by such restrictions, the risk is particularly salient in family therapy because treatment process and progress depend more on the relational dynamics of the family than on the particular diagnostic label or other formal characteristics of the presenting problem. Furthermore, as the relational dynamics are revealed, family therapists may need more flexibility than is allowed by payers to make essential treatment decisions (e.g., number and timing of sessions, which family members should be present and in which constellations).

In one case, the issue had to do with decisions about the treatment itself. Ruth, a 37-year-old mother of two male preadolescents, was referred to family therapy with her sons after her husband had left the family. This abandonment was a major crisis for Ruth and precipitated two suicide attempts. She was placed on medication, and her own mother moved into the home to care for Ruth and the children. Concerned about the safety and stability of the two boys, child protective services opened an investigation, and a mental health service did the crisis intervention. Child protective services recommended family therapy for Ruth and her mother in order to help Ruth delegate the care of the children to the grandmother; it was believed that Ruth's precarious mental health put the children at risk, and the objective was to use family therapy to facilitate the grandmother's fostering of the children, which involved moving the children to the grandmother's house. The psychiatrist in charge of Ruth's mental health treatment agreed with the need for family therapy but from a different perspective. Because he believed that Ruth needed her children to recover, he opposed the family's separation, arguing that it would have a strong negative effect on Ruth's mental health, potentially increasing her suicide risk. Starting the therapy under the pressure of these two opposing agendas created a stressful situation for—and problematic reactions in—the therapist. Although the family was open and positive about attending family therapy, the clients intuited the therapist's tension and negative emotionality. Family members attributed the negativity to the therapist's personality, became discouraged about her ability to help them, and decided not to commit to the family therapy.

The key element in managing this kind of negative reaction is locating the source of the conflict—the professional system—and seeking a solution by discussing and solving the opposing professional agendas. The family should be kept out of this process, and the therapist should avoid projecting his or her negative emotions onto the relationship with the family. The creation of a strong therapeutic alliance in these situations depends on the prior creation of a strong working relationship within the network of professionals involved in the case.

The previous example shows how a therapist's negative reactions can be projected onto the clients. This may also happen when a therapist's concern about the time allowed by the payer for treatment makes the therapist impatient with the pace of change sessions or with the family's conflict or lack of engagement in sessions. The therapist may be more aware than the clients that the "clock is ticking" and must be careful not to confound the stress and limitations imposed by the payer with the pathology or difficulty of the family. The treatment, limited as it is in scope, should be adapted to the family's needs. Good training and good peer supervision from colleagues who are used to working with these restrictions can be helpful for therapists who are new to managing negative reactions arising from multiprovider situations.

"My Community Doesn't Believe in Family Therapy"

Finally, the influence of particular ethnic, religious, or cultural communities is also an important part of the wider, extratherapy system. Negative reactions on the part of the therapist can arise when those influences are negative to or work at cross-purposes with the family treatment. In some fundamentalist Christian and ultra-Orthodox Jewish communities, for example, psychological treatment is suspect, and the therapist's and community's definitions of the family problem and beliefs about potential solutions may clash (Schnitzer, Loots, Escudero, & Schechter, 2011). Clashes of this sort can engender defensive reactions on the therapist's part.

For example, in treating the Jimenez family, who lived in a traditional and small Romani (Gypsy) community in Spain, the therapist did not originally understand the presence of the (unrelated) patriarch of the community in one session. He had not been invited by the therapist but came with the family (the parents and two children) anyway, intending to participate in the session. For the family, the presence of the patriarch was quite positive and welcome, and the clients indicated their pleasure when the therapist asked about the reason for the patriarch joining the session. Although the therapist's initial private reaction was negative, welcoming the patriarch was an exceptional opportunity to learn about the importance of collaborating with this community leader. It was also a lesson that in some cultures, the link between the family and the community is far closer than in other cultures and, in fact, the blessing and/or participation of relevant individuals from the community is crucial to the success of the therapy.

Having the understanding and flexibility to incorporate important community members into the therapy by helping them be a part of the solution, versus considering them an intrusion, can help mitigate negative reactions and the eventual fallout from those reactions. In other cases, involving community members may mean being proactive in picking up on family members' concerns that their involvement in psychotherapy may not be approved by others and addressing them tactfully. For example, a prospective client asked, "Are there Christian types of therapy?" A gentle inquiry revealed that the client had been told by her priest that psychotherapists were against prayer and other spiritual practices of healing and thus she should stay away from psychotherapy or risk losing her faith. The therapist's direct and sympathetic addressing of this concern resulted in the client feeling less conflicted and guilty about pursuing treatment, and it allowed the therapist to be more sensitive in working with the client.

A SYSTEMIC SCHEMA OF NEGATIVE REACTIONS

Our distinction between negative reactions originating within the therapist, negative reactions resulting from the family's dynamics, and negative reactions from the wider system is somewhat arbitrary. Indeed, each source of negative reactions moderates the effects of the others. For example, in treating a family with an authoritative, demanding father, a therapist who has unresolved issues with his own father may have strong negative reactions, whereas a therapist without such issues may not react in the same way. Similarly, some family dynamics (e.g., loyalty within the family combined with mistrust of outsiders) tend to be challenging when wider systems are involved in an involuntary referral but helpful later on when family members are highly involved and doing the hard work of, for example, helping a child become free of substance dependence.

This interplay can be seen in Figure 5.1, which represents a metaview of the therapeutic system in family therapy and illustrates the complexity of influences that can be sources of negative therapist reactions. The most obvious source of negative reactions, and the one that usually comes to mind, is the direct system of therapeutic interaction, which includes the therapist and the family members who regularly attend the therapy; however, indirect systems (Pinsof, 1994) also can influence the therapist's negative reactions. As we

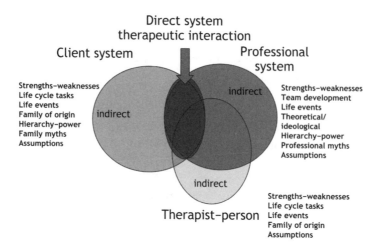

Figure 5.1. Direct and indirect systems in family therapy.

have discussed, members of the nuclear or extended family who do not participate in the therapy sessions are sometimes the source of negative reactions, as
are relevant unrelated persons (e.g., community leaders) who represent moral
authority for the family. Furthermore, as the figure illustrates, another source
of therapists' emotions and reactions toward the clients is the indirect *therapist system*, that is, the professional network connected with the case or the
therapist's work, including the therapeutic team, supervisor, and the agency
in which the therapy is taking place. The person of the therapist, his or her
idiosyncratic characteristics beyond the professional role, sometimes explains
the negative reactions. This schema may be helpful for therapists, therapists
in training, and their supervisors in thinking through the sources of negative
reactions and the reverberating effects across these sources.

MANAGING NEGATIVE REACTIONS:
SOME GENERAL GUIDELINES

In the preceding sections we have incorporated suggestions for managing negative reactions in specific kinds of situations. In this section, we provide some general guidelines for therapists working with couples and families,
and we address the ways in which thoughtful training and supervision can
help therapists manage their negative reactions.

Managing one's negative or otherwise problematic reactions to clients involves personal reflection as well as knowledge, skill, training, supervision, and consultation. Reflective practice (Orchowski, Evangelista, &

Probst, 2010) involves basic self-understanding, introspection, the ability to be aware of feelings as they arise in the moment, and a willingness to self-correct. These attitudes and skills are required for successful practice with all clients, but systemic knowledge and self-understanding are crucial when working with couples and families. It is essential to understand, for example, how interpersonal interactions in families are affected by gender and gender role expectations; cultural norms and values; and one's personal, familial history (Friedlander et al., 2006). Indeed, one of the most influential family systems theorists, Murray Bowen (1976; Kerr & Bowen, 1988), believed that the best training and supervision of family therapists required helping them differentiate from their own families of origin. Although not all reactions to families are based in countertransference, Bowen argued that therapists who are unable to "take an I-position" in their own significant relationships are in no position to help clients discover the covert dynamics that keep them stuck in dysfunctional patterns of interaction.

How do therapists recognize problematic reactions, countertransferential or otherwise? With all clients but particularly with couples and families, therapists should begin by asking themselves the following questions: How do this family's history and developmental stage compare with my own? What emotional issues (e.g., regarding parenting, violence, racism) do they bring to the table that have been problematic in my own life? Have I adequately assessed for intimate partner violence, emotional and sexual abuse, and child maltreatment? What can I learn from the family's coping style, and how can I use my personal experience to best therapeutic advantage? Am I experiencing a high level of stress in session with this family? If so, is it because the alliance is split and I am empathizing with the experience of only some family members and not that of others? What knowledge can I gain from journals and books to help me better understand this couple or family?

If self-reflection, reading, supervision, and consultation are insufficient to turn around problematic feelings, one useful strategy is to work with a subsystem of the family for a session or for a portion of a session. The family bully may show insecurities, when alone with the therapist, that she or he is unwilling to reveal in front of other family members. New information that surfaces in an individual session can be enlightening, and judicious use of that information can potentially repair an alliance in distress.

Consider, for example, a case in which a teen was consistently loud, belligerent, and unreasonable. The therapist found herself feeling very sorry for the parents and increasingly annoyed with the adolescent. When the therapist caught herself behaving somewhat passive-aggressively toward the teen, she asked to see her alone for a session. During this session, the teen revealed that she was worried sick about her mother, who had a serious medical condition, was not taking care of herself, and was drinking heavily. When the girl showed her concern for her mother and explained to the therapist—in a reasonable, measured manner—what was really going on at home, the therapist saw her own error and was able to put this new information (and her more balanced feelings) to judicious use in the subsequent conjoint family session.

Training and supervision are, of course, essential for helping entry-level couple and family therapists learn self-reflective practice and skills to manage their problematic reactions to systemic dynamics. Although most of the recognized training programs for family therapists offer or even mandate (e.g., programs recognized by the European Family Therapy Association) work on the person of the therapist as well as on the origin family of the therapist, managing one's negative reactions should be a specific goal of general training in couple and family therapy. An important precondition for the efficacy of this training is a good alliance between supervisor and trainee; it is particularly important that a high level of safety in the supervision and emotional connection with the supervisor be established prior to this work. On the basis of our own experience as trainers of family therapists, there are three therapist skills that are directly related to good detection and management of one's negative reactions:

1. *Being sensitive to differences between the content versus relational levels of communication.* Exercises to help one understand and differentiate between these two levels of communication (Rogers & Escudero, 2004) and to be able to respond to both levels can make it easier to detect difficulties surrounding one's own negative reactions. The content level is the specific topic of the conversation in therapy, what we are talking about. The relational level is how we are talking, which relates to the mutual definition of the relationship between clients and therapist. Thus, the relational level is central to understanding the process of therapeutic interaction and is fundamental to understanding the covert negative reactions of the therapists. Analysis of videotaped segments of sessions with the observational focus on the relational level (e.g., tone, nonverbal behavior, relational context) makes the trainee sensitive to his or her negative reactions at the relational level, even when the content level of communication remains correct.

2. *Developing self-awareness.* To capture the nature of the therapist's inner experience associated with specific feelings shown in therapy (e.g., anger, neglect), training and supervision should focus on the exploration of these experiences as they are associated with negative reactions. What current personal experiences could be associated with the therapist's negative reactions

during his or her interaction with the family? What experiences in the therapist's own family of origin could be associated with the negative reaction? What inner experience could be associated with a negative relational communication in which the therapist is involved? Dedicating time to this kind of self-exploration of experiences associated with particular reactions and even asking the supervisee to do a written analysis of them or to discuss them with other trainees are ways of operationalizing the training exercise.

3. *Learning to manage negative reactions by enacting them and practicing therapeutic responses.* The use of role playing to recreate the context of negative reactions by focusing on a trainee's most feared scenes is a very specific exercise to help the therapist prevent and manage his or her own reactions. Typical examples include scenes such as one partner announcing an affair, evoking fear and panic ("What do I do now?") in the therapist; a parent badly berating a child, evoking anger in the therapist; or a parent pulling a child into a marital conflict, evoking memories of triangulation in the therapist's own childhood. In our experience, the simulation of these scenes and an exchanging of the roles of therapist and client can have a strong impact on the trainees, at the cognitive as well as the emotional level.

CONCLUSION

Negative reactions can occur not just at the beginning of therapy but throughout the process of the treatment, and they can derive from multiple sources. They are to be expected, but working to understand where they are coming from and how they can be managed so that the treatment can proceed can greatly enhance the process and outcome of family therapy for all participants.

REFERENCES

Bowen, M. (1976). Theory in the practice of psychotherapy. In P. J. Guerin (Ed.), *Family therapy: Theory and practice* (pp. 42–90). New York, NY: Gardner Press.

Castonguay, L. G., Boswell, J. F., Constantino, M. J., Goldfried, M. R., & Hill, C. E. (2010). Training implications of harmful effects of psychological treatments. *American Psychologist, 65,* 34–49. doi:10.1037/a0017330

Diamond, G., Siqueland, L., & Diamond, G. (2003). Attachment-based family therapy for depressed adolescents: Programmatic treatment development. *Clinical Child and Family Psychology Review, 6*, 107–127. doi:10.1023/A:1023782510786

Escudero, V. (2009). *Guía práctica para la intervención familiar* [Toolkit for family intervention]. Valladolid, Spain: Junta de Castilla y León.

Flaskas, C., & Perlesz, A. (Eds.). (1998). The return of the therapeutic relationship in systemic therapy. In C. Flaskas & A. Perlesz (Eds.), *The therapeutic relationship in systemic therapy* (pp. 1–12). London, England: Karnac.

Friedlander, M. L., & Diamond, G. M. (2012). Couple and family therapy. In E. Altmaier & J. Hanson (Eds.), *Oxford handbook of counseling psychology* (pp. 647–678). New York, NY: Oxford University Press.

Friedlander, M. L., Escudero, V., & Heatherington, L. (2006). *Therapeutic alliances in couple and family therapy: An empirically informed guide to practice.* Washington, DC: American Psychological Association. doi:10.1037/11410-000

Friedlander, M. L., Heatherington, L., Johnson, B., & Skowron, E. A. (1994). Sustaining engagement: A change event in family therapy. *Journal of Counseling Psychology, 41*, 438–448. doi:10.1037/0022-0167.41.4.438

Haley, J. (1987). *Problem solving therapy.* San Francisco, CA: Jossey-Bass.

Heatherington, L., & Friedlander, M. L. (1990). Couple and Family Therapy Alliance Scales: Empirical considerations. *Journal of Marital and Family Therapy, 16*, 299–306. doi:10.1111/j.1752-0606.1990.tb00851.x

Higham, J., Friedlander, M. L., Escudero, V., & Diamond, G. M. (2012). Engaging reluctant adolescents in family therapy: An exploratory study of in-session processes of change. *Journal of Family Therapy, 34*, 24–52. doi:10.1111/j.1467-6427.2011.00571.x

Kelch, B. P., & Demmitt, A. (2010). Incorporating the stages of change model in solution focused brief therapy with non-substance abusing families: A novel and integrative approach. *The Family Journal, 18*, 184–188. doi:10.1177/1066480710364325

Kerr, M., & Bowen, M. (1988). *Family evaluation.* New York, NY: Norton.

Kohut, H. (1984). *How does analysis cure?* Chicago, IL: University of Chicago Press.

Madsen, W. C. (2009). Collaborative helping: A practice framework for family-centered services. *Family Process, 48*, 103–116.

Minuchin, S. (1974). *Families and family therapy.* Cambridge, MA: Harvard University Press.

Muñiz de la Peña, C., Friedlander, M. L., & Escudero, V. (2009). Frequency, severity, and evolution of split family alliances: How observable are they? *Psychotherapy Research, 19*, 133–142. doi:10.1080/10503300802460050

Orchowski, L., Evangelista, N. M., & Probst, D. R. (2010). Enhancing supervisee reflectivity in clinical supervision: A case study illustration. *Psychotherapy: Theory, Research, Practice, Training, 47*, 51–67. doi:10.1037/a0018844

Pinsof, W. B. (1994). An integrative systems perspective on the therapeutic alliance: Theoretical, clinical, and research implications. In A. O. Horvath & L. S. Greenberg (Eds.), *The working alliance: Theory, research, and practice* (pp. 173–195). New York, NY: Wiley.

Pinsof, W. B., & Catherall, D. (1986). The integrative psychotherapy alliance: Family, couple, and individual therapy scales. *Journal of Marital and Family Therapy, 12,* 137–151.

Prochaska, J. O., & DiClemente, C. C. (1983). Stages and processes of self-change in smoking: Toward an integrative model of change. *Journal of Consulting and Clinical Psychology, 51,* 390–395. doi:10.1037/0022-006X.51.3.390

Prochaska, J. O., & DiClemente, C. C. (2005). The transtheoretical approach. In J. C. Norcross & M. R. Goldfried (Eds.), *Handbook of psychotherapy integration* (2nd ed., pp. 147–171). New York, NY: Oxford University Press.

Rogers, L. E., & Escudero, V. (2004). Theoretical foundations. In L. E. Rogers & V. Escudero (Eds.), *Relational communication: An interactional perspective to the study of process and form* (pp. 3–21). Mahwah, NJ: Erlbaum.

Schnitzer, G., Loots, G., Escudero, V., & Schechter, I. (2011). Negotiating the pathways into care in a globalizing world: Help-seeking behaviour of ultra-Orthodox Jewish parents. *International Journal of Social Psychiatry, 57,* 153–165. doi:10.1177/0020764008105291

Sexton, T. L., & Alexander, J. F. (2003). Functional family therapy: A mature clinical model for working with at-risk adolescents and their families. In T. L. Sexton, G. R. Weeks, & M. S. Robbins (Eds.), *Handbook of family therapy* (pp. 323–348). New York, NY: Brunner-Routledge.

Szapocznik, J., Perez-Vidal, A., Brickman, A. L., Foote, F. H., Santisteban, D., Hervis, O., & Kurtines, W. M. (1988). Engaging adolescent drug abusers and their families in treatment: A strategic structural systems approach. *Journal of Consulting and Clinical Psychology, 56,* 552–557. doi:10.1037/0022-006X.56.4.552

Szapocznik, J., & Williams, R. A. (2000). Brief strategic family therapy: Twenty-five years of interplay among theory, research and practice in adolescent behavior problems and drug abuse. *Clinical Child and Family Psychology Review, 3,* 117–134. doi:10.1023/A:1009512719808

6

COMPASSION AMIDST OPPRESSION: INCREASING CULTURAL COMPETENCE FOR MANAGING DIFFICULT DIALOGUES IN PSYCHOTHERAPY

LAURA S. BROWN

When we enter the space of a psychotherapy encounter, myriad individuals walk into the room with us. Because each of us is a creature of multiple and intersecting identities—with a sense of self arising from our gender, culture, social class, sexuality, ability, and more—those intersectionalities and their meanings are an integral component of how we perceive and are perceived in the therapy relationship. Although in the United States we commonly require ourselves and others to pick just one part of our identities as the way we know and are known, most people experience themselves on the phenomenological plane somewhere in the places where those pieces of their social and internal worlds meet. We are Jewish men or working-class immigrants with advanced degrees from our native countries, lesbian accountants, or rural psychologists. We are everything but the checkbox on the form; the whole is greater than its parts. Likewise, our clients greet us from the places where their identities intertwine and emerge, regardless of whether we, or they, consciously perceive this. Who therapists think clients are and the aspects of their selves that are

DOI: 10.1037/13940-006
Transforming Negative Reactions to Clients: From Frustration to Compassion, A. W. Wolf, M. R. Goldfried, and J. C. Muran (Editors)

salient to the therapists may have little to no importance to them; who clients know themselves to be might be invisible to their therapists.

Multiple factors are inherent in such intersectionalities. Some of them are obvious and easily apparent. A person's phenotypic presentation (usually thought of as his or her race/ethnicity), that individual's apparent biological sex, and the presence or absence of a visible physical or emotional disability are all points of information that are usually captured at first glance. The social locations that serve as the roots of identity are, however, more numerous and often less obvious than these. Phenotype is no clear evidence of heritage; for example, a person whose father was Japanese American and mother was Swedish American will likely get the "What are you?" question for his or her entire life (Root, 1998).

It will frequently be the case that neither party has deeply inquired into those intersectionalities and their meanings. Although the psychodynamic literature on the phenomena of transference and countertransference has delved deeply and at length into the individualized microcomponents of what therapist and client represent to one another, the ways in which larger, more socially situated facets of identities and meanings become represented nonconsciously, symbolically, and interpersonally have rarely been a topic of significant focus.

The cultural competence movement in psychotherapy has noted this lacuna in the psychotherapy literature and has called attention to how the absence of attention to these variables of human diversity, as they become expressed within the therapy relationship, runs in parallel with the failures of most major schools of psychotherapy to give more than cursory notice to these topics. In this chapter, I contrast an etic paradigm for culturally competent practice that models human diversity as the specification of distinct ethnic or phenotypic categories with a model for culturally competent practice in psychotherapy that attends specifically to intersectionalities of identities and the ways in which they inform the psychotherapy encounter. Because of the focus of this volume, I then attend to the ways in which a culturally competent stance informs the therapist's response to problematic affects emerging in the context of therapy. Finally, I share a case example that illustrates how such difficult dialogues have transpired in my practice. In this example, my own struggles to implement a stance of cultural competence can be seen.

CULTURAL COMPETENCE: A JOURNEY, NOT A DESTINATION

I define *cultural competence* as a set of three therapist variables: the capacity for the therapist to be (a) self-aware in regard to her or his own intersectionalities of identities and cultural norms; (b) sensitive to the realities of human difference; and (c) possessed of an epistemology of difference that allows for creative responses to the ways in which the strengths and resiliencies inherent in identities inform, transform, and are distorted by distress and dysfunction (Brown, 2008). One does not *achieve* cultural competence. If any point has been brought home to me forcefully over the several decades in which becoming culturally competent has been a central organizing force in my practice, it is that cultural competence, like ethics, is largely aspirational in nature. Although there are some specific rules of cultural competence, just as there are multiple specific and enforceable ethical standards, the heart and soul of culturally competent practice must be seen as a stance in relationship to one's work that leaves the clinician in a state of continuous evolution, a broadening awareness of self, and an increasing willingness to accept that the more one knows, the more one knows one doesn't know much at all.

One can—and, I would argue, must—embark on this journey in order to be a compassionate and effective psychotherapist, not simply with those clients whom we code as "Other" but instead with all of the individuals with whom we work. In the following paragraphs, I outline a paradigm for culturally competent practice. It is not the only one, and it is not a universally accepted one; however, it is a model that fulfills a number of important functions that support the development of therapeutic alliances and that is consistent with the findings of research on such topics as empirically supported relationship variables and therapist characteristics.

One of the reasons why it seems that few therapists and fewer theories of psychotherapy attempt to integrate the stance of cultural competence lies in the paradigms for culturally competent practice with which most psychologists and psychotherapists are familiar. These models tend to engender feelings of guilt, shame, and incompetence, none of which are precisely salubrious affects to bring to the practice of psychotherapy. One of my students reported visiting a course on "working with diverse clients" in which the instructor told the students that "if the class was successful, the students would all have developed White guilt" (Anonymous, personal communication, October 2009). Attaching these aversive affects to the pursuit of cultural competence makes it unlikely that anyone will pursue the topic further. Worse, it makes it likely that many individuals who do pursue the matter do so to assuage these unpleasant feelings, which is a problematic motivation for developing any aspect of psychotherapy practice.

When the topic of cultural competence is not taught in ways that overtly engender distress, it is often conveyed simplistically, in ways that fail to convey the complexity and subtlety of the intersectionalities of identity. In many psychotherapy training programs the development of cultural competence has, until quite recently, been framed as the acquisition of data and algorithms about various groups of people who are "Other" to the psychotherapist.

I refer to this as the *Handbook of Psychotherapy With Alien Beings* strategy. This approach, in which students take classes in "diverse" or "special" populations, allocates segments to various groups of "Others" and commonly includes material on the characteristics and psychotherapy needs of members of different North American groups of color; lesbian, gay, bisexual, and transgendered (LGBT) people; older people; people with disabilities; and immigrants. There may be attention to groups once known as "hyphenated Americans," the Euro-American ethnic groups (e.g., Irish American, Jewish American, Polish American) that remained in some way distinctive and not fully assimilated into the dominant culture.

A powerful message of this paradigm for understanding difference is that cultural competence is about *them*: It's about the Other, the client who is diverse, and about how to address the problem of dealing with that person in psychotherapy. A strong subtext of this message is that the psychotherapist is not an Other. Working with Others is framed as requiring acquisition of specific knowledge of how to work with members of the group. Even when a psychotherapist is a member of one of the groups being studied, such training communicates an interesting metamessage about the default assumption that, similar to police who define themselves as all blue, the therapist in training who her- or himself springs from the "alien" culture has now joined the new ethnic group of psychotherapists, who are de facto members of a dominant culture.

This approach often communicates to trainees that clients who are Other do not feel safe with or understood by most psychotherapists. Although this may be true, the manner in which it is presented leads to worries about accidentally hurting feelings or saying or doing something insensitive. Psychotherapists will, at the very least, often develop anxiety about working with the Others, which can lead to problematic emotion regulation strategies when an Other is in the room.

This model for training psychotherapists to become culturally competent is known as an etic paradigm. *Etic* information is that which is "of or pertaining to analysis of a culture from the perspective on one who is not a participant in that culture" ("etic", n.d.). Etic paradigms concern themselves with so-called objective observations and categorizations of the Other that use categories of analysis and frames of meaning derived from those of the observer, not the observed. Etic paradigms can be problematic for precisely the reasons just discussed. They reduce humans to one facet of identity rather than attend to intersectionalities. They reduce work with members of the Other group into application of rules and algorithms, a sort of manualized approach that has the distinction of being much less well empirically supported than manualized approaches to treatment. Of most concern for this chapter, they emphasize understanding the client, rather than both client and psychotherapist.

Such education about diversity is likely better than none at all. When feminists, people of color, LGBT people, and other critical psychology theorists began to assail the discipline's hegemonic view of the human norm as Caucasian, male, and heterosexual, the discourse was at least joined as to how these facets of human diversity might inform behavior. When "even the rat was white" (Guthrie, 1976), psychotherapists tended to define clients who were Other as simply not amenable to psychotherapy. This was the case, of course, unless those clients were female, in which instance the very fact of their sex was seen as sufficient cause for them to require treatment. (See Chesler, 1972, for a cogent discussion of how "female" and "neurotic" were treated as equivalent conditions by the psychotherapy professions prior to the advent of feminist practice.)

There are problems inherent to the etic model, however. A therapist could read the *Handbook of Psychotherapy With Alien Beings* and become known among the local psychotherapy community as the person who got the referral when an Alien Being client showed up in their practice. This did nothing for one's competence with other varieties of Alien Being, though. The official Alien Being expert might not have learned much about gender roles in Alien culture and thus would accidentally extrapolate earthbound norms about gender to working with Alien Being women, which would be deeply erroneous. The "learn a set of rules for the space aliens" model promoted doing cultural competence by rote, in the absence of an epistemology.

The gaps in etic paradigms became more apparent as members of various Other groups jumped over the institutional hurdles and into the offices of therapists who purported to know something about human difference and diversity. Not a few of those people were refusing to follow the rules about their groups. Simultaneously, the first glimmerings of an intersectionality paradigm began to appear in the scholarly literature (e.g., Comas-Diaz & Greene, 1994; Kanuha, 1990). Such paradigms of intersectionality, which most often looked at within-individual encounters among gender, ethnicity, and sexuality, allowed psychotherapists to have a more sophisticated meta-theory of human difference to inform their work. They also began to see epistemologies of differences that allowed them to generate responses to their clients here and now, in the psychotherapy moment, rather than operate from the rote manualized versions of diversity (D'Andrea & Daniels, 2001; Hays, 2007).

Intersectionality of Identities and Culturally Competent Practice

As the protean actress Sarah Jones, who performs one-woman shows in which she becomes many characters, noted in a speech at the 2009 TED (Technology, Entertainment, Design) conference, "We are all born into certain circumstances with particular physical traits, unique developmental experiences, geographical and historical contexts, but then what—to what extent do we self-construct, do we self-invent? How do we self-identify? And how mutable is that self-identity?" (Jones, 2009). The construct of intersectionalities of identities, as briefly described at the beginning of this chapter, reflects Jones's words. Each of us has a biology that confers on us a shape, a size, a hue, a temperament, and certain abilities to process (or not) the sensory and interpersonal input of the world around us. We emerge into social, political, and historical realities that, interacting with our biological heritage, assist us in constructing identities. Our intersectional identities are a complicated tapestry. At times it appears that we are one street, running straight and true in a clear, knowable direction. At other moments we appear to others, or feel ourselves to be, a chaotic jumble of random parts. At times we believe we know who we are, only to be surprised like James McBride, who awakened one morning in his identity as an African American Baptist to discover that he was the son of a Jewish, European American woman who had been passing for African American (McBride, 1996). Some aspects of identity have been spoiled through abuse, trauma, oppression, and disempowerment; other components of identity have been rendered invisible or made too shiny through overpolishing.

Psychotherapy is in the business of inviting people to change identities from spoiled to whole. Culturally competent practice that conceptualizes people within intersectionalities enlightens all parties as to the processes of self-invention to which Sarah Jones referred. Attending to intersectionalities allows for interrogating the process of self-invention by disentangling the strands of self, including those that have generated psychological distress and problematic behaviors. This disentanglement is, to my way of thinking, central to the enterprise of psychotherapy. For many of the people who come to therapists with their misery, the process of self-construction has been one of the problematic conflation—a tangling, as it were—of negative characteristics and experiences of powerlessness and hopelessness with important aspects of self. All the while, other components of self, which might lead to a different and more functional and peaceful construction, remain in the background, ignored or unexplored.

Various acronyms developed by 21st-century cultural competence theorists function to remind psychotherapists that humans fit poorly, if at all, into the single checkboxes of life. These include Hays's (2007) ADDRESSING model, which I describe in depth shortly, and D'Andrea and Daniels's (2001) RESPECTFUL model. What these models have in common is an explicit focus on two phenomena.

The first phenomenon is a broadening of the dimensions on which human diversity might be considered. Rather than privileging ethnicity/phenotype as the sole or primary marker of human difference, these 21st-century models describe a multiplicity of the variables that I refer to as *social locations*: aspects of the social and interpersonal domain in which a person is located, some or all of which contribute to the development of identity.

ADDRESSING, for instance, stands for age, disability, religion, ethnicity, social class, sexual orientation, indigenous origins, national origin, and gender. This is clearly not an exhaustive list. In my own recent work on cultural competence in trauma practice (Brown, 2008), for instance, I expanded Hays's (2007) list to include such factors as histories of colonization (both as colonizer and colonized), relationship and parenting statuses, physical size and attractiveness, combat experience, and interpersonal violence. Hays explicitly stated, and I concur, that all humans have a stake in almost every one of these dimensions.

The second phenomenon that these models of human difference offer is the vision of human intersectionalities emerging from these multiple social locations. Such intersections are not simply additive or even multiplicative, nor are they necessarily layered. They are sometimes the sum of their parts; they are, on occasion, more than or different from that sum. Maria Root, who has been at the forefront of proposing new paradigms for theorizing the experience of people of mixed phenotype and heritage (aka "racially mixed"), has proposed, on the basis of her research on sibling pairs from such families, that there are as many as five different and equally likely trajectories of intersectional identity development that are unrelated to visible components of identity (Root, 1998, 2000).

Included in analyses of intersectionalities by culturally competent psychotherapists is their comprehension of their own intersectionalities and pathways toward identity development. In relationship to the topic of negative emotional states, culturally competent practice points therapists directly at the issue of their biases, those toward and against aspects of self and those toward and against aspects of others. Feelings about those aspects of identity that are coded as Other, the ways in which an individual relates to those identity variables, and the affects surrounding them are foundational to culturally competent practice.

Bias, Prejudice, Hate, and Self-Hate: Negative Emotions Through the Lens of Cultural Competence

Almost all current paradigms of culturally competent practice insist that psychotherapists understand their own biases, including biases toward and against aspects of the self, and engage with them mindfully rather than operate from the fantasy that those biases can be put aside in the name of objectivity, that great illusion. Bias, stereotype, and prejudice are noted compassionately as the inevitable consequences of being fully human and capable of having affect-laden associations to the Other, as well as to those aspects of self deemed Otherlike. These affect-drenched cognitions about oneself and others are construed as important variables for self-awareness and for awareness of what is transpiring in the therapeutic encounter.

This stance of compassion, also thought of as one of nonjudging, differs importantly from objectivity, which is an illusory label for what individuals in positions of power call their own subjectivities. Thus, culturally competent psychotherapists have discarded illusions of neutrality or objectivity and embrace the reality that they will have bias and will have difficult feelings about clients and themselves. Joining with Pope and Tabachnick (1993), culturally competent therapists admit to the reality of feelings of disgust, anger, fear, or hate in the presence of their clients. They learn to notice bias and to bring its realities into the foreground of models of cultural competence. Culturally competent psychotherapists eschew the stance that one would be blind to difference; after all, how can one not notice, for example, the melanin tint in the skin of someone whose ancestors did not mostly come from Europe?

A particularly salient aspect of bias and negative affect noted by the cultural competence movement is that of disowned bias, called modern or aversive bias in the scholarly literature. The term *aversive bias* refers to nonconscious biases held by individuals who consciously eschew overt expressions of bias (Dovidio, Gaertner, Kawakami, & Hodson, 2002; Gaertner & Dovidio, 2005). This form of disowned negative affect appears to have developed during the latter half of the 20th century, as the holding of overt bias became socially stigmatized and unacceptable in many social groups, including most of those occupied by psychotherapists. This paradigm posits that, as a consequence of the change in the social environment, a split developed in many individuals between their expressed, conscious beliefs, which were not biased and emphasized the value of fairness, and their well-conditioned, nonconscious, and now ego-dystonic biases, which were consciously aversive to them and which contained a plethora of negative affects about the Other. Social psychologists who have studied this phenomenon extensively suggest that approximately 85% of European American individuals hold aversive bias toward persons of color, for example, even though their consciously held attitudes and behaviors are devoid of overt bias (e.g., Dovidio et al., 2002).

The presence of aversive bias in an individual has observable impact on that person's interactions with others; thus, it is not simply a private affair but rather an intersubjective phenomenon with specific effects on the interpersonal field. Given the sensitivity of many psychotherapy clients to a therapist's own unexplored or denied feelings, it stands to reason that aversive bias can play a large part in undermining a therapeutic relationship. In consequence, culturally competent practice requires the therapist to confront the potential for aversive bias head on and to own and make conscious those problematic affects.

Aversive bias is supported by denial and undoing and leads to shame, discomfort, and distancing, all of which are destructive to a psychotherapy relationship. Members of target groups (aka "minorities") will commonly experience their interactions with such dominant group persons as crazy-making and fraught with inauthenticity, just as the psychotherapy client encountering a therapist who claims to have no angry feelings while emitting cues of angry affect feels discounted and crazy-made.

Dovidio et al. (2002), in a series of elegant experiments exploring the effects of aversive bias, paired African American individuals with European American individuals on a problem-solving task. The European American participants were assessed on measures of both overt and aversive bias and were divided into three groups: (a) low aversive/low overt bias, (b) high aversive/low overt bias, and (c) high aversive/high overt bias. Dovidio et al. found that African American participants had the most difficult time interacting with individuals in the middle group, finding it easier to relate to people who were consistently high in both conscious and nonconscious bias than to deal with the conflicting psychosocial cues emitted by individuals who were unconscious of their aversive bias. Persons in the middle group tended to behave in ways that were inappropriate for the situation; they were overly friendly, leading to suspicion regarding motive on the part of the African American participants, or they became withdrawn and almost punishing, apparently when their inauthentic attempts to create a relationship were unsuccessful. Readers who wish to assess their own levels of aversive bias on the variables of ethnicity and sex can do so for free and anonymously online (http://www.understandingprejudice.org/iat/).

The implications of these and similar findings for the psychotherapeutic relationship with survivors of complex trauma are potentially quite powerful. Psychotherapists who are unaware of their aversive bias may, like the participants in Dovidio et al.'s (2002) studies, emit interpersonal cues that undermine their conscious intentions to do well and their cultural competence. Given the heightened importance of the therapeutic alliance for clients who have anxious or ambivalent attachment styles (Norcross & Lambert, 2005), the presence of such nonconscious and disowned bias in the psychotherapist may be particularly toxic to the alliance in psychotherapy with this population. Even when a client does not have such a style, the client designated as Other may feel ambivalent or anxious in relation to the psychotherapist, assuming the presence of bias when the therapist pretends to him- or herself that this kind of negative affect is absent.

Cultural competence does not rest solely in knowing in theory that one has aversive bias, however; it also requires a willingness to acknowledge this fact about oneself compassionately, without shaming oneself or inducing guilt in oneself, as a step toward greater congruence and authenticity.

As noted above, humans are biologically wired to respond to difference and psychosocially conditioned to associate difference with negative ascriptions that are inescapable in the familial and cultural contexts in which all psychotherapists have been raised. Because virtually all humans have bias, a therapist who acknowledges that reality will have an enhanced capacity to work with clients from target groups.

Shame about bias, however, undermines effectiveness. Nathanson (1992) argued that humans have four predictable responses to shame: (a) withdrawing or distancing from the source of the shame, (b) attacking the self for being shameful, (c) attacking the source of the shame, and (d) engaging in denial. Each of these inter- and intrapersonal strategies is counter to psychotherapeutic effectiveness; ironically, the strategy of withdrawal (e.g., "I'm not trained to work with Alien Beings") has been one accepted mode of behaving in a culturally competent manner within the framework of etic models. Compassionate acceptance of the reality of psychotherapist bias and the problematic affects in which such bias is steeped allows for approach and relationship between dominant and target group members, an interpersonal style more consistent with the development of a therapeutic alliance. If I am able to accept the reality of my biases and make them conscious, then I will enact them less; distance myself less from clients who evoke these biases, because I am experiencing less shame about my own responses; and be more willing to be confronted by a client without responding in a defensive manner. Cultural competence creates therapeutic competence when it lays a foundation for awareness of and attention to negative affects and bias.

Cultural competence models do not prescribe one particular strategy for integrating awareness of bias and negative affects into psychotherapeutic practice. Rather, because culturally competent practice is a metamodel integrative with other theories of psychotherapy, it offers epistemologies with which a psychotherapist can blend these awarenesses into the therapeutic frame of her or his own primary orientations. Questions of how and whether to disclose negative affect to clients and how to assess when and whether it is appropriate to engage in direct dialogue about differences and similarities in the therapist's and client's intersectionalities cannot be answered prescriptively. Instead, culturally competent psychotherapists are likely to attend to the intersection of these factors with the realities of who else the client might be—how capable of insight, how open to direct feedback, how fearful of a loss of connection, how able to tolerate, or not, the humanity of the psychotherapist.

Cultural competence models also look closely at how therapists' own intersectionalities of identities influence their manners of integrating and expressing this kind of awareness of negative affect. As culture and context shape the ways in which we know, name, and express emotion, culturally competent psychotherapists strive to have a manner of relating to their own problematic affects that is authentic for them, rather than compliant with some kind of externally prescribed norm.

What is common to most cultural competence paradigms is that the therapist is encouraged to embrace awareness of his or her own negative affects and bias, not so as to act them out but so as to be informed by them within the larger interpersonal field of the therapy relationship. Whereas older, etic models of cultural competence adjure therapists to refer the client to another professional should such biases become apparent, current and emerging models of culturally competent practice advise precisely the opposite: Instead of distancing from the source of their shame, culturally competent therapists are invited to inquire into the levels of meaning that might be best understood if they maintain a stance of compassionate, engaged relationship with the elephant of bias in the therapy office.

Training Culturally Competent Psychotherapists

The development of cultural competence is a project of engaging both heart and mind and of engendering commitments in trainees to lifelong learning. I frequently use a story from the book *The Left Hand of Darkness* (1976) by Ursula LeGuin, an author of speculative fiction, in which a character is chided for boasting when he proclaims himself greatly ignorant, to illustrate a cardinal principle of culturally competent practice. Wisdom, for a culturally competent psychotherapist, is the embrace of one's ignorance, the acceptance that there is much one cannot know, a letting go of a false stance of authority. Moving toward cultural competence requires the acquisition of a useful epistemic model of difference and its effects in the interpersonal and psychotherapeutic realm as well as the integration of those epistemologies into one's theory of psychotherapy. Thus, as psychology professionals train culturally competent psychotherapists, they must convey to them that cultural competence is a core competency of a psychotherapist, not an add-on. Coursework on every topic can and should integrate materials pertaining to cultural competence.

Supervision from trainers who are aware of, attuned to, and committed to culturally competent practice is a must for a trainee's professional development. Such a supervisor knows that she or he must model openness of expression with regard to the presence of aversive bias as well as self-awareness of one's intersectional identities and their effects on psychotherapy practice. Thus, a culturally competent supervisor or trainer creates the safety necessary for a trainee's honest confrontation with his or her own biases and her or his own disowned or shame-filled aspects of identity. The instructor quoted at the start of this chapter who hoped to induce guilt in students represents the antithesis of the learning environment in which culturally competent psychotherapy practice is nurtured. Instructors developing courses to support culturally competent practice must take into account the ways in which preexisting guilt and shame and disowned aversive bias will be present in students. They should thoughtfully prepare a course that will offer intellectually challenging and experientially deepening educational experiences to trainees.

The maintenance of a culturally competent stance is nourished by continuing affiliation and consultation with like-minded colleagues as well as with activists, artists, theorists, and thinkers in the critical studies fields. For me, one of the great gifts of a culturally competent stance has been exposure to thinkers outside the fields of psychology and psychotherapy who are considering the meanings of intersectionalities and the development of a range of practices that challenge oppressive relationships of all kinds. Culturally competent practice is difficult to sustain in a vacuum; because dominant culture, including the culture of therapy-as-usual, does little to reward cultural competence and much to make it somewhat uncomfortable, the presence of some kind of social support and validation for this way of seeing the work of therapy is a necessary aspect of its continued integration into a psychotherapist's work.

Case Example

I have never been shy about the components of my identity and their visibility in the therapy relationship. Some of them are undeniable because they are quite visible. I have spent my adult life having strangers ask if I am someone else—and those someone elses are always Jewish women whose grandparents or great-grandparents came from the Pale of Settlement, that intersection between today's Poland and the old Russian empire where so many of the ancestors of America's Jews, including all four of my grandparents, had their homes. I am prototypically that phenotype: short, round, dark, with curly hair and pale skin. I have learned that people who know this stereotype of what Jews look like know that I am one. My social class background is expressed in markers of dress and language that are easily perceivable, should the observer know what those markers signify. Other aspects of my identity are hidden. I am a lesbian, but because my appearance largely adheres to stereotypes of femininity, my sexual orientation is invisible unless I am seen in the company of my partner, who is quite visibly not feminine. But I have written and spoken about being a lesbian in settings beyond counting, and I do nothing to hide my identity.

I make the assumption that the things that I represent—or appear to represent—to my clients are going to become aspects of our relationship over time. A philo-Semitic client raised in a fundamental Christian home felt more connection to me because I was a Jew (Brown, 2007). My lesbian clients seek me out because they reasonably assume that I will not bring homophobia or heterosexism into our relationship. My working-class clients struggle with the markers of my middle-class status. Having dialogues, and sometimes difficult ones, about these dynamics has become a norm for me in my work. The ways in which aspects of my identities represent both the good and the hard for clients are a component of the transferential and countertransferential dynamics with which I am willing to engage. I am accustomed to clients having feelings about who I am that are sometimes troubling to me.

What happens, though, when what my client represents to me is painful and challenging? What do I do when the person in the room is saying and doing things that in anyone else would lead me to distance myself and end the relationship because I find them so offensive and so pejorative to the groups that are central to my own identities? In particular, what do I do when the client is, because of her own wounds, poorly equipped to engage in discourse with me about what it might mean that she is slinging insults in my direction in an apparently unconscious manner? This is the case of someone who taught me about the limits of my cultural competence and thus gave me the gift of requiring that I stretch.

This case example is about my work with Martha, a European American woman in her early 50s who had been psychiatrically disabled by depression and posttraumatic stress since well before I met her. In some very particular ways having to do with her identities and her behaviors, she is one of the most challenging people with whom I have ever worked. Unlike the clients who challenge me because of their problems of emotion regulation and problematic self-care strategies, Martha is in many ways relatively easy to work with. She comes to sessions on time and makes no attempts to overstay at the end, is scrupulous about ensuring that I am paid, and expresses respect for me in my role as her psychologist. As much as she likes anyone, I think, she likes me. The symptoms that she brings into treatment are complicated and fascinating and require me to think several layers past manifest content almost all of the time.

Martha is in therapy largely for supportive purposes. I learned early on, as was confirmed in consultation with her previous therapist, that Martha's psychological underpinnings were fragile and somewhat primitive and that insight and Martha were strangers to one another. She had been and continues to be suicidal at times and has many conflictual relationships with the other people in her life. When these episodes of suicidality or interpersonal difficulties occur, she needs a therapist who knows her well to support her in getting past the rapids without crashing on the rocks. Most of the time, what I can offer her is an attentive listening ear, because she has historically responded very poorly to attempts to engage her in specifically empowering change processes. She is very much a dweller in the Contemplation stage of the stages of change (knowing she has a problem but not committed to doing something about it; cf. Prochaska, DiClemente, & Norcross, 1992), expressed in terms of knowing that she suffers, believing that there is nothing to be done for her suffering, and passively refusing most offers from me or her physicians to do or be otherwise. Her painfully unmet dependency needs from childhood emerge as desires to be dependent on her "parents," aka her health care providers, today.

None of this is a problem for me. I have no need to prove my power as a therapist by making people change, and I have plenty of clients who have insight and strong desires to be empowered who meet such of those needs as I have for me. So why is she the topic of this case example? I chose Martha because her heritage has left her with terrible scars of internalized domination (Pheterson, 1986), the ways in which she psychically represents oppressive currents of human history, that are specifically relevant to my own identities as Jew and lesbian. Her heritage represents anti-Semitism and homophobia in powerful and unavoidable ways. I have disguised the specifics of her heritage because they are so unusual that they would destroy any attempts to protect her identity. Suffice it to say that her parents, now long dead, were members of an organization that targeted Jews and LGBT people, among others, for discrimination. Her father, in particular, took part in activities that were lethal to Jews and LGBT people. She was raised hearing Jews spoken of in highly derogatory terms, as if we, and not those trying to harm us, were dangerous. In adult life, she joined a religion that is among those leading the fight in the United States to prevent LGBT people from gaining certain civil rights, in particular, marriage equality.

I do not know about Martha's heritage from her directly, because she has never spoken of it to me, although she has spoken of her membership in her church, which is one of her conflictual relationships. I learned of Martha's heritage when her first therapist, who is also a Jew, needed to retire from practice and asked me to take on her care. My colleague wanted me to be forewarned and to have the chance to recuse myself from the referral up front. I took the naive stance that this would make no difference to me. I do not, after all, believe in collective guilt. Martha was not responsible for her parents' behaviors, I told my colleague; I would be fine.

And fine I thought I was, until the first time that Martha let loose with a rant about "the Jews." I cannot recall what her ostensible reason was for this. Martha frequently engages in racist tirades during her therapy sessions, which are all the more strange because many of her friends and members of her social circle are people of color. Unlike the majority of European American people of her age cohort, she has a life in which people of color are her intimates and her family. I had learned to interpret these explosions of anger and racist hostility as coded expressions of her feelings of alienation and betrayal by someone, not necessarily a person who is a member of the group she was insulting. Consistent with my own paradigms for practice, I had not disclosed to her the feelings of revulsion I had at her biases, believing her not able to receive such confrontations in a manner that would be helpful to her. I was able to easily move past such feelings to a reconnected empathy for her pain at being betrayed and to respond manifestly to that deeper theme in her life narrative.

I had little to no difficulty regulating my emotions during Martha's racist outbursts. I found that I would at first feel indignant and then almost immediately think, "OK, but what does that *really* mean?" Bringing analysis to bear on her actions and using intellectual discourse and engagement as a means of staying connected in the therapeutic relationship allowed me to soothe myself and remain firmly and comfortably in the therapist role. I did not, as I might with persons who had more insight, ever ask Martha herself to interrogate the meaning or timing of her racist statements. I had found that when I asked, "I wonder what it's like to feel that way when you have so many members of X group in your immediate family," she would ignore these attempts to invite self-reflection. Her family, conflictual as it is, is her family, and the rest of the members of that group were Them, the Other about whom she was ranting.

Then came the day that the Other she was ranting about were Jews. Her rant was straight out of the propaganda of the group to which her parents had belonged, one of the versions of "Jews are rich and control the world and it's their fault that fill-in-bad-thing has been done to them." It was hate speech, about me, happening in my office.

I was massively unprepared, even knowing what I knew about her family history. It was not as if I had never encountered anti-Semitism directly before that day. I have been a target of both overt and covert anti-Semitism on many occasions. I first knew that I was a Jew when, at the age of 5, I was cast out of a play activity by two slightly older girls on the grounds that I was one of Those People; I went home crying to my mother to ask if I was really that thing. I had spent my elementary school years going mano a mano with the school principal about my unwillingness to lend my voice to the singing of Christmas carols. One of my mothers-in-law had referred to someone "Jewing me down" as I sat in front of her. And I knew my people's history, both in general from the books and in more specific detail from my grandparents, all four of whom told me tales of hiding in the cellar from the drunk Christian villagers on Good Friday afternoons after the priest had preached the story of the Crucifixion in its pre–Vatican II version.

When Martha let loose about Jews, though, I was stunned. I recall sitting silently, feeling angry. All of my hitherto-disowned feelings about her parents rose immediately to the surface. "Damn haters," I remember thinking. And then, didn't she know that I was a Jew? And that her previous therapist (also phenotypically very much the stereotype and with a much more stereotypically Jewish family name than mine as well) was also a Jew? That the physician who had been so kind to her and helped her with her complex medical problems was a Jew, too? I fumed. I remember saying something ineffectual in an attempt to stop her, which had no effect. I recall feeling detached and distanced from her. A few minutes into her rant, she switched topics, as was common for her, and went off in her new direction. After she left, I was furious and hurt. How dare she? I thought about referring her to a different therapist.

In the intervening week, after I had calmed down, I thought much about what Martha had said. At first, to be honest, I was obsessing instead of thinking. I anxiously played out the scenario in my head of announcing to her that I was a Jew. Martha was a client with whom I did very little self-disclosure, but what I had disclosed to her should have been a clue, right? My (now-deceased) therapy dog had an audibly Yiddish name, Schmulik. I had spent time teaching that previous spring in Israel, which she knew. I was absent from the office on Jewish holy days, although in her case I had never said why, only that I could not make our usual appointment that particular week. And "oh, by the way, I look like a Jew—in fact, the very characteristics that your parents' hate group had made a point of identifying as prototypically Jewish, well, that's me, your therapist," I yelled at her in my head. "The hair, the skin, the nose, the body type, me!"

This obsessing and my own level of extreme negative emotion are what finally got me to thinking and to use what I know about culturally competent practice. So what if Martha knew, not consciously but somewhere below awareness, that I was a Jew? What meaning might that then lend to her outburst of anti-Semitic verbiage? I was paying attention to my own aversive bias; what about Martha's aversive bias? What might be happening between us that she was unable to behave politely in my presence and exposed this ugly side of herself to me? This line of questioning finally allowed me to begin to settle myself and to think about our intersectionality of identities and their apparent collision somewhere in the deep unconscious in my office at her last session. It felt as if the submarine of her anti-Semitism had been hit by some inadvertent torpedo from me and, having exploded, had risen to the surface.

Thus I formed my starting hypothesis. Martha knew nonconsciously that I am a Jew. Martha did not know that I know what her father did to Jews. Or maybe she knew that the way she knew that I am a Jew: intuitively, unconsciously, through some action or omission of mine during the time we had worked together. I had been in denial that what her father did mattered to our relationship. I had, in fact, taken that part of her identity and pushed it out of my awareness, until the moment when she shoved it back in my face. Hmm. What was I doing, deciding a priori to have a dissociative relationship with this aspect of my client's history? Was it because the father who had let Jews be hurt and killed was also a father who had let Martha be terribly sexually abused by older family members and never once protected her? Had I, by making her father's identity as an oppressor to me and mine be off limits to my consciousness, engaged in a tacit abandonment and betrayal of my client?

That is where the light began to dawn. Martha's outbursts of hate speech were almost always symbolic communications about betrayal in the interpersonal realm. If I treated my hypothesis about her other episodes of hate speech as true, then what was she telling me about feeling betrayed by me that she could not voice in a more straightforward (and thus unavailable to her) fashion? How might I have betrayed her as a therapist? Something else I knew about Martha was how little the people in her life realized that she felt betrayed by them—until those moments when she would ventilate her rage at them for no apparent reason. She was a master of indirection. Like many survivors of complex trauma with attachment wounds, she feared losing relationships should she be overt in her anger toward those on whom she depended. I started to think about how I might have done something with her that she felt as a betrayal.

There was, in addition, a power differential between us as wide as Puget Sound. I was not struggling to make ends meet, having to beg at the food bank for another week's allocation. I wasn't fending off creditors. I didn't seem to be ill and suffering. She is and was all of those things. In fact, I was to her like her parents had said the Jews were to them: the fat cats, the comfortable ones, taking from them, leaving them vulnerable.

I realized that if I were going to be Martha's therapist, truly her therapist and not a support person, I would need to engage with this reality of her, not avoid or deny its meaning and existence in the room. The person who filled Martha with hatred of Jews had treated her hatefully; if I were to be her ally in healing from the wounds he cut into her psyche, I could not longer pretend that he was absent. Also, I had to deal with the anger I felt and feel at people like Martha's father, who have actively harmed my community, and with my anger at Martha for incorporating his beliefs despite his having harmed her, too. The crossroads of the therapy office in which we met was a place where the things that we did not speak of—her father's affiliation, my Jewishness— could not be ignored if our work together was to be helpful to her.

So, the following Tuesday, when Martha came into the office and sat down, I asked her, "I'm wondering if you were feeling like I was distracted or disconnected last week." I thought it would be worthwhile to test a hypothesis that I had developed in the aftermath of that session about which of my behaviors had been the catalyst for her attack. She denied this at first, then gradually, as the hour passed, made a few carefully framed comments about how busy I was. I had been a little distracted, a little on autopilot with her, the previous week. When I had done my track-back of my actions in that session, I could see it, and I imagine that she had realized it. And she had known it, as it turns out; like many trauma survivors, she is acutely attuned to whether or not I'm paying attention, and she had known how to express her anger in a way that I would be unable to ignore. That day, we began to create a place in which she could tell me a little more directly if I was doing something she didn't like or feel good about. "I really like hearing about that kind of thing," I told her. "We therapists are weird that way; we like to know when we're not being our best, because that way we could be."

Martha has made similar anti-Semitic remarks only one other time since then. I deserved that confrontation, although not its content. It was another day with too much swirling around, and my energy was not fully focused on my work. This time I was able to feel fear, then anger, and then soothe myself and, in the moment, tell her, "Martha, I get the feeling you don't think I'm listening to you very well today." I was met with another denial but an almost immediate end to the rant about the Jews.

This case example has a postscript. Soon after I completed this chapter, Martha wished me happy Chanukah. "You *are* Jewish, right?" she asked. I said yes, thanked her, and we went on. I was dumbfounded. A bit later, she mentioned that she had read my website. "I loved that part about Schmulik," she mentioned (I have posted an obituary of my canine cotherapist there); "His mommies must miss him a lot." I agreed, yes, we miss him a lot, thinking all the while, "OK, so now she officially knows that I'm a Jewish lesbian!" Somehow, our collective willingness to see and hear one another has grown. The hate speech has stopped. In fact, it seems to have stopped about just about everyone, not just Jews. This whole experience required me to see and hear and know Martha much more deeply. Perhaps that has made a difference for her.

Also around this time, Martha shared with me a dream in which she has incorporated me into her unconscious life as a powerful healing, nurturing figure. If one gives credence to the notion that bias reflects the shadow side of how a group is perceived, then perhaps the left hand of that darkness of bias in Martha is a perception that, as a person who is a member of two persecuted groups, I can understand and empathize with her pain and feelings of dispossession and alienation. I don't know; I can't ask Martha, who would find the whole thing another one of those odd therapist questions that annoy her. What she teaches me is that when I find my way to compassion for the ways in which my clients' pain is expressed, that compassion sometimes gets through the considerable contextual barriers to that ever occurring.

CONCLUSION

Psychotherapy practice is maddening, terrifying, exhilarating work in which therapists should be honored to sit in the presence of wounded human beings as they heal. Because it is a fully human endeavor, it is also one in which it is inevitable that each party will have feelings of rage, hate, hurt, and pain in relationship to the other one at some point—and sometimes many, points—along the way.

A culturally competent paradigm for psychotherapy practice empowers a therapist to think in a complex and sophisticated way about the manners in which her or his intersectionalities of identities as well as those of the client might be contributing to or generating those painful affects. This paradigm then offers a compassionate lens through which a therapist may view those experiences, in her- or himself and in clients alike. In embracing the energy of anger, pain, and hurt, we therapists can blend with it rather than fight it and, in blending, see more clearly what those expressions of distress in ourselves and our clients represent.

REFERENCES

Brown, L. S. (2007). Feminist therapy as a meaning-making practice: Where there is no power, where is the meaning? In K. Schneider (Ed.), *Existential–integrative psychotherapy: Guideposts to the core of practice* (pp. 130–140). New York, NY: Routledge.

Brown, L. S. (2008). *Cultural competence in trauma therapy: Beyond the flashback.* Washington, DC: American Psychological Association. doi:10.1037/11752-000

Chesler, P. (1972). *Women and madness.* New York, NY: Macmillan.

Comas-Diaz, L., & Greene, B. (Eds.). (1994). *Women of color.* New York, NY: Guilford Press.

D'Andrea, M., & Daniels, J. (2001). RESPECTFUL counseling: An integrative multi-dimensional model for counselors. In D. Pope-Davis & H. L. K. Coleman (Eds.), *The intersection of race, class, and gender in multicultural counseling* (pp. 417–466). Thousand Oaks, CA: Sage.

Dovidio, J. F., Gaertner, S. L., Kawakami, K., & Hodson, G. (2002). Why can't we just get along? Interpersonal biases and interracial distrust. *Cultural Diversity and Ethnic Minority Psychology, 8,* 88–102. doi:10.1037/1099-9809.8.2.88

Etic. (n.d.). In *Wiktionary.* Retrieved March 26, 2012, from http://en.wiktionary. org/wiki/etic

Gaertner, S., & Dovidio, J. (2005). Understanding and addressing contemporary racism: From aversive racism to the common ingroup identity model. *Journal of Social Issues, 61,* 615–639. doi:10.1111/j.1540-4560.2005.00424.x

Guthrie, R. V. (1976). *Even the rat was white: A historical view of psychology.* New York, NY: Harper & Row.

Hays, P. A. (2008). *Addressing cultural complexities in practice: Assessment, diagnosis, and therapy* (2nd ed.). Washington, DC: American Psychological Association. doi:10.1037/11650-000

Jones, S. (2009, April). *Sarah Jones as a one-woman global village* [Video file]. Retrieved from http://www.ted.com/talks/sarah_jones_as_a_one_woman_global_village. html

Kanuha, V. (1990). Compounding the triple jeopardy: Battering in lesbian of color relationships. In L. S. Brown & M. P. P. Root (Eds.), *Diversity and complexity in feminist therapy* (pp. 169–184). New York, NY: Haworth Press.

LeGuin, U. (1976). *The left hand of darkness.* San Francisco, CA: Ace Books.

McBride, J. (1996). *The color of water: A Black man's tribute to his White mother.* New York, NY: Riverhead Books.

Nathanson, D. (1992). *Shame and pride: Affect, sex, and the birth of the self.* New York, NY: Norton.

Norcross, J. C., & Lambert, M. J. (2005).The therapy relationship. In J. C. Norcross, L. E. Beutler, & R. F. Levant (Eds.), *Evidence-based practice in mental health: Debate and dialogue on the fundamental questions* (pp. 208–217). Washington, DC: American Psychological Association.

Pheterson, G. (1986). Alliances between women: Overcoming internalized oppression and internalized domination. *Signs, 12,* 146–160. doi:10.1086/494302

Pope, K. S., & Tabachnick, B. (1993). Therapists' anger, hate, fear, and sexual feelings. *Professional Psychology: Research and Practice, 24,* 142–152. doi:10.1037/0735-7028.24.2.142

Prochaska, J. O., DiClemente, C. C., & Norcross, J. C. (1992). In search of how people change. *American Psychologist, 47,* 1102–1114. doi:10.1037/0003-066X.47.9.1102

Root, M. P. P. (1998). Preliminary findings from the biracial sibling project. *Cultural Diversity and Mental Health, 4,* 237–247. doi:10.1037/1099-9809.4.3.237

Root, M. P. P. (2000). Rethinking racial identity development: An ecological framework. In P. Spickard & J. Burroughs (Eds.), *We are a people: Narrative in the construction and deconstruction of ethnic identity* (pp. 205–220). Philadelphia, PA: Temple University Press.

II

BORDERLINE PERSONALITY DISORDER

INTRODUCTION: BORDERLINE PERSONALITY DISORDER

A diagnosis of borderline personality disorder has become synonymous with the difficult client. Psychotherapists who are referred these clients have negative reactions even prior to the first session. These are the clients assumed to be interpersonally challenging and emotionally provocative, with strong self-destructive tendencies and pervasive problems maintaining stable relationships with others because of their erratic and overwhelming emotional states.

In this section, two very different approaches to the treatment of borderline personality disorder are presented, with different perspectives on how to understand and manage therapists' negative emotional reactions within the context of the goals of treatment and the tasks of client and therapist. Shelley McMain and Carmen Wiebe discuss dialectical behavior therapy (DBT), an evidence-based treatment, grounded in dialectical philosophy, learning theory, and Zen philosophy. John Clarkin and Frank Yeomans discuss transference-focused psychotherapy (TFP), also an evidence-based treatment, grounded in psychoanalytic object relations and attachment theory. These treatment approaches are supported by sophisticated theoretical frameworks, and their efficacy and effectiveness in treating borderline personality disorder are documented in randomized clinical trials that monitor adherence to treatment manuals. In the space allowed, the following two chapters cannot do justice to the complexity and depth of DBT and TFP; the reader is encouraged to explore in greater depth the theory, practice, and training in these two treatment modalities.

Even though DBT and TFP are grounded in very different theoretical frameworks and specify very different therapeutic techniques in their manuals, there is some common ground. For example, both emphasize the importance of establishing and maintaining a therapeutic alliance with clients. Both schools recognize the importance of therapists' awareness of their own negative reactions and the importance of seeking consultation regarding these reactions. And both emphasize how vulnerable psychotherapists are to extreme behavior and the intense affective storms that are inevitable in the treatment of this serious disorder. McMain and Wiebe, as well as Clarkin and Yeomans, vividly describe the short-term and long-term challenges of weathering these storms.

By understanding how DBT and TFP manage therapists' negative emotional responses to their clients, we also see the very striking theoretical and practical differences of these treatments. For example, in DBT, the goal of treatment is primarily to reduce rigidity and ineffective behaviors associated with intense emotions through dialectics, acceptance and skills training. The therapist's negative emotional responses are experienced in response to encountering an obstacle to a goal and are another problem that the therapist needs to solve in order to overcome that obstacle to treatment. The therapist seeks the support and encouragement of their treatment team to overcome feelings of frustration by empathizing and becoming more accepting and compassionate to the plight of the client in order to resume the work of the therapy.

In TFP, the essential goal of treatment is to help clients move from a fragmented and contradictory sense of self and others to a coherent one, with an increasing synergy between reflection, affect modulation, and relatedness to others. The therapist's negative emotional response is a signal of a disturbance in the here-and-now of the therapeutic relationship, and the task of the therapist is to understand and assist the client in repairing that disturbance as it gets played out in their relationship. The challenge for the therapist is to fully experience this emotional response as participant in the client's internal drama while simultaneously formulating a response that addresses the deeper meanings of this specific interaction. The therapist is both participant and observer in a drama that is being enacted in the therapy situation. The role of peer supervision is to help the therapist understand how his or her negative emotional responses have a depth that serves as data directly relevant to the disturbances clients experience in other areas of their lives.

7

THERAPIST COMPASSION: A DIALECTICAL BEHAVIOR THERAPY PERSPECTIVE

SHELLEY McMAIN AND CARMEN WIEBE

People diagnosed with borderline personality disorder (BPD) are challenging to treat because they frequently evoke intense countertherapeutic reactions in psychotherapists. They are one of the most stigmatized groups of individuals with mental health disorders, and they are often blamed by their clinicians for not improving. Many therapists refuse to treat this population, and those who do generally limit their practice to a few such clients.

Empirically supported approaches, such as dialectical behavior therapy (DBT), have led to a growing interest in providing treatment for BPD. The increased availability of training on current concepts of BPD and principles of effective treatment has been associated with an increase in positive attitudes, enthusiasm, and willingness to work with people with this disorder (Krawitz, 2004). Our intention in this chapter is to examine principles and strategies in DBT that engender therapist compassion. We begin by presenting an overview of DBT's etiological theory of BPD, its hypothesized mechanisms

DOI: 10.1037/13940-007
Transforming Negative Reactions to Clients: From Frustration to Compassion, A. W. Wolf, M. R. Goldfried, and J. C. Muran (Editors)

of change, and its perspective on the therapy relationship. Next, we consider the role of the treatment structure and several specific principles and strategies that enhance therapist compassion. Finally, we offer a case example to illustrate how these strategies may be used to manage negative reactions toward clients with BPD.

THEORY

DBT has a sound basis in theory and specifically focuses on three areas: (a) etiology/mechanisms of change, (b) treatment technique and the therapeutic alliance, and (c) the role of therapist self-awareness.

Etiological Theory and Mechanisms of Change

According to the biosocial theory of the etiology of BPD proposed by Linehan (1993), the core dysfunction underlying this disorder is pervasive emotion dysregulation. Emotion dysregulation develops because of a transaction between biological and social factors, in which an emotionally sensitive temperament (i.e., heightened sensitivity and intensity of emotions, and slow return to baseline) interacts with a chronically invalidating environment (i.e., one that ignores, rejects, or criticizes emotional responses). BPD criterion behaviors, which include suicidal episodes, substance use, and angry outbursts, are viewed as either a by-product of emotion dysregulation or a means to regulate emotions.

The effectiveness of DBT is assumed to involve the inhibition of dysfunctional behaviors that are associated with dysregulated emotions (Lynch, Chapman, Rosenthal, Kuo, & Linehan, 2006). The treatment strategies integrate methods derived from dialectical philosophy, learning theory, and Zen practice. Dialectical philosophy provides an overarching treatment framework, emphasizing a systemic perspective and principles of balance and interrelatedness. The core dialectical strategy in DBT consists of combining two contrasting methods: (a) cognitive behavioral change-based strategies and (b) acceptance-based strategies that stem from client-centered therapy and Zen philosophy.

Dialectical strategies can influence a client's orienting response (i.e., the reflex in responding to a change in the environment) and can thus enhance learning, attention, and cognitive processing. These strategies also help increase flexibility and decrease emotional and behavioral rigidity. Strategies such as exposure protocols, cognitive restructuring, and behavioral analysis can change the associations between stimuli. The primary acceptance strategies used are *mindfulness* and *validation*. Mindfulness promotes acceptance of experience and encourages the client to develop new associations to stimuli that elicit painful emotions and problematic behaviors. Through validation, the therapist conveys acceptance of some aspect of a client's emotions, cognitions, or behaviors and enhances emotion regulation by increasing a stable self-view, thereby reducing emotional arousal.

The four treatment modes of DBT include strategies that serve to directly or indirectly enhance emotion regulation (McMain, Korman, & Dimeff, 2001). First, *individual therapy* increases motivation to change and promotes functional behaviors through strategies such as validation, contingency management, and modeling. Second, *skills training* groups help clients learn and implement functional behaviors. Third, *telephone coaching* outside of formal sessions helps clients generalize new responses to problematic emotions across situations. Fourth and last, the *therapist consultation team* reinforces effective behavior and increases motivation on the part of the therapist.

Treatment Technique and the Therapeutic Alliance

Both therapist compassion and scientifically sound techniques are essential to the effective treatment of BPD (Linehan, 1993). The principles and strategies of DBT help to cultivate both of these. Treatment techniques and the therapy relationship influence each other: When a therapist uses effective interventions, the client is more likely to make progress; this progress increases the therapist's hope and motivation, and this in turn leads to more focused and effective application of treatment strategies.

The Role of Therapist Self-Awareness

Because working with BPD clients can evoke negative responses, the therapist's awareness of these responses is a fundamental aspect of the treatment. Individual sessions are organized according to a target hierarchy, in which therapy-interfering behaviors (including negative reactions on the part of the therapist) are prioritized above behaviors that interfere with quality of life (e.g., substance use, depression, and eating disorders), although they fall second to life-interfering behaviors (e.g., those that are suicidal or homicidal). The rationale for this is simple: The therapist must feel motivated and compassionate in order to deliver effective treatment.

Negative responses on the part of the therapist may or may not be relevant to address in treatment. At times, the therapist's reactions may parallel the reactions that other individuals have to the client and can therefore be crucial to examine. At other times, they may be due to the therapist's own personality or current life circumstances, but if they are interfering with the client's treatment, it may be important to acknowledge them.

PRACTICE

DBT encompasses several practice techniques, including an emphasis on the role of the therapy team, utilizing specific strategies to manage therapist negative reactions, and confronting any negative feelings the therapist may develop toward the client.

The Role of the Team

The DBT model puts a strong emphasis on treatment as a team approach, which is a key formula for increasing therapist compassion and sense of support. In keeping with its dialectical theory, DBT adopts a holistic perspective in which treatment occurs within the context of a community of therapists. A team is a prerequisite for the practice of DBT, the rationale being that an individual therapist cannot effectively treat BPD clients without the support of others. The team functions to help therapists stay both motivated and effective and, as such, bears the burden of responsibility for the effectiveness of the treatment.

The primary function of the team is to increase therapist motivation, enhance therapist capabilities, and help reduce therapist negative reactions toward difficult clients. The team cultivates a climate and conditions wherein compassion is nurtured. One role of the team is to ensure that therapists adhere to DBT's fundamental assumptions about clients. For example, therapists help each other adopt attitudes such as "Clients are doing the best they can," "Clients have not caused their problems but have to solve them anyway," and "The lives of suicidal individuals with BPD are unbearable." The presence of other team members and their interventions help reduce individual therapists' feelings of isolation and increase a sense of community. Team members help monitor the therapist's reactions toward clients and assist the therapist in skillfully bringing relevant issues into the therapy sessions. The practice of sharing positive and inspirational stories is common in many DBT teams and helps to engender positive feelings about work.

Consultation "team agreements" guide the interactions among team members and promote compassion toward clients. Therapists agree to be phenomenologically empathic and to search for nonpejorative, nonjudgmental, compassionate interpretations of their clients' behavior. They agree to observe their personal limits with clients and to refrain from judging other therapists for having personal limits that are broader or narrower than their own. Discussing and negotiating these personal limits directly with the clients is encouraged, because this gives both therapist and client the opportunity to resolve problems and reduce feelings of frustration. Therapists share a belief that they are fallible, which decreases defensiveness and allows acceptance of negative reactions; it also increases the likelihood that they will seek help from their colleagues when needed. Finally, the team members agree to adopt a dialectical perspective, which increases acceptance of conflict and disagreements when they occur, because conflict is normal and expected. The task of the therapist is not to avoid tension and ruptures with client or teammates; instead, a synthesis of contradictory views is pursued so that a more sophisticated understanding of a situation is attained.

Principles and Strategies for Managing Therapists' Negative Reactions

The two primary DBT strategies for managing therapists' negative reactions to clients are (a) to *observe* those negative reactions and (b) to carefully determine whether it is appropriate to *disclose* those reactions to a particular client.

Observing Negative Reactions Toward Clients

A key challenge for many therapists is recognizing and attending to negative responses before these become overwhelming and less amenable to change. Dismissing or ignoring early signs of frustration or burnout can lead to intense responses that damage the therapy relationship.

A critical component of being mindful of emotional reactions is to go beyond the labels of *frustration* or *burnout* and identify the factors that prompted the reaction. Negative emotional arousal is a natural response to encountering an obstacle to a goal, and it is important for the therapist to identify what goal is being blocked. Frustration can be a secondary reaction to other emotions, such as hurt (e.g., my client is not appreciative of my efforts), disappointment (e.g., my client is not making progress), or anxiety (e.g., my client is engaging in high-risk behavior).

As noted above, self-reflection is embedded in the structure of the treatment. The target hierarchy ensures that therapists consider their reactions toward their clients and assess whether those reactions are interfering with treatment. Team meetings provide an opportunity to reflect on and address negative reactions. Also, each therapist learns to accept his or her negative reactions by observing colleagues who share these feelings and model self-acceptance. Supervision and personal mindfulness practice are other means to increase awareness of emotional states.

Guidelines for Disclosing Reactions

In order to decide whether to contain or express a negative reaction, the therapist must consider the intensity of the reaction and its relevance to the client's treatment. In general, therapists who treat clients with BPD need to be capable of tolerating ineffective interpersonal styles. It is often useful to simply let go of frustration or irritation that is of low to moderate intensity.

Determining whether a negative reaction is relevant to treatment requires that one consider several factors. One is the relative importance of the reaction in the context of other treatment targets. In most situations, suicidal behaviors take priority; time-sensitive crises may also take priority, depending on the intensity of the therapist's reaction. If the therapy relationship and treatment are compromised by the therapist's reaction—for example, if the client destroys the therapist's property and the therapist's limits are exceeded—then it is usually considered a high priority to disclose the reaction. If the therapist's reaction is related to the client's problems and treatment goals—for example, feeling frustrated with a hostile client—this too is important to discuss. If a particular client is having difficulty maintaining other relationships because of anger, it can be useful for the therapist to disclose his or her reaction. In some cases, this disclosure should not be done if the timing is poor; for example, if the appointment may be ending, or the therapy is in the early stages and a therapeutic alliance has not yet developed.

Managing or Expressing Negative Feelings

DBT therapists use several strategies to manage and perhaps disclose negative feelings they experience in therapy.

Managing Negative Reactions

Various strategies in DBT help therapists let go of negative reactions toward clients. Team members can provide validation, encouragement, and reassurance, which serve to soothe negative emotions. Mindfully diverting one's attention from the negative reaction itself is another useful strategy.

As with the treatment of any problem, a therapist's negative reaction is viewed as simply another problem to be solved. One aspect of solving the problem involves understanding the factors that prompted the negative reaction. Frustration can develop in response to client behaviors such as phoning frequently or constantly presenting to session in crisis. Helping the client to change is one route toward changing one's own negative reaction. Frustration may arise because of factors related to a therapist's personal issues instead of the client's behavior, such as being overworked or in need of a vacation. Reducing the source of the stress may be a solution. Often, a negative reaction is prompted by an interplay between client factors and therapist factors. Sometimes, the factors that prompt a negative reaction can be modified quickly, but often they take time to resolve, and the therapist needs to use a combination of strategies in order to increase patience, tolerance, and compassion.

Because frustration can develop because of unrealistic expectations about a client's progress, it may be necessary to modify these expectations. Individuals with BPD rarely make quick and steady progress. Relapses to old, dysfunctional behaviors occur commonly, as does the resurgence of problematic behaviors around the time of treatment termination. Frustration can lead even experienced therapists to lose sight of the usual course of treatment; thus, frequent reminders from the team can be helpful.

Considering the biological and environmental factors that have contributed to a client's behaviors (i.e., the biosocial theory) can also modify a therapist's judgment and deepen feelings of empathy. Conceptualizing symptoms of BPD according to this theory implies that clients are doing the best that they can in an effort to manage their emotional distress, instead of trying to manipulate others. For example, in the case of a client who is verbally attacking, the therapist can think about this individual's lifetime of abuse and recall that this anger developed as a means of self-protection. Alternatively, the therapist may imagine the vulnerable emotion that is fueling the challenging behavior. This is especially relevant for anger, because many BPD clients attack or blame others in response to underlying fear and shame. The team may be able to further clarify the client's internal world by engaging in role play, not just to practice therapeutic techniques but also to allow the therapist to feel what it might be like to live the way the client does. Another method to increase acceptance is for team members to remind each other of DBT's assumptions about clients, such as "He is doing the best he can."

Personal practice of DBT skills can also help therapists decrease the intensity of their reactions and increase their acceptance of clients. Mindfulness practice and distress tolerance skills, such as deep breathing and imagery, can be used during or between sessions and may be particularly useful immediately prior to dreaded sessions. Examples include meditating on images that evoke empathy or compassion for the client, for example, picturing her as a powerless child being berated by her angry mother, or imagining oneself as a rock radiating warmth toward the client (K. Koerner, personal communication, 2010). As well, repeating the mantra "The client is perfect as she is" is a powerful way to reduce frustration in the moment.

Sometimes therapists need to work on addressing and solving personal issues that are compromising their ability to remain focused, compassionate, and flexible. The DBT team may give support by providing coverage for after-hours telephone consultations or skills group sessions. Teams also typically provide emotional support in the form of providing extra social contact with the therapist, ensuring that therapists are taking care of themselves (e.g., eating regularly, saying no to extra work), or offering concrete suggestions around work–life balance. Other solutions include personal therapy and mindfulness practice.

Therapist Disclosure of Negative Reactions

Negative reactions to clients should be disclosed only at moments when they are likely to be helpful (Linehan, 1993). During the early phase of treatment, before an alliance is established, this should be done with caution. Intense frustration or strong judgment on the part of the therapist should be reduced before the topic of a negative reaction is raised with the client. It is essential that the negative feelings are shared in a context of care and concern rather than in a punitive manner.

The most common type of disclosure involves discussing the effect of a client's behavior. Disclosing one's personal limits is encouraged, especially if they have been exceeded. For example, a therapist may state, "I really don't like it when you yell at me. I know this is exactly what you're working on, but I'm finding myself drained and less motivated when you yell, which is not how I want to feel and is not helpful to you!"

Personal limits will differ, and a therapist's reaction may be typical of how others react or be idiosyncratic. For example, a client who has a habit of engaging in a hostile manner may evoke irritation in the therapist. Focusing on this pattern as it emerges in the therapy relationship can be productive. Even if the therapist's reaction is idiosyncratic, it may be relevant to discuss. For example, a therapist may be very sensitive to a client using profanities and so might state, "I know many staff members in our clinic are comfortable with swearing, but personally it makes it hard for me to take in what you're saying." Or a therapist may be vulnerable because she has a new baby and is sleep deprived and so might state, "I am feeling a little a distracted and tuned out while you're talking, which has nothing to do with you, and everything to do with the fact that I didn't sleep last night."

There are several ways in which the disclosure of a reaction can be beneficial. First, the disclosure may function as an aversive contingency, such that the client stops engaging in the behavior because he or she does not like the critical feedback. Second, if the information being shared is something the client fears, its disclosure can serve as a needed exposure to the avoided stimulus. For example, if the client typically responds to critical feedback with overwhelming shame and secondary anger, the feedback discussion provides an opportunity to work on tolerating shame. Third, if the therapist's reaction is representative of how others react to the client, disclosure provides an opportunity to examine interpersonal patterns. Finally, by being direct and genuine, the therapist communicates that negative feelings can develop in any relationship and that ruptures are normal and solvable. This models effective interpersonal communication and helps develop a closer therapeutic relationship.

When therapists disclose negative reactions, it is important that they not blame clients and that they acknowledge responsibility for their reactions. For example, a therapist who allowed his personal limits to be exceeded by taking too many phone calls may say, "I realize I've been taking more phone calls from you lately than I want to, and I'm getting frustrated, which doesn't help you. I'm sorry I didn't catch this earlier, and I assure you that I'll work on observing my limits."

CASE ILLUSTRATION

The following clinical example illustrates how the principles and strategies of DBT treatment enhanced therapist compassion toward a challenging high-risk client. The client, a 23-year-old woman with BPD, identified here as Sue, referred herself for the treatment of chronic and severe suicidal and self-harm behaviors. Several factors impeded treatment, including significant chaos, homelessness, and interpersonal difficulties. The DBT treatment team felt some trepidation about treating this individual; other therapists were reluctant to be her primary therapist.

The young woman's chaotic and high-risk behaviors made it difficult to develop a therapeutic alliance. Initially, the logistics of scheduling an appointment was challenging, because Sue had an unstable housing situation and there was no means of contacting her. She missed several appointments because she was in crisis or had been admitted to a hospital. For the initial session, her individual therapist met with her on an inpatient unit in an effort to make contact and develop a therapeutic relationship. The young woman made no eye contact and showed little interest in the new therapist, leaving the latter feeling invisible. The client stated directly, "I don't want to see you; I want my old therapist." In fact, her former therapist had terminated treatment because of a lack of progress. Sue talked about her self-harm behavior in a nonchalant manner, laughing when she described how she had recently overdosed on 60 Tylenol. She appeared relaxed and comfortable in the inpatient unit and commented, "I like it here; can I stay?"

Sue appeared to be at high risk of killing herself and evidenced little motivation to change, and the therapist was immediately aware that her response was a mixture of intense fear and frustration. She also noticed a sense of depletion, not only because of Sue's high risk for self-harm but also because she felt incapable of providing the needed help. It was difficult to feel optimistic about Sue's prognosis in light of her 15-year history of intractable self-harm behaviors. Although the therapist wanted to feel motivated, enthusiastic, and optimistic, she felt a sense of dread, anxiety, and hopelessness, and she realized that these negative feelings had the potential to interfere with treatment.

During weekly consultation team meetings, the therapist discussed these feelings of frustration with her colleagues, admitting, "My client is driving me crazy! I'm afraid that she's going to die, and I feel hopeless about my ability to stop her." Validation from the team members helped therapist to increase her acceptance of these reactions and recognize that they were normal and understandable.

The therapist's frustration was identified as a problem that signaled a need for greater empathy for the client. Keeping the biosocial theory in mind, the team members helped her to reflect on the factors underlying Sue's behaviors, such as a long history of childhood sexual and emotional abuse, and to understand these behaviors as a means of decreasing strong fears of isolation and abandonment. The therapist was able to reduce her frustration by reminding herself that, taken in context, the client's behavior made perfect sense.

The first few months of work with Sue were draining, and progress was unsatisfyingly slow. Team members normalized this trying pace, noting that many clients with entrenched and unusually severe problems take longer to respond to treatment, and helped the therapist search for and reinforce all signs of progress both in Sue and in herself. They cheered when hearing that Sue had not committed any acts of self-harm for an entire week. They continuously praised the therapist for her hard work and attempts to engage Sue. At times, when the therapist felt exhausted, they provided practical assistance by offering after-hours pager coverage. Following one particularly grueling session, team members left the therapist a box of chocolates in a gesture of support and an effort to provide comfort.

After several months of therapy, there were only minimal reductions in the severity and frequency of Sue's high-risk self-harm behaviors, and the therapist was feeling hopeless and stuck. She had tried a wide range of strategies without success, and she realized that her personal limits had been reached in that she was not prepared to continue offering ineffective treatment. On the basis of the high intensity and relevance of her reaction, she decided to share her sense of frustration with Sue. She grounded herself in a sense of caring before this encounter by reminding herself of the biosocial theory and by practicing mindfulness. At the session she told Sue, with sincerity and without hostility,

> I am so frustrated by the fact that your ongoing crises make it impossible for us to do anything other than crisis management. Your self-harm is burning me out. If we don't get this behavior under control immediately, I'm not prepared to continue treatment with you.

This disclosure was very effective as an aversive contingency, because Sue very much wanted to stay in treatment and maintain the therapy relationship. Once the continuation of her treatment was made contingent on progress, Sue managed to achieve 3 months with no self-harm. This turnaround in Sue's motivation also resolved the problem of the therapist's frustration. Most important, the therapist could not have expressed her frustration effectively unless she had first balanced it with a deep sense of compassion for the client.

CONCLUSION

Two central features of dialectical philosophy as applied in DBT are (a) an emphasis on synthesizing opposites and (b) a belief in multiple truths, that is, that there is always more than one solution to any problem. The solution to a therapist's frustration may be to change it into compassion by developing greater empathy and hope, or it may be to increase acceptance and tolerance of feelings of frustration and to synthesize this reaction with compassion.

In the case illustration just provided, the therapist allowed herself to tolerate her negative reaction while integrating it with a deep sense of caring and concern for the client. In doing so, she was able to express her negative emotions directly and honestly, without hostility, irritation, or rejection of the client and in a way that conveyed her desire to help the client improve her life. This process can be described as holding on to the kernel of genuine negative emotion—and, in this case, also harnessing the energizing, motivating power of frustration—while "softening the edges" (K. Koerner, personal communication, 2010) so that frustration can be expressed in a productive manner. In the case illustration, instead of transforming frustration into compassion, the opposites were synthesized so that frustration was expressed with compassion.

REFERENCES

Krawitz, R. (2004). Borderline personality disorder: Attitudinal change following training. *Australian and New Zealand Journal of Psychiatry, 38,* 554–559. doi:10.1080/j.1440-1614.2004.01409.x

Linehan, M. (1993). *Cognitive-behavioral treatment of borderline personality disorder.* New York, NY: Guilford Press.

Lynch, T. R., Chapman, A. L., Rosenthal, Z. M., Kuo, J. R., & Linehan, M. M. (2006). Mechanisms of change in dialectical behavior therapy: Theoretical and empirical observations. *Journal of Clinical Psychology, 62,* 459–480. doi:10.1002/jclp.20243

McMain, S., Korman, L., & Dimeff, L. (2001). Dialectical behavior therapy and the treatment of emotion dysregulation. *Journal of Clinical Psychology, 57,* 183–196.

8

MANAGING NEGATIVE REACTIONS TO CLIENTS WITH BORDERLINE PERSONALITY DISORDER IN TRANSFERENCE-FOCUSED PSYCHOTHERAPY

From the moment of birth throughout the life cycle, it is a basic mammalian (Insel & Young, 2001) and human need to attach to others. The attachment process is driven by needs ranging from survival, safety, and security to affection and sexual involvement. Disturbance in these relationships is often concurrent with clinical symptoms, such as anxiety, depression (Sroufe, Carlson, Levy, & Egeland, 1999), and suicidal behavior (Van Orden et al., 2010).

The heart of personality disorders is a disturbed sense of self and dysfunctional attachments and relationships with others (Livesley, 2001; Pincus, 2005). The relationship and attachment difficulties specific to borderline pathology are characterized by dysregulation of affect, intense relations with conflict and extremes of positive and negative emotions, and fears that others will abandon one.

DOI: 10.1037/13940-008

Transforming Negative Reactions to Clients: From Frustration to Compassion, A. W. Wolf, M. R. Goldfried, and J. C. Muran (Editors)

Clients with borderline personality disorder (BPD) bring the pains, wishes, desires, and expectations of human connection to the therapeutic encounter. The therapist, an individual motivated to help others, also comes to the relationship with expectations, desires and his or her own conceptual models of how relationships operate. Although one can make generalizations across therapeutic pairs, in BPD treatment each client–therapist unit is a unique combination that takes on a life of its own as therapy progresses. It follows from the client's diagnosis of personality disorder that the psychotherapeutic relationship between clients with BPD and therapists of all theoretical persuasions will elicit disturbances in the attachment process during treatment. This is not to imply that all difficulties that emerge in the process of the treatment are attributable to the one with the diagnosis of BPD. Indeed, we would argue that clients with BPD are in the severe range of personality pathology and therefore call on special skills from the therapist to manage the relationship. Not all therapists are motivated, naturally adapted, or trained to successfully treat clients with BPD. Those who are equipped to treat these clients anticipate disruptions in the relationship between therapist and client and use effective procedures to contain their own reactive emotions in relating to these clients.

With every expectation that the treatment of a client with BPD will involve some disturbance in the relationship between therapist and client, most probably of the nature that gets the client into difficulties outside the therapeutic relationship, a therapist doing transference-focused psychotherapy (TFP; Clarkin, Yeomans, & Kernberg, 2006) can expect to experience a range of emotions in this relationship. Such emotions can be intense because of the circular intensity of the client's emotions and because of the client's proneness to negative affects and perceptions and to the opposite idealizing affects and perceptions: the frightening aspect of the client's potential to lethally harm him- or herself, and so on. This chapter focuses on how the therapist can come to the therapeutic encounter prepared for a range of emotional reactions to the client, including like/dislike, appreciation/disdain, fear/safety, and attraction/repulsion. Not only are difficulties in the relationship between client and therapist expected, but the exploration and growing understanding of the contributors to these conflicts are central goals of treatment as conceptualized in an object relations framework (Clarkin et al., 2006) and its current amplification in attachment theory.

TFP is an empirically supported treatment (Clarkin et al., 2006; Doering et al., 2010) that is based in psychodynamic object relations. As such, it conceptualizes psychological difficulties and symptoms as stemming from underlying conflicts with the psyche (e.g., conflicts between opposing affects or between urges and prohibitions to those urges) and focuses in particular on the client's internal representations (object relation, internal working model) of the self and other and on relationships as they get played out in the relationship with the therapist.

THERAPIST PREPARATION FOR A CLIENT WITH BPD

Therapists who practice TFP should be prepared for these potential disruptions in the relationship and the experience of disturbing affects in four different ways: (a) a therapy model that teaches the therapist to use his or her emotional responses to the client to better understand the client in depth and to anticipate intense reactions, (b) assessment of the individual client, (c) knowledge of one's typical reactions to threat, and (d) peer supervision of the treatment of the individual client.

Theoretical Model and Expectations

Psychoanalytic object relations theory views an individual's sense of self and others as stemming from internalized representations or images of self and others as experienced in moments of intense affect in the course of development. In successful psychological development, the myriad and disparate images of self and other that have been internalized merge into complex, nuanced, and realistic images of self and other. In the conflictual development characteristic of clients with BPD, the internal images of self and others remain segregated into those of an extreme negative emotion (e.g., persecutor in relation to victim) and those of an ideally positive nature (e.g., perfect provider in relation to totally satisfied charge). These extreme and unrealistic images are projected onto experiences in the present, leading to distorted and emotionally charged experiences.

These experiences will occur in the therapy, and a central part of the therapist's work is to help the client observe, gain awareness of, and modify internal images that interfere with successful adaptation to present situations. The client's projection of internal images onto the present situation is called *transference*. Transference is not limited to the therapeutic setting, but TFP therapists are trained to focus on it as the window into the client's internal representational world. The therapist's emotional responses to the client are referred to as *countertransference*. Therapists are trained to be aware of these responses and to understand them as a reflection of images and emotions within the client's mind that are affecting the interpersonal field. In brief, the therapist is trained to function as a barometer of the client's emotional state, including aspects of that state of which the client may not be consciously aware but may instead express in acting-out behaviors or experience as originating in others by the process of projection. Central to the TFP treatment model is therapists' use of awareness of their emotional responses to guide clients in broadening their own conscious grasp of the makeup of their minds and the conflicts therein. Teaching therapists to use their emotional responses in this way helps them use negative reactions therapeutically and avoid harmful reactive responses.

For example, in supervision a therapist in training may describe feeling guilty and worthless after a client harshly criticized him for canceling a session. Although the therapist's spontaneous urge was to defend himself against the accusation, which would have risked a nonproductive standoff, the supervisor helped him understand that he was being made to feel what the client feels as part of the client's internal world: the hapless victim of an unfairly critical judge. The supervisor thus helped the therapist empathize with a dynamic within the client of a relation between a harsh judge and the judge's unfairly accused victim. The therapist's awareness of this relationship, or *object relations dyad*, that was regularly played out within the client's mind, as well as between the client and others, helped the therapist engage the client in observing and becoming more aware of it. This process of increasing awareness of the characters within his own mind helped the client gain mastery over the previously unfettered harsh judgment and thus become both less harsh toward the self as well as toward others and less angry and defensive as he understood that some of the harshness of criticism he perceived from others stemmed from the projection of his internal harsh judge onto others.

Assessment of the Individual Client

TFP assessment should focus not only on the client's symptomatic emotional states and behaviors but also on his or her typical ways of conceptualizing the self and relating to others, including prior therapists (Caligor & Clarkin, 2010). There exists both a clinical interview (Kernberg, 1984) and a related semistructured interview (Stern et al., 2010) to aid therapists in this crucial phase of treatment. Clients with BPD often have an intense desire to rush into treatment, despite many previous failed attempts, exactly replicating their propensity for attaching rapidly with high expectations, which often is followed by severe disappointment and contempt for the other that does not fulfill the client's needs.

It is important to emphasize that clients with BPD, who are similar only in that they meet at least five of the nine BPD criteria (American Psychiatric Association, 1994), are dissimilar in many clinically important ways. This is why the focus of the clinical assessment cannot be dominated by the examination of the BPD criteria alone.

Most important to the theme of this chapter, and to therapists' affective reactions to clients, is the client's individual attachment style. How does this particular client attach to and relate to others? This would include relationships with bosses, parents, acquaintances, friends, lovers, and prior therapists. Beyond the likelihood of disturbance in these relationships, what is the quality, over time, of these relations? Are any of these relations long lasting, despite conflicts?

Therapist's Self Knowledge

With clinical experience, therapists begin to know the conditions under which they react with intense emotions toward a client, although every new client brings unexpected events. The intense emotions on the part of the therapist toward the client can be ones of attraction (liking, warmth, nurturance, erotic excitement) or ones of repulsion (fear, anger, disgust, rejection). Therapists also begin to know how they can manage the momentary intense negative affect, as well as the internal mechanisms they can use to manage their own affect and maintain a therapeutic relationship with the client—not one that discards or avoids their reaction but instead one that makes use of information about the client that the reaction provides.

Peer Consultation

There is no senior therapist working with clients with BPD who does not need peer consultation and supervision at times, especially on cases that involve conflicts and intense affect activation in the therapeutic relationship. As the clinical illustration we provide next suggests, treatment with clients diagnosed with BPD can be very involving and intense on the part of the therapist. An actively suicidal client can frighten the therapist and create a gnawing sense of unease. An angry client who verbally attacks the therapist and the treatment can create therapist self-doubt, discouragement, and guilt.

CLINICAL ILLUSTRATION

Client

The client was a 25-year-old single woman, the second of three daughters born to a father who was a shoemaker and a mother who was a nurse. She grew up in a low-income neighborhood and graduated high school with some subsequent college courses. She reported some emotional and sexual abuse in her developmental years. She met the criteria for BPD as well as some criteria for histrionic and dependent personality disorder. She first sought professional help when she was 18, feeling a vague sense that something was wrong, and made two suicide attempts before age 22. She was currently working and sharing an apartment she rented with her female cousin.

Therapy Situation

The following are excerpts of a TFP session. Commentary on the therapeutic exchange is interspersed throughout the dialog.

> *Client:* I have a real problem at home. We have a new roommate and she called me, on the verge of tears. I feel guilty! We tried to resolve it. There are bedbugs in the apartment, the majority in my room. It's very frustrating. We got an exterminator, and we did all they said to do. I'm spending money and time, and it's much better. But the new roommate, she's freaking out. I feel bad for her.
>
> *Therapist:* How is it better?
>
> *Client:* It's gotten better, there are not so many [bug] bites. I felt awful for her. Our landlord did not want to pay for the exterminator. Finally, after months, we got the exterminator. And on top of this, I go to work today and my boss asked me to do a stupid assignment. They asked me to call a competitor for information; I called them and lied to them about who I am. I don't want to get paid for such stupid junk! I've been crazy all day.

This early session in TFP (within the first 3 months) starts with intense affective arousal on the part of the client, who is disturbed and preoccupied about two events that are happening in her current life. TFP focuses on the present, including both the client's relationship with the therapist and current relationships in her life. In the individual session, TFP focuses on the dominant relationships in the client's life that are the most affect laden, and so in this session the therapist begins to follow the client's lead and focus on the two events outside the therapy relationship that are upsetting her, while also paying attention to her own reaction to the client's remarks, in particular, her discomfort (anxiety, anger) concerning the mention of bedbugs that she imagines the client might have transported to her office.

> *Client:* Our roommate called me, crying. She's getting like I get, focused on bad things, just staring at things all day.
>
> *Therapist:* Had you told the boarder about the bedbugs?
>
> *Client:* We did not have them in her room. The exterminator did our room.
>
> *Therapist:* Not hers?

Client: No. It's just one thing after another. We have to spend $25 on a bed cover. I feel so tired of trying, and it's one problem after another.

Therapist: You were worried about losing your job last time, but that might be something that you might have a role in, as you've suggested yourself when you talk about some of your angry reactions.

Client: On the way over here, I did not want to come. I just wanted to sit alone and run away from things.

Therapist: That's why you are here—to talk about those kinds of urges instead of repeating the pattern here by running away.

Client: I just want a temporary fix, (to) run away.

Therapist: You can run if you choose. It's up to you.

Client: You're right. Something always happens to me, or I do it to myself. I feel horrible the whole day. I get so tired. I just want to die.

Therapist: If you choose that path, you are in charge of that, too.

The client now links the upsetting events outside the therapy session with the therapy situation itself, that is, her wish to not come to therapy today, a comment that may have been partly provoked by her therapist's mention of her role in job difficulties. A TFP therapist is alert both to any affect expressed in the session and to the issue the client brings up of not wanting to come to the session. The therapist will be alert to any references the client makes to what is going on between the two of them. In addition, the TFP therapist is mindful of anything that suggests the client might drop out of treatment in this early phase. Most clients with BPD are ambivalent about treatment, wanting treatment and the opportunity for change and the relationship with the therapist that it involves and yet having little trust that relationships are helpful. They fear that efforts to change are too painful and won't really succeed and are anxious in situations where their habitual way of viewing the world, as maladaptive as it may be, is challenged.

Client: Yes, it's just where my mind goes. Sometimes I don't want anyone's help. I'd rather everyone gave up on me, and then I would be at liberty to kill myself.

Therapist: I can help to the best of my ability. But, you say that as if it's my problem rather than yours.

Client: I'll convince myself that this is not working and then not come. I know this is for me, but I could say "screw it." Things are going bad, and it's driving me crazy.

Therapist: What's your worst fear about what is happening today?

Client: The roommate will leave in her anger at us. If she does leave, I worry about the finances. I'm trying to be positive about it.

Therapist: You fought with the landlord about paying for the exterminator?

Client: Yeah, we threatened to move.

Therapist: Had you thought about mentioning this problem here before today? [Long silence]

The TFP therapist brings the focus to the difficult transaction that is going on in the room between the two of them. It occurs to the therapist that this is the first time she has heard from the client about the bedbug difficulty, and the question to the client implicitly raises the issue of the client's resistance to or difficulty in bringing the problem to the therapy as well as the issue of withholding information, in this case information that might concern the therapist, who has begun to worry that the client has brought bedbugs into her office.

Therapist: Are you uncomfortable here today? You are folding your arms, like you are closing up.

Client: I feel like killing myself.

Therapist: I'm wondering how angry you are now?

Client: Today I felt like killing myself, and I came here hoping on the other side.

In TFP, the therapist is cognizant of three sources of information about the client: (a) the verbalizations made by the client, (b) the nonverbal body language from the client, and (c) his or her own feelings toward the client. In this situation with this client, the therapist is very anxious that the client might have infested her office with bedbugs and that this emotional reaction—if not understood and used as information—would distort her ability to see the client clearly. The therapist gives herself time to reflect on the situation and her emotions internally, to avoid slipping into a reaction to the client that is too emotional. In her fear and anger, the therapist is in danger of asking questions that are thinly disguised criticisms, to which this client, who is very self-critical and always alert for rejection, might react strongly and hence leave treatment. The therapist is, despite the mixed feelings, alert to the client's nonverbal behavior, which suggests that the client is feeling defensive and criticized.

Therapist: You do have problems going on in your life, but is there any hope, or are you seeing only problems now?

Client:	I got job issues! And home issues!
Therapist:	We have two options. If you are suicidal, hospitalization is an option. The other is to work here to understand what's motivating these feelings right now.
Client:	You wouldn't care if I killed myself.
Therapist:	You are here because part of you knows you should stay. What you just said might be the most important thing for us to think about.
Client:	It's wrong to feel this way, but maybe I'm supposed to die. I keep hoping it'll get better, but it doesn't . . . You're staring at me, looking at me. What do you assume I'm thinking? I don't want to think anymore. [Begins crying]
Therapist:	Should we consider the hospital?
Client:	I'm not going home, but I'll call my cousin.

The therapist once again notes nonverbal behavior on the part of the client that suggests the client feels criticized and also, now, rejected by someone in a caretaking role who she believes is indifferent to her. The therapist wants to surface these thoughts and attitudes so that the client does not just suppress the feelings and act on them by prematurely ending treatment or killing herself. The following excerpt is from the next session.

Therapist:	How did it go?
Client:	I came here last time on a bad day, and it got worse and worse. I'm not anticipating that today.
Therapist:	We have an opportunity to look at how it got worse that day, how it got worse as our session went on. Any thoughts about that?
Client:	When I think about things, it gets worse. My life is no better now than it was a couple years ago. All therapy does not work.
Therapist:	What about what is going on between you and me?
Client:	I want to be here but . . .
Therapist:	During the session you got more upset. Afterward, I had the feeling you experienced my questions about the bedbug situation as criticism and that you saw me as critical about how you handled the situation.
Client:	I guess.
Therapist:	What are you feeling now?

Client: I just felt bad, and talking about it made it worse.

Therapist: I was struck by your feeling that I was staring at you as if I was uncaring and unconcerned.

Client: When I have therapy, and when I don't say anything I feel you're disappointed.

Therapist: Are there signs that I'm disappointed? [Silence] Would it make sense if I'm quiet because I want to listen and observe and learn what is in you?

The therapist introduces the notion that there may be a difference between what the client thinks the therapist is thinking and feeling and how the therapist reads her own thoughts and feelings. This is extremely important because the therapeutic relationship is an opportunity for clients with BPD, who often have a sense that others are critical and that relationships are not productive and helpful, to perceive other possibilities.

Client: What goes on here does not affect my life. Therapy is separate from my life. I have emotional reactions toward my boyfriend which impact on me. But feelings here, I don't know if that is going to help.

Therapist: After the last session, I thought I saw how critically you see yourself. You might leave your job because you're not doing a good job. Dealing with the roommate, feeling that you are not doing a good job of that. I couldn't tell if you thought I felt that way too. You feeling that I was critical of you too.

Client: I thought you cared more about me possibly bringing bedbugs into your office than about me.

The client verbalizes her fear that the therapist is concerned about bedbugs in the office and gives evidence of her awareness that not having mentioned that situation before may have been an avoidance that was based on fear of rejection but that included some hostility. Her fear is an accurate reading of what is likely going on in the therapist's mind. This is an opportunity for the two of them to experience a difficulty in the relationship and find a way to overcome it by sharing perceptions of each other and what they mean.

Client: You barely know me. Therapy feels . . .

Therapist: What would make the therapy feel more personal? Is there no connection between us?

Client: I'm crazy and you're not! [Laughing]

Therapist: Do you think I think you are crazy?

Client: Not horrible crazy, but I do have the diagnosis.

Therapist:	You use the word *crazy* as if I think something is wrong with you, that I am critical and rejecting of you.
Client:	Well, what difference would it make if I left the country or my boyfriend left me? Why would you be concerned?
Therapist:	That's a good question. Yes, I did wonder about the bedbugs here. You took that as my only concern, concern about myself.
Client:	Yes, I did.

Discussion

The therapist's response of fear at the hands of threatened or feared behaviors of the client can be seen as falling into a class of similar situations. Therapists often report being fearful when clients threaten suicide, threaten to break something in anger in the therapist's office, stalk the therapist between sessions, or make threatening phone calls to therapists or their office personnel, all situations we have observed in years of clinical research with the treatment of clients with BPD.

Clients with BPD handle crises with emotional arousal that overwhelms task-oriented solutions. This client (i.e., the one in the case illustration) is also self-blaming and prone to see others as critical of her and then paradoxically somewhat irresponsible in her way of dealing with the bedbug situation in therapy. This is part of the *splitting* or defensive black-and-white thinking that will be addressed in the therapy. The client's reaction to the real-life crisis is to isolate herself (e.g., avoiding the therapy session) and look for a quick solution, such as suicide.

Within this context, the therapist also has needs. She does not want the client to abandon treatment, or to commit suicide, and she does not want her office infested with bedbugs. A crucial step is for the therapist to control her own immediate reaction to this possibility that the client has brought in bedbugs to the office and to use her reaction to understand corners of the client's mind of which she is not so aware, such as her capacity—in the context of seeing herself as a victim—to be threatening, both to her therapist and the new roommate (via the bedbugs) and to herself (via suicide). The therapist—as neutrally as possible—asks questions about how the client and her boyfriend dealt with the bedbugs. It does not appear that the therapist is outwardly alarmed or questions the client in a critical or accusing manner; however, the client, extremely sensitive to self-blame and perceived blame from others, becomes more agitated as the session goes on. In the second session, the client states her perception/fear that the therapist is critical of her and fearful she might contaminate her office space. Her suspicions are, in part, accurate, and the therapist acknowledges her fear, so the two of them can openly discuss and assess their views or representations of each other.

CONCLUSION

In an acute therapeutic disruption, it is important for the therapist to use the situation as an opportunity to explore the client's view of the therapist and to consider the possibility that the client can reach some flexibility and increased awareness in his or her view of the other as well as of the therapist. The view of the therapist that the client forms over time is probably the most important aspect to consider. A developing positive view of the therapist not only bodes well for continuing in treatment but also may be a sign that the client can form a human relationship that is positive, despite disagreements.

We and our colleagues have used the Adult Attachment Interview (AAI; George, Kaplan, & Main, 1985) in modified form to examine the evolving conception of the therapist in the client's mind, and the evolving perception of the client in the therapist's mind (Diamond, Stovall-McClough, Clarkin, & Levy, 2003). One client with BPD, when asked on the modified AAI to provide five adjectives to describe her relationship with her TFP therapist, selected *reliable, dignified, important, mildly frustrating,* and *confusing.* She illustrated the adjectives with clear examples from the treatment, which was of 1 year's duration. She described feeling at the beginning of the treatment that the therapist would forget her in between sessions. She had perceived him as cold, and interested only in his academic career and not in her. Her reaction to that perception of him was to act "tricky" with him, but she began to realize this was wasting her time. Gradually, she began to trust him more, and respect grew. She no longer tried to outsmart him, and "all the bullshit parts of me" went home to rest. She said that she felt a little more secure in general because the therapist had been so reliable and a steadying influence, the kind of security one might find in "a home when you're a kid."

An optimal therapy milieu provides a secure base for clients with BPD, who often have been raised in conflicted, frightening, unpredictable environments. A therapist who is consistent, supportive without being intrusive, and relatively affectively balanced despite disturbing moments, is probably one of the common elements across effective treatments (Bateman & Fonagy, 2009; Clarkin, Levy, Lenzenweger, & Kernberg, 2007; Linehan et al., 2006). If the experience with the therapist stimulates a more balanced and benign view of others, the client may be able to form more satisfying relationships in her extratherapy life in tandem with achieving more affective stability.

REFERENCES

American Psychiatric Association. (1994). *Diagnostic and statistical manual of mental disorders* (4th ed.). Washington, DC: American Psychiatric Association.

Bateman, A., & Fonagy, P. (2009). Randomized controlled trial of outpatient mentalization-based treatment versus structured clinical management for borderline personality disorder. *The American Journal of Psychiatry, 166*, 1355–1364. doi:10.1176/appi.ajp.2009.09040539

Caligor, E., & Clarkin, J. F. (2010). An object relations model of personality and personality pathology. In J. F. Clarkin, P. Fonagy, & G. O. Gabbard (Eds.), *Psychodynamic psychotherapy for personality disorders: A clinical handbook* (pp. 3–35). Washington, DC: American Psychiatric Publishing.

Clarkin, J. F., Levy, K. N., Lenzenweger, M. F., & Kernberg, O. F. (2007). Evaluating three treatments for borderline personality disorder: A multiwave study. *The American Journal of Psychiatry, 164*, 922–928. doi:10.1176/appi.ajp.164.6.922

Clarkin, J. F., Yeomans, F. E., & Kernberg, O. F. (2006). *Psychotherapy for borderline personality: Focusing on object relations.* Washington, DC: American Psychiatric Publishing.

Diamond, D., Stovall-McClough, C., Clarkin, J. F., & Levy, K. N. (2003). Patient–therapist attachment in the treatment of borderline personality disorder. *Bulletin of the Menninger Clinic, 67*, 227–259. doi:10.1521/bumc.67.3.227.23433

Doering, S., Horz, S., Rentrop, M., Fischer-Kern, M., Schuster, P., Benecke, C., . . . Buchheim, P. (2010). Transference-focused psychotherapy v. treatment by community psychotherapists for borderline personality disorder: Randomized controlled trial. *The British Journal of Psychiatry, 196*, 389–395. doi:10.1192/bjp.bp.109.070177

George, C., Kaplan, N., & Main, M. (1985). *Adult Attachment Interview.* Unpublished manuscript, University of California, Berkeley.

Insel, T. R., & Young, L. J. (2001). The neurobiology of attachment. *Nature Reviews Neuroscience, 2*, 129–136. doi:10.1038/35053579

Kernberg, O. (1984). *Severe personality disorders: Psychotherapeutic strategies.* New Haven, CT: Yale University Press.

Linehan, M. M., Comtois, K., Murray, A., Brown, M., Gallop, R., Heard, H., . . . Lindenboim, N. (2006). Two-year randomized controlled trial and follow-up of dialectical behavior therapy vs. therapy by experts for suicidal behaviors and borderline personality disorder. *Archives of General Psychiatry, 63*, 757–766. doi:10.1001/archpsyc.63.7.757

Livesley, W. J. (2001). Conceptual and taxonomic issues. In W. J. Livesley (Ed.), *Handbook of personality disorders: Theory, research, and treatment* (pp. 3–38). New York, NY: Guilford Press.

Pincus, A. L. (2005). A contemporary integrative interpersonal theory of personality disorders. In M. F. Lenzenweger & J. F. Clarkin (Eds.), *Major theories of personality disorder* (2nd ed., pp. 282–331). New York, NY: Guilford Press.

Sroufe, L. A., Carlson, E. A., Levy, A. K., & Egeland, B. (1999). Implications of attachment theory for developmental psychopathology. *Development and Psychopathology, 11*, 1–13. doi:10.1017/S0954579499001923

Stern, B. L., Caligor, E., Clarkin, J. F., Critchfield, K. L., Horz, S., MacCornack, V., ... Kernberg, O. F. (2010). Structured Interview of Personality Organization (STIPO): Preliminary psychometrics in a clinical sample. *Journal of Personality Assessment, 92*, 35–44. doi:10.1080/00223890903379308

Van Orden, K. A., Witte, T. K., Cukrowicz, K., Braithwaite, S., Selby, E., & Joiner, T. E. (2010). The interpersonal theory of suicide. *Psychological Review, 117*, 575–600. doi:10.1037/a0018697

III

MANAGING NEGATIVE REACTIONS ACROSS OTHER DISORDERS

INTRODUCTION: MANAGING NEGATIVE REACTIONS ACROSS OTHER DISORDERS

The previous section compared two different approaches to the understanding and management of therapists' negative reactions to clients diagnosed with borderline personality disorders, a diagnostic category synonymous with difficult cases. Both transference-focused psychotherapy and dialectical behavior therapy acknowledge the need for therapist self-awareness and self-regulation of negative reactions to clients, but they advocate very different approaches in the management and expression of these reactions. These chapters and the preceding chapters on theoretical orientations emphasize that a comprehensive account of therapists' negative reactions needs to specify both therapist factors, such as theoretical orientation, and client factors, such as how symptoms manifest during the therapy session. Symptomatic behaviors associated with other diagnostic categories present their own unique challenges for the therapist. Remaining therapeutically present while clients recount episodes of abuse and trauma, not becoming caught up in the power struggles that may occur when interacting with antisocial personality disorders, and the frustrations of working with the seriously mentally ill can deplete even the most resilient and compassionate of therapists. All cases present their own challenges, and while it is important not to identify a client with a diagnostic label, a practitioner needs to be mindful that specific problems impact them in predictable ways.

The following three chapters discuss the personal challenges of therapists treating problems frequently encountered in clinical practice: depression, narcissistic personality disorder, and substance abuse. These chapters are written by experienced scholar–practitioners who have thought deeply about how personal reactions influence the process and outcome of therapy. They describe how specific behaviors and labels can elicit automatic responses from the therapist that are often predictable, perhaps even inevitable, reactions when treating these clients. Hanna Levenson describes how the humorlessness, social isolation, and sense of worthlessness of chronically depressed individuals elicit a host of negative reactions in others, including their therapists, and beget a response that promotes more depression. Jeffrey Magnavita's articulation of a unified biopsychosocial model emphasizes how a therapist needs to understand his or her feelings of helplessness, inadequacy, and frustration in treating narcissistic personality disorders at the intrapersonal, interpersonal, familial, and cultural levels. Frederick Rotgers, using the principles of attribution theory drawn from social psychology research, describes how therapists are vulnerable to the deeply ingrained cultural stereotypes and prejudices of substance abusers as morally corrupt.

9

TIME-LIMITED DYNAMIC PSYCHOTHERAPY: WORKING WITH REACTIONS TO CHRONICALLY DEPRESSED CLIENTS

HANNA LEVENSON

"Gloria," a new client, sits down in my office and immediately tells me in a barely perceptible voice that she does not see a reason for living—no one cares about her, and she cares for no one. She goes on to say, in a painstakingly halting manner, that she has been feeling this way for as long as she can remember—the entire 45 years of her life. She has little hope that coming to therapy will do any good, but her neighbor (who is studying to become a psychologist) urged her to see someone professionally. "This is my last resort. I doubt anyone can help." As I stare at the thinning hair on the top of her head (I cannot see her face because her head is cast downward at her hands, which rest listlessly in her lap), I can feel my mouth go dry and my stomach clench. An image of her dangling from a rope invades my consciousness. I become aware that I am thinking of someone to refer her to and that I am angry with myself for agreeing to see her. What did she mean this was her "last resort"? Would I have to hospitalize her? Could I help her? I glance at the clock on

DOI: 10.1037/13940-009
Transforming Negative Reactions to Clients: From Frustration to Compassion, A. W. Wolf, M. R. Goldfried, and J. C. Muran (Editors)

my table and notice the minute hand clicking. Only 45 seconds have passed. I let out an audible sigh and at that very second Gloria looks up. I can tell by the dejected expression on her face that I have already disappointed her.

This vignette captures the essence of what I hope to address in this chapter—how working with clients who have chronic depression can result in very negative thoughts, feelings, and behaviors on the part of the therapist, which then get communicated to these clients, often activating in them the very thoughts, feelings, and behaviors that maintain or even increase their depression. From an interpersonal point of view, a cyclical, transactional pattern emerges in which the behavior of one person affects the emotional reactions of the other person, which in turn affect that person's behavior, which then triggers the emotional reactions of first person, leading him or her to react in some way, and so on. In addition, these patterns involve inference, anticipation, expectation, and encoding that are partly due to the individuals' temperament and learning (a function of their idiosyncratic histories and cultural backgrounds) as well as to innate capacities within the human mind. Of course, these types of transactions occur in every relationship, not just therapeutic ones, but in this chapter I concentrate on an attachment-based, psychodynamically relational, experiential model of treatment (time-limited dynamic psychotherapy; TLDP) for understanding why therapists are often in danger of reacting negatively (antitherapeutically) to someone who manifests the signs and symptoms of chronic depression. I hope this model will also provide suggestions for helping therapists deal with such reactions and guide them from frustration to compassion.

DEPRESSION

Almost every book or chapter on depression as a clinical problem or issue begins with a description of the magnitude of the problem. It is one of the most common and devastating of psychological disorders, "affecting 10 to 15 percent of the population at some point in their lives" (Segrin, 2011, p. 425). The incidence for women is even higher, with upper estimates indicating 1 in 4 women will be affected by a major depressive episode (American Psychiatric Association, 2000). Although there are many diagnoses that contain depressive symptoms, in this chapter I focus on what may happen to the therapist's thoughts, feelings, expectations, wishes, and behaviors and to the ensuing transactions between client and therapist when clients show evidence of some depressed affect, while understanding that depression encompasses a large and heterogeneous range of disorders, subtypes, and presentations (Carragher, Adamson, Bunting, & McCann, 2009; Segrin, 2011). In general, I focus on the therapist's negative reactions to clients who present with depressed affect (e.g., humorlessness), behavior (e.g., social isolation), and/or cognition (e.g., worthlessness) while acknowledging that such negative processes will not necessary occur in all cases in which depression is involved. Before I get into how therapists are affected by the presentation of depression in its various forms, I present the interpersonal lens through which readers can understand these reactions.

THEORY

In this section I discuss how to understand therapists' negative reactions through a specific interpersonal model—TLDP. The general mechanisms of change as well as the assumptions and theoretical underpinnings of TLDP are covered along with a brief introduction to TLDP formulation and intervention strategies.

Mechanisms of Change

Over 25 years ago, Hans Strupp and Jeffrey Binder (1984) developed TLDP as a way to help therapists with clients who evidenced difficulties forming positive therapeutic alliances as a result of their lifelong dysfunctional interpersonal difficulties. The goal of TLDP was to examine and shift clients' recurrent dysfunctional interpersonal patterns that came to the fore while trying to forge a relationship with the therapist. It was thought that if the therapist could help the client see his or her maladaptive style and how self-defeating it was, then change could occur.

A critical aspect of TLDP as outlined by Strupp and Binder (1984) was that

> the patient–therapist relationship is conceived of as a *dyadic system* [emphasis added] in which the behavior of *both* [emphasis added] participants is continually scrutinized by the participants themselves. The overarching goal of TLDP is to mediate a constructive human experience which results in improvements in the quality of the patient's interpersonal relations. (p. xiv)

Thus, TLDP privileged here-and-now processing as a pivotal way to create shifts in interpersonal functioning and for understanding their meaning. Therapy was seen as "basically a set of interpersonal transactions" (Strupp & Binder, 1984, p. 29).

A decade later, I wrote *Time-Limited Dynamic Psychotherapy: A Guide for Clinical Practice* (Levenson, 1995). As the title indicates, that book was designed to translate TLDP principles and strategies into pragmatically useful ways of thinking and intervening for the practitioner. In that book, I placed a major emphasis on the power of experiential learning (as opposed to insight) for achieving change. By focusing on client–therapist transactions within therapy sessions, the client could be helped to have his or her worst fears about what could be expected from another person disconfirmed.

In my most recent book on TLDP (Levenson, 2010), I incorporated *attachment theory* and *experiential–affective* approaches into an integrative framework. Attachment theory helps explain why people behave as they do—what motivates them. An experiential–affective emphasis focuses the therapeutic process of change—what needs to shift for change to occur.

Integrative View of TLDP

From an attachment point of view, the individual is seen as innately motivated to search for and maintain human relatedness. Bowlby (1988), in his monumental work on attachment, separation, and loss, viewed "the human infant's reliance on, and emotional bond with, its mother to be the result of a *fundamental instinctual behavioral system* [emphasis added] that, unlike Freud's sexual libido concept, was relational without being sexual" (Mikulincer & Shaver, 2007, p. 7). In this framework, certain attachment patterns learned from caregivers in childhood result in unconscious representational models of the self and attachment figures—expectations of how one will be treated by others and concomitantly how one treats oneself.

Those internalized working models of how the interpersonal world works result in attitudes, perceptions, feelings, and behaviors that then invite others to respond in ways that serve to reinforce the working model. For example, a child who has grown up with authoritarian, punitive parents might adopt a helpless, hopeless attitude about the world because his or her behaviors do not bring about desired outcomes (e.g., love, attention, attunement). Such a child could easily grow up to be a depressed, hopeless, and helpless adult.

Like Bowlby, the interpersonal psychiatrist Harry Stack Sullivan focused on what was transpiring in the room between therapist and client. Sullivan was one of the first to take into account what was being contributed both by client and by therapist in the therapeutic endeavor. "The psychiatrist cannot stand off to one side and apply his sense organs, however, they may be refined by the use of apparatus, to noticing what someone else does, without becoming *personally implicated* [emphasis added] in the operation" (Sullivan, 1954, p. 3). Sullivan coined the term *participant observer* to underscore how the therapist in each session occupies two roles simultaneously—that of an expert, trained observer as well as that of an emotionally involved participant.

From an experiential-affective point of view, importance is placed in this model on the process of becoming aware of, experiencing, and processing feelings and emotions (Fosha, Siegel, & Solomon, 2009; Greenberg, 2002). From an emotionally focused point of view, clients need help not only to get more in touch with their feelings in the sessions and in their lives but also to learn how to reflect on and reprocess their emotions. Work from the cognitive neurosciences suggests that reflecting on one's feelings, sensations, and imagery may actually foster healthy brain processes and structures (Siegel, 1999).

TLDP Principles and Goals

In the integrated version of TLDP, the search for and maintenance of connections with others is a major motivating force. From early experiences with caregivers, mental structures and processes are either inhibited or facilitated. They affect one's capacity for emotional regulation, self-reflection (mentalization), a felt sense of security (Sroufe & Waters, 1977), and the development of coherent narratives about one's life (Fonagy, Gergely, Jurist, & Target, 2002). Such schemata help one to interpret the present, understand the past, and anticipate the future; they also lead to many of the presenting symptoms (such as depression) clinicians see in therapy.

TLDP also holds that although a dysfunctional pattern of interaction may have (in most cases) begun in the past, it is maintained in the present in relationship to others and oneself. According to the principle of circular causality, one person's message to another "imposes a condition of emotional engagement" (Kiesler, 1996, p. 209) that then results in a corresponding (complementary) response imbued with emotion that gives the other a sense of intention, giving rise to another affective response, and so on. For example, a depressed, helpless client has learned that what he or she does has little consequence and so engages with others in his or her life in a passive, unenergetic manner. Others respond to his or her lack of engagement with them as disinterest and experience him or her as a "deadweight." At first they might try to lift his or her spirits, but then they would be likely to pull away from him or her. Being aware of this rejection, he or she would probably pull back more with an increased sense of worthlessness.

Thus, from a TLDP perspective, clients are seen as "stuck" in maladaptive patterns that they originally developed as self-protection and as an adaptive reaction to their treatment by others. But now these security operations (*defenses*) have become part of a vicious cycle (Wachtel, 1982) in which individuals recreate the very situation that they most fear. To shift these maladaptive relationship patterns, the TLDP therapist needs to become aware of relationship themes in the person's life as well as what it is like to relate to the client.

This is of particular importance for clients who have rigid and pervasive dysfunctional strategies and/or extreme difficulties in affect regulation, because often the very issue that is problematic in the outside world is played out within the client–therapist relationship. In such cases there is likelihood that the therapist will become "hooked" (Kiesler, 1996) into responding to the client in ways that make complementary sense, given the client's presentation (e.g., hostility begets hostility). I have termed the reenactment of this pull on the therapist's part as *interactive countertransference* (Levenson, 1995). Of course, it is critical that the therapist eventually unhooks him- or herself from this dysfunctional dynamic (and by so doing also helps the client unhook from his or her lifelong dynamic), but as a first step it is necessary to examine how one might be co-creating the harmful transactional pattern in the session. Thus, the therapist's own feelings (both the positive and the negative ones) are a powerful signal (and not noise or a warning sign). It is an example of what has been called *implicit relational knowing* (Stern et al., 1998; for more on the premises of TLDP, see Levenson, 2010).

There are two main goals for TLDP: (a) to provide new experiences (of self and other) and (b) to provide new understandings (of self and other). Change occurs experientially and cognitively and within and between (Levenson, 2010). To achieve the experiential goal, the therapist fosters feelings, thoughts, and actions that will result in a more functionally adaptive, authentic manner of being in the world rather than the client's more typical inflexible, constricted repertoire. This means that clients are encouraged and invited (in the process of relating to their therapists and to significant others in their lives) to have transactions that will disconfirm their life experiences and expectations. In addition, the therapist can promote an emotion that is incompatible with a dysfunctional emotion— thereby changing emotion with emotion (Greenberg, 2002).

It should be noted that the therapist does not "provide" new experiences to the client in a mechanical fashion (as in a meal served to a guest). Rather, the therapist begins by listening to the client's story, discerning repetitive interpersonal and intrapersonal themes in the story, validating the ways (i.e., security operations) the client has learned to cope, and then helping the client become aware of deeper emotions linked to these themes while also promoting their emotionally regulated expression. I used to see the goal of a new experience as minicorrective emotional experience. Now I see it not only as disconfirming the past but also as creating moment-by-moment emergent experiences (cf. Stern, 2004) that give rise to future possibilities.

For example, I treated a 74-year-old man, Mr. Johnson, for problems of depression (I describe his case in more detail at the end of this chapter). As a boy, Mr. Johnson was treated by his father in a harsh, violent manner, and as a consequence he grew up taking on a placating, submissive stance in life (i.e., secondary emotional responses). When I saw him he was isolated; he was drinking and feeling depleted and hopeless. My goal was to help Mr. Johnson have a series of experiences (within my office and outside) in which he could be assertive without incurring the retribution he had come to fear and in which he could experience himself as empowered and engaged with life.

My initial reaction to Mr. Johnson's deferential, hapless manner was frustration and impatience. In a particular session, when he expressed feeling lonely and worthless because his daughter was ignoring him, I amplified (through validating, heightening, reflecting, and reframing) glimmers of his nascent anger at the way he was being treated by her. As he began to voice his own needs in a more wholehearted, less anxious way, I felt myself becoming increasingly more engaged in the sessions and feeling more compassionate about Mr. Johnson's plight in the twilight of his years. Similarly, Mr. Johnson's less subservient, more assertive stance was more inviting for his daughter, who actually enjoyed being around him more, which is what he wanted in the first place.

The second goal of TLDP focuses on helping clients cognitively to make meaning of their emotional-relational experiences and to reflect on them. By tracking moment-to-moment feeling states that are being evoked and expressed in sessions, clients come to see how they have disowned parts of themselves that they previously had to relinquish to stay attached to caregivers (and thereby stay safe). Metacommunicating about what is happening in the sessions as client and therapist attempt to relate to one another enables the client to see how his or her lifelong pattern is emerging in the here and now of the sessions.

Again, going back to the case of Mr. Johnson, in the third session he said he was having trouble concentrating because he was hungry, but he also talked about his family's going on a vacation without him over the weekend. I thought if he could tell me he was ending the session early to get something to eat (i.e., literally go for what he wanted), he could have a new experience (i.e., not being the "good client"). However, he characteristically was not able to take this step and instead kept complaining that he was not up to the session as the session continued. When I asked him what would keep him from deciding "to get something in your stomach right now," he replied that he couldn't think of leaving "unless you'd let me go." This interchange allowed us to discuss (metacommunicate) how his lifelong pattern was being played (reenacted) in our session.

Formulation and Intervention

In TLDP the therapist needs to ascertain what is the cyclical maladaptive pattern (CMP) for each individual. To do so, the therapist uses a specific method to delineate such patterns (Strupp & Binder, 1984). The *dynamic focus* or CMP contains four categories that are used to organize information about the client's interpersonal story. In addition, I (Levenson, 1995) have a fifth category—the therapist's interactive countertransference, which is of particular importance for the present chapter.

1. Acts of the self. This category includes the client's thoughts, feelings, motives, perceptions, and behaviors of an interpersonal nature. For example, "I believe other people have the answers" (thought). "I feel sad when my daughter forgets about me" (feeling). "I start drinking when I am alone" (behavior). Sometimes these acts are conscious, and sometimes they are out of awareness, but usually they are relevant to primary emotions that are disowned, disavowed, and/or distorted as a result of underlying attachment needs.

2. Expectations of others' reactions. In this group go all the statements and inferences having to do with how the client imagines others will react to him or her. "If I let people know how angry I am inside, they will reject me." Often the attachment fears and longings of clients are revealed in terms of what they expect will occur if they are more fully themselves.

3. Acts of others toward the self. This category consists of how the client perceives he or she was and is being treated by others. "My wife dominated me completely."

4. Acts of self toward the self (introject). In this section go the client's thoughts, feelings, and behaviors concerning him- or herself when the self is the object of the action. "When others get upset with me, I berate myself for being a failure." According to TLDP, the way someone treats him- or herself is largely a function of how the person was treated by others.

5. Therapist's interactive countertransference. For this category, the therapist needs to focus on his or her reactions to the client (at behavioral, cognitive, and affective levels). The clinician's self-awareness is central here. What is the clinician aware of feeling as he or she sits in the room with the client? What is the clinician pushed or pulled to do? What is going on at a visceral level? What is the clinician thinking? What images come to mind?

Once he or she has sufficient data for each of the CMP categories, the therapist begins to listen for redundant themes emerging in the material. The clinician then links the components together to tell a story—a story of how the client manifests inflexible behaviors that lead to self-defeating expectations that lead to dysfunctional interactions with others that lead to and have been perpetuated by negative self-appraisals that ultimately lead back to the client's inflexible behaviors. The CMP should be a plausible narrative delineating aspects of the client's internalized working model to better understand historical and contemporary factors.

With regard to intervention strategies, TLDP does not use "disembodied techniques" (Butler & Strupp, 1986); interventions are seen as relational acts embedded in the client–therapist relationship (Norcross, 2002). Pragmatically, therapists can use whatever strategies they feel competent in to achieve the idiosyncratically derived experiential and cognitive goals. For example, I would feel free to use imagery, behavioral rehearsal, and psychoeducation if I thought they might foster the therapeutic objectives. At any one point, intervention strategies can be directed toward (a) facilitating the therapeutic alliance, (b) accessing and processing emotion, (c) exploring empathically, (d) building the therapeutic relationship, (e) examining cyclical patterns, (f) promoting change directly, (g) discussing the time-limited aspects of the therapy, and (h) inquiring in a focused manner (see Levenson, 2010, for an explication of each of these).

DEPRESSION FROM A RELATIONAL, ATTACHMENT-BASED, EXPERIENTIAL PERSPECTIVE

Many theoreticians from a variety of theoretical orientations have commented on the role of interpersonal transactions in understanding the etiology and course of depression. Coyne's (1990) interactional theory of depression outlines how people with depression presumably elicit a negative feeling state in others, which then results in rejection.

Interpersonal Antecedents and Consequences of Depression

From a relational, attachment-based perspective, depression is often a normal reaction to a loss of connection with significant figures in the person's life. There is a considerable clinical and empirical literature describing the early childhood experiences of people who are at risk for becoming depressed later in life. Death of a parent early in the child's life is a well-known indicator for vulnerability to depression in adulthood, as are parental abuse, neglect, and overprotection (Cummings & Davis, 1995). There are also abundant empirical data that *exit events* are often followed by a depressive reaction.

From an interpersonal perspective one can see how depression is the gift that keeps on giving. It has been found that children of depressed parents are at 2 to 5 times greater risk for developing some form of psychological problem or symptom (including depression) than those of nondepressed parents (Beardslee, Bemporad, Keller, & Klerman, 1983). Using attachment theory, Cummings and Davis (1995) developed an emotional security hypothesis for understanding the impact of parental depression on child mental health. They emphasized how insecure attachments and marital discord can affect the child's emotional arousal and a capacity for emotional regulation that then leads to a greater likelihood of the child becoming depressed.

Horowitz (2004), writing on the interpersonal foundations of psychopathology, discussed two manifestations of depression. "Two people, each vulnerable to depression, may have different templates. For one, interpersonal loss, loneliness and sadness may be central; for the other, failure, self-criticism, and sadness may be central" (p. 154). Similarly, Summers and Barber (2010) elucidated that those clients who have an abandonment-related depression manifest a dependent transference and tend to see their therapists as rescuers; whereas those with a more angry transference experience their therapists as critical and rejecting.

These two templates may differentially affect one's self-concept and behavior toward others. For example, Mongrain, Vettese, Shuster, and Kendal (1998) found that self-critical women consider themselves less loving and more hostile, and their boyfriends and objective raters observed such behavior. Mongrain (1998) found that self-critical people (compared with those who are more dependent) are less likely to expect, ask for, and receive social support. Not surprisingly, the facial (e.g., little eye contact), postural (e.g., slumped shoulders), verbal (e.g., hesitations, slow speech), tonal (e.g., monotonous), and self-involved behaviors (e.g., self-touching) of people with depression, in addition to the often repetitive, self-critical content of their speech, send out messages to others that push them away. Segrin and Abramson (1994) reviewed some of the literature on what they called the *behavioral indexes of social skill*, outlining what those with depression do or fail to do in social interactions that leads to negative reactions from others.

Segrin and Dillard (1992) conducted a meta-analysis of the research literature to test Coyne's theory. Their results strongly supported the interactional proposition that depressed people (as compared with nondepressed people) do elicit rejection from others. In addition, the more depressed some people were, the more they were seen as having fewer positive personality traits (e.g., sociability, agreeableness) and more negative traits (e.g., detachment, abrasiveness).

However, their findings with regard to depression and induction of negative mood in others are more complex. It appears that the relationship is curvilinear. The more depressed someone is, the more he or she produces increasing levels of negativity in others up to a point, but then higher depression scores result in decreasing levels of negative mood. Segrin and Dillard (1992) conjectured that people avoid interacting with people who have severe depression rather than having negative feelings about them.

One can see how these interactive patterns can precipitate, define, and maintain depression. This, then, is the "double whammy" of chronic depression. The very presentation of depression begets a response that promotes yet more depression. The prototypic transactional sequence goes something like this. A person experiences some type of loss of connection with others and/or with aspects of the self. He or she displays sadness and withdrawal and communicates a helpless and/or submissive stance in both a verbal and a nonverbal manner. In the beginning, others might genuinely react to the neediness of depressed person with concern and offers of help. Trying to cheer up the person is quite common. However, these responses may only serve to trigger or aggravate further self-condemnation and loss of agency on the part of the depressed person, causing even more depressed affect. Others then become frustrated (and irritated) with that person's seeming intransigence and lack of initiative. But these others are often inhibited from directly expressing their annoyance and negative affect with the depressed person because he or she is already feeling so down. So they "leak their hostility" (Kiesler, 1996, p. 145) or just avoid the person altogether, which the depressed person (correctly) interprets negatively, experiencing more loss and inadequacy and ultimately more depression to complete the CMP.

Therapist Experiences of Clients' Depressed Affect

Now what happens when a person with chronic depression goes to a therapist for help? From an interpersonal point of view, do the same CMPs occur between therapist and client? In the clinical literature, it is well established that certain diagnostic groups or psychiatric symptoms do engender negative countertransferential reactions in their therapists (Benjamin, 1993b). Beck, Rush, Shaw, and Emery (1979), some of the founders of cognitive therapy, well understood the process whereby negative reactions could be engendered in therapists:

> Too often, therapists view depressed patients as "willfully" passive, indecisive, and manipulative. The therapist becomes frustrated and the patient feels criticized; his condition may deteriorate or he may drop out of treatment. These interactions are described in the analytic literature in the context of transference and countertransference reactions. (p. 58)

In the empirical literature, however, there are few studies to inform therapists regarding therapist countertransference reactions toward specific client populations, syndromes, or symptoms. Schwartz and Wendling (2003), in reviewing the literature, concluded "there is a dearth of empirical, generalizable work in this area" (p. 653). In one of the few investigations in an actual therapeutic setting, Rossberg, Karterud, Pedersen, and Friis (2010) found that the depressive symptoms of day treatment center clients were positively related to therapists' feelings of being overwhelmed and having lower confidence. In addition, their results indicated there was a strong correlation between the degree to which clients changed and negative countertransference reactions. "It is reasonable to believe that, from a symptom perspective, both parties in a less than successful relationship would be disappointed, and so the therapist would feel less important and confident, and more bored, on guard, overwhelmed, and inadequate" (Rossberg et al., 2010, p. 193). Exhibit 9.1 contains a list of therapists' negative reactions to working with people with chronic depression frequently mentioned in the literature.

The assumption in TLDP (well supported by empirical evidence) is that to a large extent the therapist does not have a choice in whether to contain or express negative (or positive) affect states. These emotional responses are automatically (and universally) manifested in the tone of one's voice, the turn of the mouth, the dilation of the pupils of the eyes, gestures, and more (Ekman, 2003). Often one does not even know what is being experienced until one observes oneself in the action. The idea in TLDP is not to try to suppress these automatic responses (as if this were possible) but to become aware of them and have them inform the formulation and intervention strategies. The pull from people experiencing chronic states of helplessness, hopelessness, and worthlessness can be quite overwhelming and dysregulating.

TRAINING

One of the major foci of training is on helping those learning TLDP see how they can use their reactions to clients (especially the negative ones) to understand the case and to create change events. Given this potential, how does the teacher–supervisor help trainees recognize, manage, and use these reactions? (Helping them acknowledge and use positive feelings is also quite

EXHIBIT 9.1
Common Therapist Interpersonal Reactions to Working
With Chronically Depressed Patients

Advice giving	Cheerleading	Overwhelmed
Angry	Critical	Reassuring
Annoyed	Depressed	Rejecting
Avoiding	Frustrated	Scared
Bored	Hostile	Sucked dry
Caretaking	Inadequate	
Cautious, careful	Overly responsible	

powerful, but I am confining my comments to the focus of this book on negative reactions.) I address three aspects that I have found relevant in answering this question: self-awareness, use of theory, and empathy.

Self-Awareness

In a direct parallel to helping clients become aware of and express their emotions, the TLDP supervisor helps trainees become aware of their emotional experience as they attempt to form a helping relationship with clients. I do most TLDP training in a small group format of five to seven trainees, usually with predoctoral psychology students and third-year psychiatry residents (see Levenson, 1995, 2003, 2010, for more specifics). We meet for a 3-hour block of time weekly for 6 months. Some of this time is spent in didactic instruction, during which I illustrate specific points of TLDP theory and practice using edited videotaped segments of actual sessions with me or previous trainees as therapists. I edit these video segments not to find snippets of brilliant demonstrations of "here's how to do it" but rather to illustrate therapeutic opportunities. I have often found that showing how I made a "mistake" (e.g., a reenactment of a dysfunctional interaction with a client) and then tried to repair it (e.g., metaprocessed what was happening) can be very educative on several fronts. Also, revealing these missteps to trainees demystifies the process and conveys to them that the acting out of the negative countertransference with difficult cases is part and parcel of the TLDP model. Trainees, in their developmental idealization of supervisors' and teachers' skills, sometimes have trouble actually recognizing when their supervisors make mistakes—getting emotionally pushed or pulled in sessions. For example, when I play a particular video segment for my class that shows me becoming irritated with a "yes-butting" client, the students put forth circuitous rationalizations for reframing what they are seeing as an example of planned, incisive work, rather than noticing I have gotten hooked into playing out a dysfunctional dynamic.

At various junctures during these segments, I stop the video and ask the trainees to say what is going on, to distinguish between relevant and irrelevant material, to propose interventions, to justify their choices, and to anticipate the moment-to-moment behavior of the clients (Levenson & Strupp, 1999, 2007). I particularly focus on eliciting what the trainees are feeling and thinking at these moments, imagining that they are the therapist. I also share what was going on in my mind and gut, both while I was doing the therapy and now while reflecting on it. This form of anchored instruction (Binder, 1993) and modeling has been shown to be most relevant for learning clinical material.

After the didactic portion, which involves the trainees' active participation, each trainee shows a small portion (e.g., 10 minutes) from that week's videotape of his or her session with a client. (Trainees are assigned to work with one client and videotape a maximum of 20 sessions using TLDP. They are to watch each session privately prior to class and select a portion to show in the group supervision.) As they show their tapes, they or I can stop it at any place in that segment to reflect on what was happening, how they were feeling, what they were thinking, what was the intention of their intervention, and more. We also discuss what they felt and noticed while they were reviewing their video.

I cannot overstate the importance of using video for teaching and supervision purposes. Compared with process notes or even audio, video provides a vivid account of what actually occurs in therapy. Supervisors and supervisees alike tend to portray their therapies as more coherent and cogent than they were in real life—confabulating details and smoothing out the rough spots (Levenson & Strupp, 1999). Furthermore, when trainees review their entire hour on video, they can be in a more reflective state of mind. This allows them to have some emotional distance (more on the observer end of the participant–observer spectrum) so they can more easily identify reenactments and their own reactions that they were not aware of during the session.

Critical in this endeavor is my creating a safe space to foster the trainees' emotional awareness and experience. I am trying to create a supervisory alliance and a healthy group process in direct parallel to the trainees' trying to create therapeutic alliances and facilitative processes in their work with clients. (For more on the parallels between TLDP and TLDP supervision, see Levenson, Butler, & Bein, 2002.) This *safe enough* atmosphere opens up the trainees' exploration of their own visceral reactions, somatic sensations, reveries, nonverbal behaviors, autobiographical resonances, and more.

There are some helpful exercises that can be used to foster students' awareness of their own sometimes subtle mental and somatic processes. The "raisin experience" (to encourage mindful eating), as outlined in Jon Kabat-Zinn (1990) in his work on the practice of mindfulness in everyday life and used by Safran and Muran (2000) in training students to learn brief relational therapy, is one such example. Ekman's (2003) emotional recognition skill-building training videos (how to distinguish between minute facial changes displaying various emotions) are another. Role plays in which the trainees take on the role of their clients are also very effective.

Quite often at the beginning of the training year, when I ask what a trainee is aware of feeling at a particular place on the tape (usually when there was some evidence of an emotional shift or stalemate), I might hear a description of the client (e.g., "The client is very resistant here") rather than something about the trainee's own emotional reactions (see Levenson, 1995, for transcripts of trainee–supervisor interactions). Somewhere in their training the students have learned they should have positive regard for clients at all times, or if they do feel something negative, it must be a sign they have not worked through their own personal conflicts. In other words, trainees come to label their own feelings as *bad*—evidence that they are incompetent at best and unfit at worst. Consequently, even when they are aware of negative reactions, they censor revealing these reactions in public. This has serious consequences for the practice of TLDP because countertransferential reactions must be recognized, processed, and used for understanding and intervening, especially when the clinical presentation is so powerful (e.g., as often is the case with chronic depression).

One nonthreatening way to promote more self-awareness is, as I have previously indicated, to model that for the students. When I show portions from my own work, I talk about how I was feeling toward the client at the time. I highlight and comment on my awareness of what was happening in my body and in my mind. I reflect on my formulation to see if I have become a participant (Sullivan, 1953) in an interactive drama with the client. Do my reactions make sense given what the client says about how he or she is treated by others? Helping trainees hear my emotional reactions and see my behavior on the video often gives them additional permission to tap into their felt experiences. In addition, I have found that asking the other trainees in the group for their reactions while they are watching a colleague's tape can be quite freeing. Often other trainees feel more implicit permission to say what is getting evoked for them as they watch a colleague's work with a difficult client or situation ("I feel really frustrated. You seem so calm. I just want to shake him!"). Here again, the video is invaluable for putting all trainees in the therapist's position to hear and see the nitty-gritty of what transpires in a session. As the presenting supervisee hears the reactions of his or her peers, more safety is created to acknowledge previously censored or warded-off feelings. Also, because they are not directly involved, trainees can be very perceptive in discerning what is going on with their colleagues ("Your voice sounds really tense there").

Another way I try to promote self-awareness is to help trainees have a new experience of themselves and others within the context of the group supervision. Quite often our educational system creates a shaming experience for students (Alonso & Rutan, 1988). By creating a positive supervisory alliance (Efstation, Patton, & Kardash, 1990) and supportive group processes (e.g., validation), students can have new, more enlivening experiences (both educationally and personally), much as the goal of TLDP is for clients to have new experiential learning.

Use of Theory

Trainees can also better learn to recognize and manage their negative reactions toward clients through reliance on TLDP theory. Because attention to countertransferential feelings, thoughts, and behaviors is built into the principles of TLDP, trainees are encouraged to use their emotions to inform their case conceptualizations, intervention strategies, and assessment of progress. Developing the CMPs for each client permits trainees (and experienced therapists as well) to grasp the complementary reactions that are evoked in people with whom their clients interact. Trainees are then taught that similar reactions within themselves are what would be expected, given that transactions in the therapy might be a microcosm of relationships with others. In this way, countertransferential reactions contribute to an understanding of the client and what might need to shift for a good therapeutic outcome. By reframing one's own negative feelings as somewhat predictable and potentially helpful, one lessens the harmful impact of such reactions.

However, I do not want to convey that TLDP blithely views all therapist feelings and behaviors as examples of interactive countertransference. Therapists and trainees still need to be vigilant for signs of classic countertransference in which their own life history, defenses, biases, stereotypes, and more come forth and need to be dealt with through consultation, therapy, and/or their own deep reflection (Gelso & Hayes, 2007; Levenson, 1995). Having said all this, I am very much in agreement with Maroda (2004), who discussed the impossible difficulties in making clear "distinctions between the 'real' and the imagined, projected, displaced, or distorted" (p. 98).

Because the transactional frame of TLDP acknowledges that the therapist is likely to act out various dynamics with clients who have rigid modes of relating, it is easier for students to conceptualize that their own negative reactions are acceptable. Furthermore, by focusing on the attachment theory base of TLDP, students are reminded that the clients are doing the best they can with what they have. As Benjamin (1993a) stated, "Every psychopathology is a gift of love." This aspect leads directly to the next section on empathy.

Empathy

The third component of helping trainees manage negative reactions to clients is to focus on an empathic understanding of the adaptive function of the client's interpersonal behavior. Building empathy for the client involves imagining walking in that client's shoes as though they were the trainees' shoes. When trainees can have an emotional sense of how clients (especially the so-called difficult ones) had to give up aspects of themselves (e.g., curiosity, vitality, healthy entitlement) to stay attached to caregivers, they begin to have some compassion for them.

One of the specific suggestions I offer to trainees when they are getting frustrated, irritated, or experiencing some other negative emotion during a session is to imagine the client as a 3-year-old child. This is not done to be patronizing toward the client but rather to help the trainee get a sense of how styles of relating are not conscious choices by passive-aggressive clients who stay up nights thinking of ways to drive their therapists to distraction. Seeing the 3-year-old child sitting before you is a way of deeply understanding the emotional compromises that that person made, often at great personal cost.

Related to empathy for clients is fostering less negative judgment toward oneself. In research I and my students recently conducted (Montagno, Svatovic, & Levenson, 2011), we found that training in an attachment-based, emotionally focused model resulted not only in more competency in the model but also in more openness to processing the therapists' own emotions, which in turn led to more self-compassion (i.e., kindness, mindfulness, and identification with greater humanity). Work from TLDP research (Henry, Schacht, Strupp, Butler, & Binder, 1993) similarly indicates that those therapists who had more hostile introjects were more likely to treat clients in a disaffiliative manner. It is my experience in training hundreds of future clinicians that learning TLDP helps them not only to have empathy toward the people they work with but also to have increased self-acceptance for all the ways they themselves are human.

CASE ILLUSTRATION

I have written about my client whom I called Mr. Johnson in my first book on TLDP (Levenson, 1995), and he provided the basis for a professional video (http://www.psychotherapy.net) using an actor to role play Mr. Johnson. However, I have never before written in depth about my therapy with this client from the point of view of my countertransference and how it shifted from frustration and irritation to compassion and fondness during our 20-session brief therapy. I have decided to focus on Mr. Johnson for this chapter because my experience with him epitomizes therapist reactions to clients with chronic depression. As I relate significant portions of my work with Mr. Johnson, I include my uncensored thoughts, feelings, and actions (in italics). Readers can see how sometimes I was trying to formulate what was going on with Mr. Johnson and intervene (as an observer), and sometimes I was neck-deep in unwittingly co-creating his life's script with him (as a participant), and sometimes both.

At the time I saw Mr. Johnson I was working in an outpatient clinic of a large medical center. I wanted to video a complete 20-session TLDP therapy to use for training purposes. Because I did not want to be biased toward searching for the ideal brief therapy case, I asked the person in charge of triaging to assign me the next person who was up for therapy, although I soon regretted this decision. *When I saw Mr. Johnson's intake form, my heart* sank, and the thought crossed my mind that I would not be able to use this as a training case. Mr. Johnson was a 74-year-old man who was about to be discharged from an inpatient psychiatry unit where he had been hospitalized for a month for major depression and binge drinking. *That one sentence triggered many of my cultural and personal stereotypes. Was he too old to learn "new tricks"? Was he cognitively impaired because of his age, because of his alcoholism? He was hospitalized such a long time! Would a brief therapy really be helpful? I was not an expert on the treatment of alcoholism. I felt relieved that I had only offered to do an evaluation to judge his appropriateness. I reassured myself that there was no commitment on my part other than to do a session or two.* I also was informed that Mr. Johnson was a widower, retired, with four grown children. The sparse notes indicated that he had been "compliant" with his treatment (on both psychiatric and alcohol inpatient units), which consisted of individual sessions with a psychiatrist, antidepressant medications, an alcohol education group, and milieu therapy. *Thank goodness for that, at least.*

A segment from the first few minutes of our first session follows.

Therapist: Maybe the best way to get to know you is to have you tell me what brought you into the hospital, what's been going on, and how I can be of help. *I noticed that Mr. Johnson sat slumped in his chair—a dumpy looking man in a plaid shirt appearing to be his stated age but with jet-black hair. He stared at the floor with flat affect and a monotone voice. Periodically he took off his glasses, stared off into the distance, and sighed audibly. Whatever part of me hoped he looked better than his write-up was disappointed.*

Client: [speaking very slowly] Well, it started in June. We were living in San Carlos, my daughter and I. We have four children. *OK, right away I was confused by the "we"—certainly he does not mean he and his daughter have four children. And I was also feeling a bit put off by his lack of expression and the singsong nature of his voice.* But Susan, the youngest, lived with me the longest. We just got a notice from the landlord one day that he was going to move into our apartment, and we would have to get out and look for another place. So I started looking. We had a cat too. *I am a dog person, but I nonetheless have empathy for the struggle pet owners have in finding a place to rent.* I started looking all over San Carlos and, ah, down that whole area. My daughter was working down there. And, ah, we just couldn't find a place at all that would take animals. So they decided somebody has to take care of our cat—a relative. *"They?" more confusion; I was feeling burdened by the anticipation of working hard in this therapy to understand what he is talking about.* But we still couldn't find a two-bedroom apartment for less than $700 or $800. *That was a lot of money back then.* It was just terrible. [uh-huh] *I'm saying uh-huh, but I could feel myself wishing for another client—someone with more energy and focus. There was a sinking feeling in the pit of my stomach.* What happened was I started getting depressed and nervous and exhausted and started drinking. We finally found a place that we could afford, you know, $700, which was way out in Tilton, and it was at the end of a dead-end street—way up on a high place. *I smiled inwardly at the irony of its being a dead-end street. Metaphor is truly a gift to therapists.* It was very isolated. *I noted another parallel with his own psychology. I saw the themes in Mr. Johnson's life becoming apparent, and this realization helped ground me and keep me more engaged but only on an intellectual level.* Anyway, I knew something was wrong. I was really behaving weirdly, so I came over here, and they started taking me at the Day Treatment Center. *I continued to be in my head as I noted his tendency to phrase things in terms of others acting on him. Significant for his CMP I thought, and I became more alert to similar themes.* I would come here every day to the Day Treatment Center. That was in October. Anyway, I was taking Librium and a sleeping pill [longer than usual pause], but I was still drinking. *Uh-oh. I didn't like the sound the sound of benzodiazepines and alcohol, especially in someone his age. I made a mental note to consult with the resident who was prescribing medication. That's the last thing I need, for him to accidentally overdose.* And I . . . so my daughter complained to Betty, the nurse, down there about it, and Betty had me admitted to the Psychiatry Inpatient Unit. *There was the lack of agency again. People are doing to him and for him. And I have joined the group—I was already worried and taking charge.* And I was there a couple of weeks. And then they convinced me I should go to the Alcoholic Inpatient Unit. So I spent a month in there, and I quit drinking. Ah, but I was depressed. So I came back one day for this depression to the admissions, and they admitted me again. *Now I was aware of becoming annoyed with him. His voice and phrasing had a whiny quality. Whining was not approved of in my family, where it was considered a moral flaw— as in "don't complain because you have no new shoes; there are people who have no feet." So I was unclear in the moment if what I was experiencing was more a product of my own unique family dynamics (that is, classic countertransference), or was my negative reaction similar to how others in Mr. Johnson's life might respond (that is, interactive countertransference)?*

Therapist: Back to the Alcohol Inpatient Unit? *Now I was feeling exhausted, and we were only a few minutes into the first session.*

Client: No, to Psychiatry. And I was there through June. Well, that's about it.

Although I am not proud of all of my reactions to Mr. Johnson, from a TLDP point of view, examining these feelings, thoughts, and behaviors is a critical part of formulating the case, setting the goals for the therapy, and even choosing the interventions most likely to be of help. Being aware of these countertransferential reactions enabled me to see their potential for co-creating Mr. Johnson's CMP in the here and now of the session, allowed me to anticipate ruptures in the therapeutic alliance, made me more alert for recognizing therapeutic impasses when they did occur, and in general prepared me to capitalize on opportunities to maximize new experiential learning. In brief, I felt held by the tenets of TLDP and its scope in taking into account my reactions.

In this first session (and throughout the therapy) I learned more about Mr. Johnson's history. He was treated in an authoritarian and harsh manner by his father, who physically abused him when drunk. My client had memories of sitting at the dinner table afraid to say a word or draw any attention to himself. His mother was sympathetic but passive. He described her as a "saint." Consequently, as a young boy, Mr. Johnson became a placating and anxious child. By being meek he could avoid punishment from his father and get attention from his mother. Later in life, Mr. Johnson married a woman who was described in the inpatient notes as "domineering." He felt he was always disappointing her ("She wanted me to be more of a man"), which led to his being more careful and compliant. This further infuriated his wife and left Mr. Johnson feeling like a helpless failure, causing him to become depressed and withdrawn. By the time I saw him, his internalized working model of how the interpersonal world worked had been repeatedly confirmed in his day-to-day experiences.

My preliminary CMP for Mr. Johnson sounded something like this. Mr. Johnson was a very isolated, depressed, dependent man who expected others to know best what he should do. He pressed them to assume responsibility for his life. Others did seem to step in and direct him perhaps because they felt sorry for him, they got worn down by his whiny passivity, or they felt guilty for not wanting to do more. However, eventually they got frustrated and irritated by his hapless stance and defeatist attitude; they felt he was treating them in a passive-aggressive manner. The end result was that they became annoyed with a nonverbal "leakage of hostility" (Kiesler, 1996, p. 145) and/ or withdrew from him. Although Mr. Johnson initially seemed to comply with others' directives and demands, he often ended up feeling not helped but rather rejected, unloved, and worthless. He was unable to feel effective and nurtured, and his sense of abandonment, helplessness, and hopelessness led to his increased drinking, isolation, and depression, completing the cycle. My goal was to help Mr. Johnson feel more empowered and become more assertive and to incorporate an awareness of the adaptive function of his submissive style.

I saw Mr. Johnson the following week. This excerpt is 15 minutes into the second session. The client has just finished telling me that his daughter Susan decided to move in with her friends when he got evicted from the family home.

> Therapist: Do you think Susan's sorry she moved? *I did not realize when I said this but caught it later when watching the video that I was identifying with Susan here. I was feeling that if I were his daughter, I would have been delighted to have a good reason to move away from him.*

> Client: I don't know. [plaintively] She still calls me Daddy. But then when she's gone, you know, she's with her friends. I guess she's forgetting me, and it hurts. [emphatically] It hurts. I don't see her. She says, "Oh, Dad, I have things to do." I ask her to come over—I say, "Let's meet and have an afternoon." She says [mimicking his daughter], "I have other things I have to do." One of her friends has a boat in College View. They go out on the bay [pejoratively] "bay-ing it." And I just feel left out.

> Therapist: [matter-of-factly] Well, you are! *Although I meant to validate Mr. Johnson's experience of feeling left out, my phrasing was stark and patronizing. Here again, I was imagining that his daughter would definitely prefer to be out with friends sailing than at home with her sad sack father. My efforts to empathize with him were undercut by my tone, which was more aggressive and distancing—just the very reaction he was used to getting from others.*

> Client: I am. [lamenting] Yeah, I'm really left out. So, I don't know . . . [resigned tone, voice trails off] *I was aware of the pull to tell him to "get a life!" His plaintive tone seemed designed to pull me to jump him and save him and yet it had the opposite effect; I felt I was getting more irritated.*

> Therapist: The least she could do after you went to all the trouble of raising her and giving her things was stick around for the rest of your life. *Wow! As I said this, I was immediately struck by the tone in my voice and the phrasing of my words.*

My intention was to put on the table what I thought he was saying in so many words but was afraid to say. I was trying to give him the space to be angry with his daughter for abandoning him in his moment of need when he had been there for her throughout her life. But as the sentence came out of my mouth, it sounded sarcastic. I certainly was having some countertransferential feelings about his woe-is-me stance! Whereas I was unaware of feeling dismissive when I asked about Susan's moving out a few minutes earlier, here I was very aware of my mocking tone. Because I had already developed a rudimentary formulation, I reminded myself that my negative reaction was consistent with what Mr. Johnson experienced from so many people. Thus, I was able to reflect on what was happening in real time and reverberate between the observer and participant stance. It was a bit of a roller-coaster ride, but this is a concrete example of how the TLDP formulation helped keep my emotions regulated. (This "reflection-on-action" is an advanced skill [Schon, 1983] that involves interpersonal pattern recognition, self-reflection, and self-monitoring [Binder, 2004].)

Client: Anyway, I guess these are the things, the fears . . . *I was struck by how quickly he moved away from what I said without even acknowledging it. I didn't want to miss an opportunity to process what was happening between the two of us, so I interrupted him.*

Therapist: How do you feel about what I just said?

Client: What did you say? [pause] *I just knew he heard me, so I didn't say anything. I realized I might have been giving him a mini new experience of not rescuing him, but it also could have been a manifestation of my irritation.* At least she could have stuck around? [pause] I'm not that possessive. Really, I'm not that possessive to want her to stick around. I just want her in the same household. That's what I really want.

Therapist: [nodding] OK. *I found myself chuckling inside. Yeah. He did want her to stick around—even in the same household. I felt like I had his number, and although I was engaged intellectually, I still was not feeling his pain.* How do you feel about the fact that I said the least she could do is not move out?

Client: I don't know. If I answer that, it would seem like a selfish answer. If I just said, well, I feel that she's unjust or she's unfair, it would be a selfish answer on my part because I know kids have to grow up and go their own way.

Therapist: Oh, OK. I am beginning to understand. *He was afraid of being seen as selfish. At this point I felt myself starting to soften inside. I could begin to sense how he lost or perhaps never had a sense of healthy entitlement. He wanted more, but that was selfish. I began to have some empathy for his plight. This man feared being labeled (and labeled himself) for his authentic feelings of wanting more of a connection with his daughter. He gave me some evidence of nascent anger by using words such as unjust and unfair. I decided to validate and heightened these. They were glimmers of a forthright protest—not characteristic of his usual depressed and depressing lament. I am pulled to support this small voice of protest.* Well, you know that in your head, but I'm really asking you how your gut feels.

Client: [begins crying] I don't want her to go! I want to be with her. She's my little kid. [pause] If Susan goes, I don't really have anybody. [pause] Well, I'm feeling sorry for myself, but that's the truth of the matter. [sighs] Anger at myself for making [pause], you know, for getting rid of a house that could have kept us all together. *There were so many thoughts and feelings I was having as Mr. Johnson was talking. I was wondering if in part his tears were relief that someone wanted to hear about his true feelings. I heard his plaintive cry, "I don't want her to go! I want to be with her." He sounded like a child who is being abandoned, softening my heart more. Also his tears spoke volumes about his deep longing and fears of loneliness. "If Susan goes, I don't really have anybody." If Mr. Johnson had been crying inauthentic, crocodile tears, I probably would not have been moved emotionally and may have even felt manipulated. But instead his sorrow touched me, and I was aware that my negative reactions were subsiding. We were implicitly getting to know one another.*

By the end of the 20-session therapy, I was feeling quite positive toward Mr. Johnson. As he owned his feelings more (especially those that were empowering), I felt more engaged. And as I felt more present, he was able to take more and more risks to be his true self who could be righteously angry without worrying that I would punish him or that he would overwhelm me. We were developing a functional cyclical transactional pattern.

As Mr. Johnson came forward more in his life with less depression and anxiety, those around him (particularly his children) responded differently ("My daughter came down to visit me the other day, and I was mowing the lawn, and she wanted to mow"). In addition to his having new interpersonal experiences, Mr. Johnson demonstrated an understanding of the adaptive value of his nonassertiveness.

A 1-year follow-up of Mr. Johnson indicated that he was not clinically depressed. He described his children as well and his relationships with them as improved. He was not drinking and, in consultation with his physician, had discontinued his antidepressant medication. Although this therapy took place many years ago (and I have since learned that Mr. Johnson died), I still think of him warmly and with gratitude for teaching me so much.

CONCLUDING COMMENTS

Because of their helpless, hopeless presentation, depressed clients in particular can activate strong negative emotional, cognitive, and behavioral reactions in their therapists. TLDP can help therapists treat such difficult clients by focusing on a maladaptive dynamic system of interactions that gets maintained in present relationships. The goals are to disrupt these transactional patterns and to alter the client's internal working models of self and other. This chapter focused on seeing how the therapist can move from negative reactions to compassion using a revised integrative view of TLDP that strengthens its interpersonal focus by being more explicit about its attachment theory base and the centrality of dyadically created, experiential, emotionally based learning. A method of formulating, strategies for intervening, and a training model were described, along with a case illustration.

REFERENCES

Alonso, A., & Rutan, J. S. (1988). Shame and guilt in supervision. *Psychotherapy: Theory, Research, Practice, Training, 25*, 576–581. doi:10.1037/h0085384

American Psychiatric Association. (2000). *Diagnostic and statistical manual of mental disorders* (4th ed., text rev.). Washington, DC: Author.

Beardslee, W. R., Bemporad, J., Keller, M. B., & Klerman, G. L. (1983). Children of parents with a major affective disorder: A review. *American Journal of Psychiatry, 140*, 825–832.

Beck, A. T., Rush, J. A., Shaw, B. F., & Emery, G. (1979). *Cognitive therapy of depression.* New York, NY: Guilford Press.

Benjamin, L. S. (1993a). Every psychopathology is a gift of love. *Psychotherapy Research, 3*, 1–24. doi:10.1080/10503309312331333629

Benjamin, L. S. (1993b). *Interpersonal diagnosis and treatment of personality disorders.* New York, NY: Guilford Press.

Binder, J. L. (1993). Is it time to improve psychotherapy training? *Clinical Psychology Review, 13*, 301–318. doi:10.1016/0272-7358(93)90015-E

Binder, J. L. (2004). *Key competencies in brief dynamic psychotherapy*. New York, NY: Guilford Press.

Bowlby, J. (1988). *A secure base: Clinical applications of attachment theory*. London, England: Routledge.

Butler, S. F., & Strupp, H. H. (1986). "Specific" and "nonspecific" factors in psychotherapy: A problematic paradigm for psychotherapy research. *Psychotherapy: Theory, Research, Practice, Training, 23*, 30–40. doi:10.1037/h0085590

Carragher, N., Adamson, G., Bunting, B., & McCann, S. (2009). Subtypes of depression: Results from a nationally representative survey. *Journal of Affective Disorders, 113*, 88–99.

Coyne, J. C. (1990). Interpersonal processes in depression. In G. I. Keitner (Ed.), *Depression and families* (pp. 31–54). Washington, DC: American Psychiatric Association.

Cummings, E. M., & Davis, P. T. (1999). Depressed parents and family functioning: Interpersonal effects and children's functioning and development. In T. Joiner & J. C. Coyne (Eds.), *The interactional nature of depression: Advances in interpersonal approaches* (pp. 299–327). Washington, DC: American Psychological Association. doi:10.1037/10311-011

Efstation, J. F., Patton, M. J., & Kardash, C. M. (1990). Measuring the working alliance in counselor supervision. *Journal of Counseling Psychology, 37*, 322–329. doi:10.1037/0022-0167.37.3.322

Ekman, P. (2003). *Emotions revealed*. New York, NY: Holt.

Fonagy, P., Gergely, G., Jurist, E. L., & Target, M. (2002). *Affect regulation, mentalization, and the development of the self*. New York, NY: Other Press.

Fosha, D., Siegel, D., & Solomon, M. (Eds.). (2009). *The healing power of emotion*. New York, NY: Norton.

Gelso, C. J., & Hayes, J. A. (2007). *Countertransference and the therapist's inner experience*. Mahwah, NJ: Erlbaum.

Greenberg, L. S. (2002). *Emotion-focused therapy: Coaching clients to work through their feelings*. Washington, DC: American Psychological Association. doi:10.1037/10447-000

Henry, W. P., Schacht, T. E., Strupp, H. H., Butler, S. F., & Binder, J. L. (1993). Effects of training in time-limited dynamic psychotherapy: Mediators of therapists' responses to training. *Journal of Consulting and Clinical Psychology, 61*, 441–447. doi:10.1037/0022-006X.61.3.441

Horowitz, L. M. (2004). *Interpersonal foundations of psychopathology*. Washington, DC: American Psychological Association. doi:10.1037/10727-000

Kabat-Zinn, J. (1990). *Full catastrophe living*. New York, NY: Delta.

Kiesler, D. J. (1996). *Contemporary interpersonal theory and research*. New York, NY: Wiley.

Levenson, H. (1995). *Time-limited dynamic psychotherapy: A guide to clinical practice*. New York, NY: Basic Books.

Levenson, H. (2003). Time-limited dynamic psychotherapy: An integrationist perspective. *Journal of Psychotherapy Integration, 13,* 300–333. doi:10.1037/1053-0479.13.3-4.300

Levenson, H. (2010). *Brief dynamic psychotherapy*. Washington, DC: American Psychological Association.

Levenson, H., Butler, S., & Bein, E. (2002). Brief psychodynamic individual psychotherapy. In R. Hales, S. C. Yudofsky, & J. Talbot (Eds.), *American Psychiatric Press textbook of psychiatry* (pp. 1133–1156). Washington, DC: American Psychiatric Press.

Levenson, H., & Strupp, H. H. (1999). Recommendations for the future of training in brief dynamic psychotherapy. *Journal of Clinical Psychology, 55,* 385–391.

Levenson, H., & Strupp, H. H. (2007). Cyclical maladaptive patterns: Case formulation in time-limited dynamic psychotherapy. In T. D. Eells (Ed.), *Handbook of psychotherapy case formulation* (2nd ed., pp. 164–197). New York, NY: Guilford Press.

Maroda, K. J. (2004). *The power of countertransference*. Hillsdale, NJ: Analytic Press.

Mikulincer, M., & Shaver, P. R. (2007). *Attachment in adulthood: Structure, dynamics, and change*. New York, NY: Guilford Press.

Mongrain, M. (1998). Parental representations and support-seeking behaviors related to dependency and self-criticism. *Journal of Personality, 66,* 151–173.

Mongrain, M., Vettese, L. C., Shuster, B., & Kendal, N. (1998). Perceptual biases, affect, and behavior in the relationships of dependents and self-critics. *Journal of Personality and Social Psychology, 75,* 230–241. doi:10.1037/0022-3514.75.1.230

Montagno, M., Svatovic, M., & Levenson, H. (2011). Short-term and long-term effects of training in emotionally focused couple therapy: Professional and personal aspects. *Journal of Marital and Family Therapy, 37,* 380–392. doi:10.111/j.1752-0606.2011.00250.x

Norcross, J. C. (Ed.). (2002). *Psychotherapy relationships that work: Therapist contributions and responsiveness to patients*. New York, NY: Oxford University Press.

Rossberg, J. I., Karterud, S., Pedersen, G., & Friis, S. (2010). Psychiatric symptoms and countertransference feelings: An empirical investigation. *Psychiatry Research, 178,* 191–195. doi:10.1016/j.psychres.2009.09.019

Safran, J., & Muran, J. (2000). *Negotiating the therapeutic alliance*. New York, NY: Guilford Press.

Schon, D. A. (1983). *The reflective practitioner*. New York, NY: Basic Books.

Schwartz, R. C., & Wendling, H. (2003). Countertransference reactions toward specific client populations: A review of the empirical literature. *Psychological Reports, 92,* 651–654.

Segrin, C. G. (2011). Depressive disorders and interpersonal processes. In L. M. Horowitz & S. Strack (Eds.), *Handbook of interpersonal psychology* (pp. 425–448). New York, NY: Wiley.

Segrin, C. G., & Abramson, L. Y. (1994). Negative reactions to depressive behaviors: A communication theories analysis. *Journal of Abnormal Psychology, 103,* 655–668. doi:10.1037/0021-843X.103.4.655

Segrin, C. G., & Dillard, J. P. (1992). The interactional theory of depression: A meta-analysis of the research literature. *Journal of Social and Clinical Psychology, 11,* 43–70. doi:10.1521/jscp.1992.11.1.43

Siegel, D. J. (1999). *The developing mind: Toward a neurobiology of interpersonal experience.* New York, NY: Guilford Press.

Sroufe, L. A., & Waters, E. (1977). Attachment as an organizational construct. *Child Development, 48,* 1184–1199. doi:10.2307/1128475

Stern, D. N. (2004). *The present moment in psychotherapy and everyday life.* New York, NY: Norton.

Stern, D. N., Bruschweiler-Stern, N., Harrison, A. M., Lyons-Ruth, K., Morgan, A. C., Nahum, J. P., . . . Tronick, E. A. (1998). The process of therapeutic change involving implicit knowledge: Some implications of developmental observations for adult psychotherapy. *Infant Mental Health Journal, 19,* 300–308. doi:10.1002/(SICI)1097-0355(199823)19:3<300::AID-IMHJ5>3.0.CO;2-P

Strupp, H. H., & Binder, J. L. (1984). *Psychotherapy in a new key.* New York, NY: Basic Books.

Sullivan, H. S. (1953). *The interpersonal theory of psychiatry.* New York, NY: Norton.

Sullivan, H. S. (1954). *The psychiatric interview.* New York, NY: Norton.

Summers, R. F., & Barber, J. P. (2010). *Psychodynamic therapy: A guide to evidence-based practice.* New York, NY: Guilford Press.

Wachtel, P. L. (1982). Vicious circles: The self and the rhetoric of emerging and unfolding. *Contemporary Psychoanalysis, 18,* 259–273.

10

PATTERN RECOGNITION IN THE TREATMENT OF NARCISSISTIC DISORDERS: COUNTERTRANSFERENCE FROM A UNIFIED PERSPECTIVE

JEFFREY J. MAGNAVITA

Narcissistic personality, in spite of its severity and increasing prevalence in North America (Dingfelder, 2011), is one of the least studied of the personality disorders (Russ, Shedler, Bradley, & Westen, 2008). Our understanding of this spectrum of disorders has evolved considerably since Freud (1914/1957) first introduced the concept of narcissism in 1914 and since the groundbreaking work of Heinz Kohut, who wrote the now classic volumes *The Analysis of the Self* (1971) and *The Restoration of the Self* (1977). Although Freud introduced the concept of narcissism, before Kohut there existed only vague theoretical constructs on this spectrum of often difficult to treat clients who were not highly responsive to traditional psychoanalytic methods of free association, development of a transference neurosis, and analysis of transference. Kohut shifted the emphasis from Freudian drive theory to a depiction of the dyadic nature of self-regulation, which was seen as both a theoretical and clinical leap in the conceptualization and treatment of narcissistic disorders.

DOI: 10.1037/13940-010

Transforming Negative Reactions to Clients: From Frustration to Compassion, A. W. Wolf, M. R. Goldfried, and J. C. Muran (Editors)

Kernberg (1984) also made significant advances by elaborating an object-relational model of narcissism.

In this chapter, I examine transference and countertransference from a unified framework using conceptual tools that have been developed for complex pattern recognition. First, I review some of the basic conceptual issues regarding narcissistic spectrum disorders to orient the reader. Then I focus attention on how to use complex pattern recognition tools to understand how countertransference can be used to better conceptualize the clinical phenomena and strategize treatment using a unified perspective.

To better comprehend the material that follows, it is useful to begin with some definitions of *countertransference*, which was first introduced by Freud in 1914.

> Countertransference refers to emotions, associations, and defenses triggered by the patient in the clinician, whose etiologies are in a true sense unconscious or difficult to bring to conscious awareness. When true countertransference feelings have crystallized, the clinician begins to re-experience past relationships in the current relationship with the patient. (Shea, 1998, p. 549)

A contemporary definition offered by Gelso and Hayes (2007) describes countertransference as "the therapist's internal and external reactions that are shaped by the therapist's past or present emotional conflicts and vulnerabilities" (p. 130). They further elaborated that "in general, countertransference refers to the therapist's feelings, cognitions, and behaviors that occur in response to dynamics occurring in the counseling relationship that stem from either the therapist's unresolved issues or from maladaptive behaviors elicited by the client" (see Hofsess & Tracey, 2010, p. 52). Countertransference reactions of the therapist when understood can be a useful pattern recognition tool in the diagnosis and treatment of narcissistic disorders.

CONCEPTUALIZATIONS OF NARCISSISM

The origins of the term *narcissism* come from Greek mythology, specifically, the figure Narcissus, a young man who, when looking into a pool of water and seeing his reflection, falls in love with himself. He remains unable to love others and is possessed by his own image. This mythological story became the basis for the clinical conceptualization of individuals who are stuck at what is generally considered a normal stage of development beyond the time that is usual for most people. In psychoanalytic terms, the individual has not moved beyond fixation on the self, which becomes the primary object of love rather than shifting to others. This means that there remains an excessive fixation on self and a lack of achieving an optimal balance between self–

other functions, which allow for more flexible and adaptive functioning and the capacity for intimacy and closeness on the one hand and the capacity to experience autonomy on the other.

The term *narcissism*, as well as other psychological constructs, evolved along different branches of clinical science whereby clinical theorists using different terminology describe similar phenomena. According to Ronningstam (2005), the description *Narcissus-like* was first introduced in psychiatry by Ellis in 1898. Clinical theorists and researchers have devoted considerable attention to the elaboration of the concept of self-esteem that can help one achieve a clearer picture of the clinical phenomena. Abundant literature demonstrates the importance to psychological well-being of having a positive and stable self-esteem and the difficulties when someone has negative self-esteem. If clinical theorists and researchers shine the illuminating light of this literature of self-esteem on this topic, clinicians can better orient themselves when working with conditions of narcissism. They can readily see that when self-esteem is low, this is not an optimal state. When too low, individuals may use their internal negative self-schemata to project on the external world and in so doing have their negative expectations generally fulfilled. Clinicians can reasonably say that individuals who have excessively inflated self-esteem are experiencing a kind of protective grandiosity characteristic of narcissism whereby they use whatever means available to shape their relational matrix to support their over-rated self-conception. Dyadically they select people and careers that affirm their overinflated sense of self.

Before discussing how transference and countertransference evolved in the treatment of narcissistic disorders, some background seems central to an appreciation of this topic. The reader has probably already experienced some type of personal reaction to the topic of narcissism. Clinicians may recall a particularly challenging case and reactivate feelings of frustration, powerlessness, and a variety of other emotions. Narcissism, as it is used both clinically and in general parlance, has many meanings and implications. In terms of general culture in North America, the word *narcissism* is often used as a pejorative term in movies and literature as well as in daily conversation to describe an individual who is preoccupied with his or her status to the point of doing what is necessary to preserve his or her elevated sense of self. Movie stars are those most often described as narcissistic, and although many may be, there are a variety of other professions that can claim their share of individuals who lack a certain level of empathy for others and seem to do best when they can use their considerable charm to further their own means. Often depicted in literature and movies, these characters do not age gracefully as they attempt to seek eternal youth and power. There are a number of examples from movies, including Madonna's character in *Desperately Seeking Susan* and Natalie Portman's mother in *Black Swan*, as well as historical figures such as General George Patton. Many politicians and business tycoons are also branded with this pejorative label, which may very well be apt given the dual lives they lead and the discrepancy between their private and public selves. There seems to be a rise in the prevalence of narcissism (Twenge & Campbell, 2009). Some experts believe that America is becoming an increasingly narcissistic society, and there is some evidence to suggest that narcissism is on the rise, especially in young people (Dingfelder, 2011). But concerns about American society becoming increasingly narcissistic are not new. Lasch (1979), a sociologist, believed that American culture mirrors narcissistic traits in its emphasis on materialism, achievement, and the pursuit of pleasure. Narcissistic personality traits may even be adaptive in a culture that values individualism.

Clinically, when psychologists refer to narcissism, they also use it in a variety of loose ways that do not always serve them well because they lack precision. The most commonly used definition of narcissistic personality disorder, of course, is the standard categorical description used in the *Diagnostic and Statistical Manual of Mental Disorders* (DSM) of the American Psychiatric Association (2000) in which a number of criteria have to be met and then clinicians may apply the diagnosis. Although this conceptualization has been useful in some ways by making the criteria standard and the diagnosis seemingly easy for researchers to verify and code, nevertheless, it has limited application to clinicians who treat clients with narcissistic spectrum disorders. In fact, narcissistic personality disorder may be eliminated from the next edition, the *DSM–V*, although this decision remains controversial (Dingfelder, 2011). There is a great deal of variability in personality that the term *narcissistic* cannot capture fully. Applying the label to a particular individual does little in terms of suggesting a course of treatment because the extreme variation among those who might receive this diagnosis is considerable, and treatment implications may vary dramatically from case to case. Millon (1999) provided a crisp description of the central features of narcissistic "personality style as an overevaluation of self-worth and a grandiose sense of self-importance and uniqueness. In seeming contradiction to the inflated self-concept is an inordinate need to be loved and admired by others" (p. 433). Rather than try to use solely the *DSM* diagnostic criteria of narcissistic personality disorder as a guide to the appropriate treatment approach, I suggest that an understanding of the variations in narcissistic configurations can be illuminated and refined using transference and countertransference phenomena as a pattern recognition tool to guide to diagnosis and treatment. However, I "modernize" these conceptions to fit unified theory, which I hope provides a less theoretically biased set of clinical constructs and tools to examine the complexity of the treatment of narcissistic spectrum disorders.

NORMAL VERSUS PATHOLOGICAL NARCISSISM

For this discussion, the concept of narcissism can be conceptualized for heuristic purposes on a spectrum from normal to pathological. Normal narcissism allows for a healthy love of self, necessary for identification of needs, self-assertion, and maintenance of stable self-esteem. Although one might be hurt or shamed by criticism or inappropriate behavior, there is a tolerance for these feelings and an ability to metabolize them and change behavior if this proves adaptive. There exists a realistic appraisal of the self and an acceptance of one's limitations. For example, one man seen for consultation described how he felt like he was a failure in his life because he always thought that he would become president of the United States, and although very successful by most standards, he truly experienced himself as failing. This overvaluation of self and inability to adjust might be a valid perspective for a little boy but seems maladaptive for an adult at his phase of life. When narcissism is in the healthy range, there is an optimal balance between self–other functions. In other words, there exists a simultaneous interest in others as well as self. All people experience oscillations between these two polarities, but in narcissistic disorders the individual is stuck too much at the self end of the continuum. This capacity to attune to others' needs is a critical function for the development and maintenance of intimacy and closeness. Individuals with healthy narcissism are capable of empathy for others and sensitive responding to the plight of others.

As one moves on the spectrum from normal to pathological narcissism, there is an increasing shift in the ability to have empathy for others while at the same time a shift from self–other balance to primarily self. In the extreme in these individuals, there exists what Kernberg (2005) termed a "syndrome of malignant narcissism" (p. 43) characterized by antisocial behavior. Sometimes these traits are evident in executives who have reached the pinnacle of success, and there are abundant stories of how the combination of narcissistic functions leads to antisocial behavior that is all too often justified and minimized. Gordon Gekko from the movie *Wall Street* exemplifies this type. Lacking an integration of self–other representations, narcissists are primarily concerned with how others can be used in the service of maintaining their fragile self-function and esteem regulation. There also may exist a lack of what Fonagy termed *mentalization* (Fonagy & Target, 2003), or *self-reflectiveness*, thus making the person prone to self-defeating behaviors without the benefit of correction that learning from one's mistakes affords.

As with all personality dysfunction, there are repetitive maladaptive patterns in operation whereby the individual engages in the same behavior even though the results are less than optimal. Self-esteem becomes less stable and more prone to destabilization as one continues toward the extreme end of the spectrum of pathological narcissism. The individual may attempt to compensate for feelings of inadequacy and insecurity by maintaining a grandiose sense of self ungrounded or poorly grounded in a realistic self-appraisal. This may present as haughtiness, arrogance, and entitlement in some individuals. There may exist an indifference to others and a lack of deep emotional involvement.

Affectively, as one moves from healthy to pathological narcissism there is a heightening of sensitivity to perceived humiliation with strong feelings of shame resulting in the more malignant cases in interpersonal aggressive and violent behavior (Ronningstam, 2005). Interestingly, narcissistic individuals may be superficially socially adept but display a sense of entitlement emanating from the belief that they are special. However, in extreme forms of narcissism, esteem may actually be quite stable, but maintaining this homeostasis requires increasingly higher levels of self-distortion.

Now that I have established a basic conceptual framework to understand narcissism, I next examine the concept and process of countertransference. There is some empirical support that indicates narcissistic disorders can be placed on a spectrum on the basis of their severity. Using the Shedler–Westen Assessment Procedure—II, Russ, Shedler, Bradley, and Westen (2008) suggested that there are three subtypes of narcissistic personality disorder, which they labeled as *grandiose/malignant*, *fragile*, and *high-functioning/exhibitionistic*. The narcissistic/malignant exploit others with little regard for those they use, and their grandiosity appears to be primary, not used as a defense. The fragile narcissists have a defensive type of grandiosity, which is seen under stress, whereas, the high-functioning narcissists tend to be more comfortable and competent and achievement oriented. Next, I return to the topic of transference and countertransference, two related concepts useful in the clinical process.

CLASSICAL VIEWS OF TRANSFERENCE
AND COUNTERTRANSFERENCE

The concept of transference emerged from Freud's experience with patients and his keen observations of his clinical cases. Freud's patients predictably expected him to act in certain ways toward them and in so doing attempted to reenact the relationships they experienced with their primary attachment figures. The reader should remember that Freud did not have the well-elaborated conceptualization and empirical evidence showing the veracity and the fundamental nature of attachment. Nor did he have the contemporary understanding of relational and cognitive schema, so the scientific underpinnings of what was occurring in clinical practice could not be understood as they can be today. He wrote about patients developing a transference neurosis, which he then believed was vital to analyze for a cure. He strove to present himself as a blank screen whose neutrality would encourage this transference phenomenon to fully develop. Researchers and clinicians know now that the transference reenactment patterns will occur in relational contexts. Freud then was able to analyze the transference neurosis using interpretations to assist the patient in realizing that this process was really projection of unresolved issues (Magnavita, 2003).

Only later did it emerge—when other theoretical advances had been achieved—that transference was not a psychology of one mind projecting itself on a neutral other; rather, a much more intricate bidirectional process was occurring whereby the mind of the client was interacting with the mind of the psychotherapist to create something unique. The countertransference phenomenon became critical to understanding and pioneering later interpersonal conceptualizations as well as intersubjective perspectives. What is important in this regard is that there was an acknowledgment that as much as individuals who completed psychoanalytic training wanted to believe that they were no longer "contaminated" by the analysis of their clients, in fact, they were often experiencing powerful internal processes in response to their clients' experiences and projection. This process represents the push and pull of transference–countertransference activation. Clearly, psychotherapists have "bad" days and do not really feel neutral toward all, if any, of their clients. The real breakthrough, I believe, came when countertransference, instead of being viewed as an untoward side effect of treatment, could serve as a powerful clinical tool and be used in service of treatment of the client. Wachtel (1997) wrote, "Where once countertransference was very largely viewed in terms of error, of ways in which the therapist's unconscious was leading her astray, now countertransference is viewed as an essential tool of the therapy" (p. 395). Thus, transference is just one aspect of a complex dynamic system that expresses itself in various configurations and patterns in various relational units.

TRANSFERENCE AND COUNTERTRANSFERENCE THROUGH THE LENS OF A UNIFIED FRAMEWORK

It is generally accepted that the construct of transference–countertransference represents a powerful interpersonal force extant in all psychotherapeutic endeavors and in all relationships to a large degree (Anderson, Reznik,

& Glassman, 2005). Experimental research has shown support for the following conclusions:

1. Significant–other representations are activated automatically in transference.
2. Affect arises relatively automatically in transference when the significant self–other representation is activated.
3. The relational self is activated relatively automatically when the significant self–other representation is activated.
4. Some self-regulatory processes in the relational self are evoked in response to "threat" (e.g., negative cues) in transference and are automatic (Anderson et al., 2005, p. 423).

It is a natural process as science evolves for constructs that are useful to be repackaged in contemporary scientific parlance and for those for which empirical support has been weak to disappear. To most effectively make use of the original concepts of transference and countertransference in the service of clinical practice, researchers can assimilate new conceptual developments, as well as converging lines of evidence, that strengthen and expand the original conceptualizations. Countertransference–transference may be conceptualized using a systemic model that views the entire personality as a system embedded in various matrices. In this system, affect is an attractor state that forms the human attachment system and creates the dynamic tension in all levels of the system. This unified relational framework is described by Ham and Tronick (2009):

> We believe that the human being is an open, nonlinear dynamic system consisting of many interrelated domains of functioning (physiological, emotional, cognitive/symbolic, and social/behavioral). This system is thought to move toward more complex and coherent states of self-organization as it interfaces with itself and the outer environment. We refer to this self-organization as a "state of consciousness." This state expresses the entire system of meanings, intentions, and purposes through which one operates and experiences the self in the world. As in all complex systems, there are multilayered, hierarchically organized domains of functioning, and each domain is related to and affects the other. A more coherent state of consciousness occurs when "all" domains are organized into greater (but never complete) harmony with other levels. Coherence is a function of organization, complexity, and flexibility in adapting to different environmental conditions. (pp. 620–621)

Drawing from an evolving framework of unified clinical science and psychotherapy (Magnavita, 2005a, 2005b, 2006), clinicians can incorporate four clinical constructs, which are also useful clinical tools. Because of the limited scope of this chapter I provide a very brief description of the levels of this model, and readers may refer to previous work, which delineates this metatheoretical framework. Incorporating a multilevel system relational framework allows clinicians to understand and enhance their treatment of narcissistic spectrum disorders.

In this system there are four interrelated nested subdomains that can be depicted as triangular configurations to depict the process and structure. This framework is based on the concept of personality systematics, which posits that the personality system is a dynamic system with component parts that are constantly evolving and exist in configurations alternating between organized chaos and stabilization that allows for flexibility, adaptation, and growth. Personality may be viewed as an emergent phenomenon. Schwartz and Begley (2002) described this term: "An *emergent phenomenon* is one whose characteristics or behaviors cannot be explained in terms of the sum of its parts; if mind is emergent, then it cannot be wholly explained by brain" (p. 350). The four domain levels are (a) *intrapsychic–biological* or what occurs in the mind–brain system, (b) *interpersonal–dyadic* or what transpires in two-person configurations, (c) *relational–triadic* or what occurs in three-person relationships, and (d) *sociocultural–familial* or what occurs in larger relational systems. These represent the entire system moving from the microscopic to the macroscopic structures and processes. The basic units or molecules of human functioning are dyads, triads, and larger family and social systems in which they operate. Patterns occur in the ways in which dyadic, triadic, and larger systems operate.

FOUR DOMAIN LEVELS USEFUL FOR TRACKING TRANSFERENCE–COUNTERTRANSFERENCE USING COMPLEX PATTERN RECOGNITION

The unified framework briefly described previously portrays the four-level domain and component subsystems ranging in perspective from micro-sytem to macrosystem processes. Psychotherapists generally orient their work to one or two levels. Personality dysfunction, in whatever expression, is evidence of a system in which the adaptive value derived from earlier developmental experiences in the relational matrix has lost its adaptive value.

At the intrapsychic–biological level, a personality system may be conceptualized using a computer analogy. A computer has hardware, which is equivalent to the human brain, and sets the genetic and biological parameters for the system, but the software is the operating system, which is necessary to have a functional system. If the personality operating system is encoded with maladaptive beliefs, dysfunctional schema, and immature defenses, then the personality system as it operates throughout the various levels of the biopsychosocial system will be maladaptive or dysfunctional. As one moves from the intrapsychic–biological to the sociocultural–familial, the perspective widens and is embedded in mutually interactive feedback processes. For example, narcissistic disorders will express themselves dyadically in the way interpersonal processes occur, but this style may also be supported socially and culturally. Evident in popular culture, the continual iterations of narcissism interacting with culture can be seen in magazines and television shows reinforcing a culture of narcissism (Lasch, 1979).

At the intrapsychic–biological level, in narcissistic spectrum individuals there is a preponderance of inhibiting affects, primarily shame, which is related to a core belief that one is defective, bad, not good enough, or unlovable. Clients in treatment may respond with a hypersensitivity to perceived slights, such as the therapist running late for a session or being tired or less attentive than usual. At the defensive level of operations, grandiosity is used to protect one from these feelings, and efforts are made to seek admiration to avoid the unbearable affects associated with being unlovable, bad, or defective, which may be linked to abandonment and survival terror (i.e., without these attachments one will not survive when a child). The therapist may be the recipient of powerful projections resulting in feeling powerless, guilty, anxious, or despairing. These feelings are often signs that the client is intolerant of these affects. Empathy can be enhanced when these dysphoric affects are projected and stimulated in the therapist. The therapist can actually experience what it is like to try to fend these feelings off and the effort required to maintain equilibrium under the force of great internal pressure.

In this way the countertransference experience of frustration can be concerted to empathy. It is often useful to imagine what it was like as a child and to be the receptacle of parental affect, which was overwhelming. Perceived abandonment may occur when the psychotherapist goes on vacation or has to cancel an appointment, at which time a crisis might ensue for the client and a destabilization from the disruption of the attachment. The major pattern recognition tool available to the psychotherapist is the unique way in which the client uses defenses to create a character defense system. The client's unique constellation of defenses can be catalogued in the initial phase of treatment by observing all defenses used in the intrapsychic and interpersonal domain (Magnavita, 1997).

The organization and type of defenses unique to an individual create a response in others. Many times an immediate reaction is noted, such as a desire to protect, care take, and relate cautiously, and so forth, that provides an initial view of the intrapsychic structures and process. This rapid pattern recognition enables the therapist to more carefully calibrate the intensity of treatment. Clients with primitive defenses such as projective identification, acting out, and splitting should not have their anxiety raised precipitously or they may become flooded and regress dramatically (Magnavita, 1997).

An overreliance on transference interpretations for higher functioning clients may cause disruption in the alliance. Therefore, when considering sharing countertransference reactions, the therapist must proceed with caution with personality dysfunction. The unique constellation of defenses exerts an interpersonal force to which the psychotherapist reacts. For example, more primitive defenses generally create a level of cautiousness, whereas higher level defenses such as intellectualization and detachment may induce boredom or tiredness.

In one case, a young man with a superior intellect was extremely suicidal and believed that because he had not achieved his goal to become part of an elite military special operations unit, he should end his life. His grandiosity was unable to be transformed into other possibilities that were attainable when this one no longer was a possible goal. This pattern activated a concern for the integrity of this young man's inner resources, which was used to inform treatment. The concern led to an intensive course of outpatient psychotherapy until the grandiosity could be transformed into other possibilities.

At the interpersonal–dyadic level the therapist will hear reports of difficulties with current attachments representing the pattern of behavior that is recurrent in relational reenactments. Themes of hurt, injury, and distress when sufficient and excessive supplies to regulate self-function are not provided by significant others and achievements at work. Classic transference phenomena are observed in the expected relationship with the psychotherapist. The client immediately begins to exert interpersonal influence on the psychotherapist to pull toward treatment that his or her schema have been structured to expect. "Often the narcissist projects guilt feelings that the therapist is the cause of the narcissist's vulnerability and wounded self-image. Feeling that we do not appreciate them or that we are being too critical, narcissists respond with hurt feelings" (Lachkar, 2004, p. 90). The therapist who notes his or her action tendency can use this as a critical pattern recognition tool by asking how this might represent an early attachment schema being reactivated in the therapeutic context.

A common countertransference theme experienced in the psychotherapist is a mixture of resentment and annoyance at the demands being made to validate the client even when they are challenging and demanding. An ability to recognize these feelings and balance affirmation with selective feedback is critical to maintain. In one case a client relentlessly exhorted his wife to meet his excessive demands for validation and reassurance and attempted to convince the psychotherapist that something was indeed inadequate about her. The pull to validate his distorted perception in an attempt to avoid the pain of taking responsibility for his self- regulation stimulated a feeling of being "hammered for love." This countertransference response was shared at the appropriate time with the client and used to illustrate how his spouse might feel.

When working with couples, the therapist may experience *couple transference,* which "refers to the mutual projections, delusions, and distortions, or shared couple fantasies, which become displaced onto the therapist" (Lachkar, 2004, p. 92). When using couples therapy with clients with narcissistic disorders it is not uncommon for them to be paired with someone on the borderline spectrum. These couples may "evoke reactions that convey the message that we must provide immediate solutions and that unless we do, we are disregarding the couple" (Lachkar, 2004, p. 90).

At the triadic–relational level, there exist family patterns that are common in dysfunctional family systems (Magnavita, 2000). An important pattern recognition tool is observing and experiencing triangulation. Human relationships tend to form triangles especially when there is an unstable or undifferentiated dyad. The psychotherapist can be pulled into these triangles in a variety of ways. Donaldson-Pressman and Pressman (1994) described characteristics of two subtypes of narcissistic family systems: overtly and covertly narcissistic. In the volume *Relational Therapy for Personality Disorders* (Magnavita, 2000), 10 family systems that may lead to personality dysfunction in their members were elaborated. The various subtypes share common themes, communication patterns, and relational issues.

Two types of narcissistic family systems were described on the basis of Donaldson-Pressman and Pressman's (1994) work using this typology of the covertly or overtly narcissistic family. A sense of entitlement often predominates the family system and an air of superiority covers an essential deficit. Members of these systems may be prominent members of the community or society and may appear to "have it all" and elicit admiration from those who are not too close to them. Achievement is expected of all members regardless of the cost. Marital dysfunction is a common aspect of these systems, and infidelity is commonly observed in clinical practice. These families almost immediately activate countertransference reactions in the psychotherapist because of their level of dysfunction, chaos, and entitlement. They may expect special treatment and stimulate feelings of inadequacy in the psychotherapist. The psychotherapist may never feel he or she is expert enough for the family. Children in these families may be expected to achieve in extraordinary ways or risk losing their connection.

A second type of family system is the covertly narcissistic family. In this type, the reversal of the parent–child subsystem has a much more subtle feel to it because the dynamics are more covert than the overtly narcissistic. The basic dynamic is that the children, but most often one child, become a mirror for the incomplete self-system of a parent. There is a deficiency in the nurturing, mirroring capacity of the parental figures and the expectation that the child will inordinately satisfy the validation needs of the parental figures. Members of these family systems may appear to be highly functioning in the world, but in their personal and family lives they may be dramatically dysfunctional.

Transference and countertransference themes in these family systems will regularly include expectations of being treated as if they are special, which may induce resentment in the psychotherapist. Expressions of entitlement and special treatment, which cannot be attained, may make the psychotherapist feel inadequate or not good enough. These families may transfer from one practitioner to another looking for the "right" therapist who has the special qualities needed to understand and help them. In one case a 40-year-old physician was in treatment for anxiety and depression but more importantly had never found a mate and married, even though she longed to have a family. When speaking of her father and his treatment, she evoked anger in the psychotherapist, although she idealized and wanted to protect her father by rationalizing the treatment she endured. This alerted the psychotherapist to substantial nonmetabolized anger that needed to be processed.

At the sociocultural–familial level, strong forces shape people's view of narcissism and its societal meaning. Social and political subsystems can create a culture in which narcissism is stimulated. Athletes, movie stars, and rock singers are idealized, and popular culture combined with technological advances encourages the seeking of fame for fame's sake, often without the expectation of a life of discipline necessary to advance in one's profession or career. Narcissistic individuals may catalyze social groups and lead to destruction, such as occurred when the minister Jim Jones led his community to a mass suicide by drinking Kool-Aid laced with poison. Narcissistic individuals may highjack entire countries that they control by force of their narcissistic drive and heavy-handed control of the population.

EMPIRICAL EVIDENCE ON COUNTERTRANSFERENCE AND PERSONALITY DISORDERS

There is a dearth of empirical studies on countertransference with personality disorders. In a study by Rossberg, Karterud, Pedersen, and Friis (2007) using a sample of 71 clients, the researchers found that clients with Cluster A and B compared with Cluster C personality disorders stimulated greater negative countertransference and fewer positive countertransference reactions in a cohort of 11 therapists. Additional findings indicated that clients who dropped out of treatment had countertransference reactions that from the start of treatment were significantly different than those who completed treatment. After only 2 weeks of treatment, negative countertransference reactions were evident, suggesting that at the start of treatment the therapist already was feeling overwhelmed and inadequate. Furthermore, there was a strong correlation between positive countertransference reactions and improvement in clients' Global Assessment of Functioning scores. Conversely, negative countertransference reactions were correlated with less improvement.

Countertransference measures have been developed to empirically rate countertransference responses in substance abusers (Najavits et al., 1995) as well as for personality disorders (Betan, Heim, Conklin, & Westen, 2005). The Countertransference Questionnaire is an instrument developed by Betan et al. (2005) with eight empirically derived factors, which are independent of clinicians' theoretical orientation. These include (a) overwhelmed/disorganized, (b) helpless/inadequate, (c) positive, (d) special/overinvolved, (e) sexualized, (f) disengaged, (g) parental/protective, and (h) criticized/mistreated. This 79-item questionnaire is a psychometrically valid instrument for both clinical and research use. This instrument was used to create prototypes of reactions commonly experienced by therapists in clinical practice. The descriptions of responses to clients with narcissistic personality disorder were reported. These included "feeling anger, resentment, and dread in working with narcissistic personality disorder clients; feeling devalued and criticized by the client; finding themselves distracted, avoidant, and wishing to terminate treatment" (Betan et al., 2005, p. 894). One important conclusion the researchers reported is as follows:

> Although every clinician and every therapeutic dyad is distinct, the significant correlations between the countertransference factors and personality disorder symptoms suggest that countertransference responses occur in coherent and predictable patterns. To put it another way, patients not only elicit idiosyncratic responses from particular clinicians (based on the clinician's history and the interaction of the patient's and clinician's dynamics) but also elicit what we might call average expectable countertransference responses, which likely resemble responses by other significant people in the patient's life. The associations between countertransference patterns and personality characteristics support the broad view of countertransference reactions as useful in the diagnostic understanding of the patient's dynamics, particularly those involving repetitive interpersonal patterns. To the extent that patients shoring diagnostic features on axis II have similar ways of thinking, feeling, and behaving interpersonally, one would expect them to evoke similar reactions from others, including therapists, and this appears to be the case. (Betan et al., 2005, p. 895)

In support of using a unified framework, the researchers also concluded that the unique countertransference responses are not colored by the therapist's theoretical orientation. Coherent patterns emerge independent of the theoretical lens that the therapist uses and even if he or she is not trained to observe these phenomena.

TECHNICAL ASPECTS OF TRANSFERENCE AND COUNTERTRANSFERENCE IN THE CLINICAL PROCESS WITH NARCISSISTIC SPECTRUM DISORDERS

In the next sections, I review some of the technical considerations when treating clients with narcissistic spectrum personality dysfunction. It should be evident that embarking on a course of treatment requires specialized skills and should not be undertaken without the appropriate training and supervision (Magnavita, 2004).

Containing and Expressing Negative States

In the treatment of narcissistic disorders, whether in individual, couple, family, or larger system settings, it is inevitable that the psychotherapist will be emotionally activated, and this awareness can be used to assist the treatment process. Personality-disordered clients stimulate greater affective response in the psychotherapist because of the difficulty they have with their affective experience and emotional regulation as well as the disturbances in their interpersonal relationships. This results in a greater tendency to project these nonmetabolized affective complexes on those around them. Clients with narcissistic disorders will stimulate a spectrum of emotional responses in the psychotherapist. Clients with narcissism may enter treatment in a collapsed state after experiencing what seems like a massive assault on their self-esteem. This might be due to the loss of a job, public scandal, or divorce.

In these situations, the sources that previously fed the narcissistic system can trigger a clinical depression when withdrawn. At the beginning of treatment, this intensely painful affect will stimulate compassion and nurturing in the psychotherapist. When clients enter treatment as the result of pressure from others, the client's mode of interacting may stimulate negative feelings in the psychotherapist. High-achieving narcissistic individuals may act in a demeaning way to a psychotherapist who they perceive to have less social status, achievement, intelligence, and so forth. It is always beneficial when negative emotions are activated to bear in mind that the client is using strategies he or she learned early in life, which have lost their adaptive value. Being able to tolerate the affects generated in the treatment is essential for helping the client metabolize these feelings. Reacting inappropriately engenders further distress in the client.

Therapeutic Management When Working With Personality Dysfunction

One of the greatest developmental tasks of the psychotherapist treating clients with personality disorders is that of emotional tolerance. This tolerance necessitates an ability to experience one's own affective states as well those of the clients in treatment. The experience of the range of emotion if blocked may unduly strain the therapist. It is much better to acknowledge to oneself and choose when and if the emotional activation should be shared. Psychotherapists need to have a comprehensive approach to handle working with clients who are often in high states of distress. The psychotherapist should have appropriate self-care skills so that any toxic effects that may occur from vicarious traumatization can be managed. The psychotherapist benefits from working in a team and being able to share his or her reactions with others.

Making Therapeutic Use of Countertransference Awareness

Awareness of states experienced, which is in resonance with the client, represents a valuable part of the treatment process. How a therapist's awareness is used is a central technical concern of the treatment process. The first step is to accept that all therapists resonate with the client's affective communication. Although one can ignore these affective reactions, they can also be used to deepen the understanding of the client's phenomenology and unique emotional experience. Affective communication will occur at both a subliminal level of and conscious level of awareness through microfacial expressions, tone of communication, prosody of speech, and possible state resonance between the limbic systems of client and therapist. The basic stance, in a word, is mindfulness. This necessitates openness to experience and willingness to experience "not knowing," vulnerability, and states of induced dysphoria.

Self-Disclosure at Different Phases of the Treatment Process

Self-disclosure, when used judiciously and appropriately, can be a powerful technique at any stage of treatment. Self-disclosure can be used to normalize the client's self-perception. The key is not to use the therapeutic process for the therapist's own therapy, and if the therapist finds him- or herself talking too much about him- or herself, it might be time for that individual to seek out his or her own therapist. Sharing feelings when appropriate can also be a powerful way of modeling emotional expression and creating a bond. As previously discussed, in a unified psychotherapeutic approach, affect is an attractor state. Too little affect and the treatment process is deadened, and too much can flood the process. Premature termination or regression may result if the affect is too high to be managed and held by the therapist–client dyad.

A thorough discussion of the factors that lead therapists to express or restrain their expression of their internal experience is far beyond the scope of this chapter. A fundamental principle is that the self-disclosure of sharing of countertransference information should be done when it is in the service of the client's growth as opposed to fulfilling the needs of the therapist. As with any therapeutic strategy or technique, what may benefit one client may harm another, so the best thing a therapist can do is have a solid understanding of the client's personality system and the way in which it operates. The other important point is that it is best to ask permission before sharing one's countertransference reaction. The phrasing can be individualized but saying, "I am not sure if you are interested or if it would be helpful to share my reaction with you, but if you think it might, I will share this with you." This communicates collaboration and choice, which is an important part of creating a partnership in treatment, something that most people with personality dysfunction have not had a sufficient experience with.

Phase of Treatment and Management of Negative Affective States

The therapist will generally have more difficulty when negative states are regularly induced as a result of the treatment process and the unique configuration of each client as it interacts with the psychotherapist's personality system. Various clients will place greater demands on the therapist at different stages of treatment. For the clients who fall more on the severe spectrum of narcissistic dysfunction, the initial stage of treatment may be when more negative affect is generated because the client's anxiety is high and more primitive defenses may be operating as a result of the level of disorganization. With other clients, the challenge may come later in treatment when progress seems to be at a standstill and the client questions the therapist's effectiveness. During this phase, states of boredom, irritation, and impotence can cause the psychotherapist to question his or her effectiveness. This might indicate that the focus has been lost, and inquiry may result in a discussion of taking a break or termination.

Managing Anger Toward the Client in the Early Phases of Treatment

Anger is often induced in the psychotherapist and is a naturally occurring phenomenon. The experience of strong affective states, including anger, does not necessarily indicate the need to transfer to another psychotherapist. The first step is being open and aware of one's affective states and responses. Once anger toward the client is recognized, how it is handled is critical.

Anger may be an appropriate response when someone is intruding on one's boundaries or making unrealistic demands. In this case, the anger serves to alert the therapist to what may be a demand situation that is quite high. In this case, it is often necessary to seek colleagues to debrief and discuss the therapist's reactions so his or her feelings can be appropriately metabolized. In other cases, the experience of anger in the therapist might be the result of projected affect, which the client cannot bear and which is being stirred in the therapist.

For example, a client who reports a history of abuse or neglect or current mistreatment may elicit anger in the therapist. This may be therapeutic to share with the client. With some clients, allowing oneself to express the anger may be highly therapeutic and model appropriate expression of affect. In other cases, this may be counterproductive, and instead, being able to appropriately hold the anger allows the client to reclaim his or her dissociated affect. Many clients with narcissistic disorders have a history of parental neglect, which sometimes is quite dramatic. In these instances, when anger toward major attachment figures is aroused, it is sometimes appropriate to show this personal reaction in a spontaneous manner, which can model appropriate expression of affect and create more self-compassion. In other cases, exploring the nature of the therapeutic disruption is the best course.

Using Negative Emotional States to Enhance Compassion Toward the Client

Therapists working with narcissistic spectrum clients will enhance their compassion when the client is in touch with his or her painful affect related to the relational trauma or other trauma experienced. The more quickly the therapist can help the client contact affect, the better the chance the therapist's compassionate response will be activated. When an individual is using narcissistic defenses, it may be hard to empathize with his or her suffering. The suffering is not a felt experience but rather contains defenses, which are often seen as antagonistic to others.

Role of Training in Therapists' Self-Awareness

Training therapists to trust their response system is critical to being effective. Although self-awareness cannot be taught, a deliberative process can be modeled, which encourages contemplation, examination of one's responses, and the creation of a safe relationship to explore uncritically the range of human responses that are encountered in the consultation room. Positive emotional responses may also be disturbing to the psychotherapist.

These include love, protectiveness, and sexual arousal. The most important part of this countertransference, of course, is that these should never be acted on in any inappropriate or boundary-violating manner but should be used for deepening understanding of the client's reenactment and the natural forces in the healing process.

Acknowledging the Role of Negative Affect in Supervision as a Source of Treatment Data Versus the Need for a Trainee to Seek His or Her Own Therapy

It is critical that therapists in training understand that negative affective experiences are part of the therapeutic process. Negative affective states in the therapist should be delineated from a negative therapeutic alliance. If a therapist finds that he or she is reacting to the client in a way that is causing discomfort in the client, this should be a sign that there may be issues that the therapist has not addressed in his or her life that would benefit from some therapeutic attention.

CASE ILLUSTRATION USING A UNIFIED FRAMEWORK

Countertransference Awareness and Management in the First Session

Incorporating a unified framework affords the psychotherapist the opportunity to shift perspectives and understand dynamic forces as they operate in the intrapsychic, dyadic, triadic, and larger sociocultural domain systems. In this case, the client was a prominent physician who came to treatment after pressure from his wife that she was going to initiate a divorce if he did not make some changes.

The initial session included the physician and his wife, who were in their late 40s. The client had spent most of his adult life pursuing a demanding career as a specialist for which he received many accolades from his peers and patients. He was a well-known figure in medicine for his contributions to the field. However, according to the wife's description, home was another matter. At home he was prone to fits of rage over minor interpersonal disruptions and her expression of reasonable expectations of a husband and father. After having an episode of rage, it was not uncommon for him to retreat to his office and isolate himself from his family for days. His wife would have to cajole him to resume his family relationships. His presentation seemed to best match the fragile narcissist previously described and depicted by his tendency to use his grandiosity to ward off painful feelings of "inadequacy, smallness, anxiety, and loneliness" (Russ et al., 2008, p. 1479). He felt "important and privileged, and when defenses are operating effectively" (p. 1479), he functioned well.

During the first session, his attitude toward his wife was demeaning and contemptuous. He saw the problems resting with her in that she did not realize how her behavior justified his anger. At the intrapsychic level, he seemed to have issues with emotional dysregulation evident by his rapid escalation and agitation. This engendered a sense of caution in the psychotherapist, which is often indicative that the client has a fragile ego structure whose anxiety must be modulated and down-regulated. This is achieved by the use of empathic understanding (Trujillo, 2002) and pacing the interview so that the client does not become flooded by too rapidly moving into conflicted areas (Magnavita, 1997).

The dyadic pattern could be mapped by witnessing the dynamic process as it unfolded between husband and wife. He was emotionally intimidating and bullying, and she was not able to set appropriate boundaries and clear limits. Her intrapsychic process indicated that she was traumatized, possibly dissociating, and going into a freeze response. As the session intensified, the wife said that she was at the end of her rope and that the final straw was that he had hit her, which he had never done before.

At the triadic level, there was a powerful pull to take sides, with each member of the couple looking toward the psychotherapist for validation of his or her position and placing the blame on the other. Experiencing a strong pull to triangulate is usually a countertransference indication of dyads that are poorly emotionally differentiated and of individuals who have a low level of self–other differentiation. She used the therapeutic context to find her voice and set a boundary. This disclosure resulted in an immediate rise in the husband's anger and his adamantly denying that any such thing had happened and asking where in the world could this be coming from and why she was doing this to him.

The level of rage and the faltering of his ego defenses generated fear in the therapist. This fear was a sign that things were escalating and getting out of control. This pointed to the need for a comprehensive assessment of his ego-adaptive capacity. Recognizing this fear as a sign that there was ego fragility, which can result in a loss of control, the therapist decided it was necessary to bring the level of anxiety in the session down. Anxiety regulation is an important aspect of any therapeutic endeavor, but it is essential when treating individuals with personality dysfunction, who may have a very low tolerance for emotional experience and quickly become flooded, at which time a loss of impulse control might result.

Clearly, in this session fear was being aroused. It was noticeable in the wife when her husband's behavior started to escalate. She began to demonstrate a fear reaction by freezing and not responding, which is a sign that this situation had been going on for a while. Her limbic response was telling her not to fight with him, which the therapist trusted to mean he might potentially resort to violence. As the therapist recognized his own fear, he realized that this man's narcissistic defensive structure was quite brittle. She was accusing him of something, which he could not believe he was capable of doing to her. Moving away from this emotionally laden topic was imperative to bring the anxiety down to a manageable level.

Countertransference in the Middle Phase of Treatment

After a few marital sessions with some continued episodes of emotional dysregulation on the husband's part, a recommendation was made to see them each individually for a session after which a recommendation for a phase of individual work with the husband along with a psychopharmacological consultation was accepted. This suggestion was met with protest on the client's part. He felt that this must mean that he was the one with the problems. The force of his belief that he was being treated unfairly induced a sense of guilt in the therapist and greater reflection on the treatment recommendations.

It was clear that the husband's level of emotional dysregulation must be lowered before couples therapy could be tolerated. However, the guilt and doubt induced in the therapist that he was being unfairly treated, which went against his special status, was tolerated and the therapist's position held. This "holding of the guilt" in the transference allowed the husband's mixed feelings to emerge and be expressed rather than reenacting transference dynamics that mimicked his early control battles with his father. Using the example of his "impotent rage" with his wife and in the transference provided in vivo experience to process and proved productive.

Standing firm with one's therapeutic belief can be difficult, but eventually doing so in this case allowed the husband the forum he needed to begin to examine the perspective of his wife and children and to see his behavior through their eyes. He began to see and own the fact that he was an emotional tyrant bullying those around him and that this led to feeling alienated instead of feeling closeness. He disclosed that his father viewed him as a "bad son" and treated him as if he was never good enough. The fact that it was recommended that he undergo psychotherapy reactivated this core belief, reactivating deep shame that he was never good enough for his father.

As an increasingly collaborative relationship was being formed, the level of compassion on the part of the therapist increased. The husband's willingness to experience his vulnerability and own his behavior showed courage and strength. Positive feelings of admiration for this man who had overcome great difficulties and entered a career in which he devoted himself to helping ill people became prominent. It was easier to truly admire him.

He began to bask in the glow of genuine acceptance, and appreciation for his positive qualities resulted. As his ability to regulate his emotion and self-function improved, his wife was brought back for more intensive couples work. Because she felt safer, she was able to identify issues of abuse from her childhood that allowed her to accept his behavior and promoted her entering into therapy for resolution of her trauma. A unified framework provides pattern recognition tools useful for dealing with complex cases.

CONCLUSION

The treatment of clients on the spectrum of narcissistic disorders is a complex therapeutic endeavor, which can be enhanced by an understanding of transference–countertransference phenomena as expressed in the personality system. Using personality systematics and unified framework, clinicians can understand how transference–countertransference represents dynamic patterns for four domains of the human ecological system. As part of dyadic, triadic, family, and cultural responses, experiences stimulated in various therapeutic contexts can be used for complex pattern recognition. When transference–countertransference is seen as a resonant state stimulated in relational contexts, this information if received and processed can be used to sharpen diagnostic formulations and enhance psychotherapeutic effectiveness.

REFERENCES

American Psychiatric Association. (2000). *Diagnostic and statistical manual of mental disorders* (4th ed., text revision). Washington, DC: Author.

Anderson, S. M., Reznik, I., & Glassman, N. S. (2005). The unconscious relational self. In R. R. Hassin, J. S. Uleman, & J. A. Baragh (Eds.), *The new unconscious* (pp. 421–481). New York, NY: Oxford University Press.

Betan, E., Heim, A. K., Conklin, C. Z., & Westen, D. (2005). Countertransference phenomena and personality pathology in clinical practice: An empirical investigation. *The American Journal of Psychiatry, 162,* 890–898. doi:10.1176/appi.ajp.162.5.890

Dingfelder, S. F. (2011, February). Reflecting on narcissism: Are young people more self-obsessed than ever before? *Monitor on Psychology, 42*(2), 65–68.

Donaldson-Pressman, S., & Pressman, R. M. (1994). *The narcissistic family: Diagnosis and treatment.* New York, NY: Lexington Books.

Ellis, H. (1898). Auto-eroticism: A psychological study. *Alienist and Neurologist, 19,* 260–299.

Fonagy, P., & Target, M. (2003). *Psychoanalytic perspectives on developmental psychopathology.* London, England: Routledge.

Freud, S. (1957). On narcissism. In J. Strachey (Ed.), *The standard edition of the complete psychological works of Sigmund Freud* (Vol. 14, pp. 69–102). London, England: Hogarth Press. (Original work published 1914)

Gelso, C. J., & Hayes, J. A. (2007). *Countertransference and the therapist's inner experience: Perils and possibilities.* Mahwah, NJ: Erlbaum.

Ham, J., & Tronick, E. (2009). Relational psychophysiology: Lessons from other-infant physiology research on dyadically expanded states of consciousness. *Psychotherapy Research, 19,* 619–632. doi:10.1080/10503300802609672

Hofsess, C. D., & Tracey, J. G. (2010). Countertransference a prototype: The development of a measure. *Journal of Counseling Psychology, 57,* 52–67. doi:10.1037/a0018111

Kernberg, O. F. (1984). *Severe personality disorders: Psychotherapeutic strategies.* New Haven, CT: Yale University Press.

Kernberg, O. F. (2005). Identity diffusion in severe personality disorders. In S. Strack (Ed.), *Handbook of personology and psychopathology* (pp. 39–49). Hoboken, NJ: Wiley.

Kohut, H. (1971). *The analysis of the self.* New York, NY: International Universities Press.

Kohut, H. (1977). *The restoration of the self.* New York, NY: International Universities Press.

Lachkar, J. (2004). *The narcissistic/borderline couple: New approaches to marital therapy* (2nd ed.). New York, NY: Brunner-Routledge.

Lasch, C. (1979). *The culture of narcissism: American life in an age of diminishing expectations.* New York, NY: Norton.

Magnavita, J. J. (1997). *Restructuring personality disorders: A short-term dynamic approach.* New York, NY: Guilford Press.

Magnavita, J. J. (2000). *Relational therapy for personality disorders.* Hoboken, NJ: Wiley.

Magnavita, J. J. (2003). Psychodynamic approaches to psychotherapy: A century of innovations. In F. W. Kaslow (Ed.-in-Chief) & J. J. Magnavita (Vol. Ed.), *Comprehensive handbook of psychotherapy: Psychodynamic/object relations* (Vol. 1, pp. 1–12) Hoboken, NJ: Wiley.

Magnavita, J. J. (2004). Toward a unified model of treatment of personality dysfunction. In J. J. Magnavita (Ed.), *Handbook of personality disorders: Theory and practice* (pp. 528–553). Hoboken, NJ: Wiley.

Magnavita, J. J. (2005a). *Personality-guided relational psychotherapy: A unified approach.* Washington, DC: American Psychological Association. doi:10.1037/10959-000

Magnavita, J. J. (2005b). Systems theory foundations of personality, psychopathology, and psychotherapy. In S. Strack (Ed.), *Handbook of personology and psychopathology* (pp. 140–163). Hoboken, NJ: Wiley.

Magnavita, J. J. (2006). In search of the unifying principles of psychotherapy: Conceptual, empirical, and clinical convergence. *American Psychologist, 61*, 882–892. doi:10.1037/0003-066X.61.8.882

Millon, T. (1999). *Personality-guided therapy.* Hoboken, NJ: Wiley.

Najavits, L. M., Griffin, M. L., Luborsky, L., Frank, A., Weiss, R. D., Liese, B. L., . . . Onken, L. S. (1995). Therapists' emotional reactions to substance abusers: A new questionnaire and initial findings. *Psychotherapy: Theory, Research, Practice, Training, 32*, 669–677. doi:10.1037/0033-3204.32.4.669

Ronningstam, E. F. (2005). *Identifying and understanding the narcissistic personality.* New York, NY: Oxford University Press.

Rossberg, J. I., Karterud, S., Pedersen, G., & Friis, S. (2007). An empirical study of countertransference reactions toward patients with personality disorders. *Comprehensive Psychiatry, 48*, 225–230. doi:10.1016/j.comppsych.2007.02.002

Russ, E., Shedler, J., Bradley, R., & Westen, D. (2008). Refining the construct of narcissistic personality disorder: Diagnostic criteria and subtypes. *The American Journal of Psychiatry, 165*, 1473–1481. doi:10.1176/appi.ajp.2008.07030376

Schwartz, J. M., & Begley, S. (2002). *The mind and the brain: Neuroplasticity and the power of mental force.* New York, NY: HarperCollins.

Shea, S. C. (1998). *Psychiatric interviewing: The art of understanding* (2nd ed.). Philadelphia, PA: Saunders.

Trujillo, M. (2002). Short-term dynamic psychotherapy of narcissistic disorders. In F. W. Kaslow (Ed.-in-Chief) & J. J. Magnavita (Vol. Ed.), *Comprehensive handbook of psychotherapy: Psychodynamic/object relations* (Vol. 1, pp. 345–364). Hoboken, NJ: Wiley.

Twenge, J. M., & Campbell, W. K. (2009). *The narcissism epidemic: Living in the age of entitlement.* New York, NY: Free Press.

Wachtel, P. L. (1997). *Psychoanalysis, behavior therapy, and the relational world.* Washington, DC: American Psychological Association. doi:10.1037/10383-000

11

NEGATIVE REACTIONS TO SUBSTANCE-USING CLIENTS: WHERE THE REACTIONS COME FROM, WHAT THEY ARE, AND WHAT TO DO ABOUT THEM

FREDERICK ROTGERS

Substance users are among the most stigmatized of persons suffering from behavioral disorders in our society. In addition to carrying the same stigma often attached to those with mental illnesses, substance users are much more likely to be viewed not only as "mad" but "bad." Substance use disorders are the only psychiatric disorders that we, as a society, have elected to address largely as a criminal justice problem rather than as a health care issue. In addition, substance use disorders are often viewed as an individual choice, and some clinical writers have emphasized this view in their work (Schaler, 1999). This view is, as we will see later, one still held by many people in our society, a view that has not been overcome by the strenuous efforts of organizations such as the National Council on Alcoholism and Drug Dependence to shift public thinking toward a view of substance use disorders in the medical model—that is, as a disease. The multifaceted and nearly universal stigma attached to persons with these disorders presents unique challenges to clinicians who both

DOI: 10.1037/13940-011
Transforming Negative Reactions to Clients: From Frustration to Compassion, A. W. Wolf, M. R. Goldfried, and J. C. Muran (Editors)

specialize in working with these individuals and to those who encounter them in general practice settings (Rasinski, Woll, & Cooke, 2005).

In this chapter, I address this stigma and its impact on clinician reactions to substance-using clients from several perspectives. First, I review some of the literature on the origins of the stigma attached to substance use in contemporary American society. The specifics of that stigma are somewhat different from how substance users and substance use disorders are viewed in other parts of the world. Second, I review some of the most common negative reactions to substance-using clients that I have experienced or that have been reported in the literature and anecdotally to me by colleagues and supervisees. Finally, I discuss some ways that clinicians can reduce their negative responses to these stigmatized individuals and become more effective therapists when working with them.

In this chapter, I avoid terms such as *addict, addiction, alcoholic,* and *substance abuse(r)*. As is seen in the next section of the chapter, the labels we apply to phenomena or people have a tremendous impact on how we view them and how we believe they should be dealt with therapeutically or otherwise (J. F. Kelly & Westerhoff, 2010). In addition, many of these and similar terms, although popular in colloquial usage, are so vague in their meanings as to be virtually useless in precise professional or scientific discourse. For example, there is an old joke among clinicians who work in college counseling settings that the college student's definition of an "alcoholic" is "anyone who drinks more than I do."

Another example of the confusion over the precise meanings of these terms comes from a central philosophy in American treatment for substance users: the twelve-step program derived from Alcoholics Anonymous (AA). In AA, the term *alcoholic* is left largely undefined in a specific sense. Rather, an alcoholic is someone who is "like us"—those who have encountered AA and have decided that their drinking experiences are similar enough to those of the people whose stories are in the "Big Book" (Alcoholics Anonymous World Services, 2001) to self-label as *alcoholic*. Although it is possible, upon careful reading, to derive specific characteristics that the author of the Big Book, Bill Wilson, includes in this definition, nowhere does Wilson actually propose a formal, dictionary or *Diagnostic and Statistical Manual of Mental Disorders* (DSM)–like definition. This vagueness has led, for example, to an overapplication of that label to persons whose drinking may be quite dissimilar to the drinking experiences detailed in the Big Book. The term *alcoholic* has become to those in AA akin to "pornography" as defined by U.S. Supreme Court Justice Potter Stewart, who famously quipped that he couldn't define it, but he knew it when he saw it. I believe scientific and professional discourse demands more of us with respect to defining our terms.

There is so much subjectivity, bias, and stigma associated with these terms that using them, in itself, serves to perpetuate that bias and stigma.

In place of these terms, I use the terms *substance user, substance misuse*, and *substance dependence*. I also refer to the individuals who are the consumers of the services of therapists as *persons with* [substance use issues or substance dependence]. It is my belief that because of the strength of the stigma that has developed with respect to these individuals, we need to remind ourselves regularly that the individuals sitting in front of us in the therapy office are people, not diagnoses. They are people who have experienced difficulties associated with their substance use in various degrees, but they are first and foremost human beings who deserve our respect as such. I firmly believe that one important act in addressing our own negative reactions to clients who use substances is to change our own language when discussing them.

A final note is in order about references and the scholarly/scientific basis for this chapter. Having worked with substance users for more than 3 decades, I have much clinical experience on which to draw. I have been fortunate enough to have had the full range of clinical experiences in the field, from doing clinical research, to running a therapeutic community and an outpatient treatment program, to working in correctional facilities where substance use is a major clinical issue, to training clinical psychologists in how to work with persons who have substance use issues. I draw on this experience extensively in this chapter.

However, as a therapist committed to the use of empirically supported treatments in the context of evidence-based practice (Norcross, Beutler, & Levant, 2005), I recognize the limitations of local and personal clinical experience, especially with respect to how generalizable that experience is to other therapists and settings. For that reason, I had hoped to provide a solid basis in research findings for my chapter. That was not possible. In searching the literature in preparation for writing, I was able to locate only two significant research studies related specifically to the negative reactions that therapists have to substance-using patients and the impact those reactions might have on treatment (J. F. Kelly & Westerhoff, 2010; Najavits et al., 1995). The findings of these studies are discussed later in this chapter. Unlike the literature on psychotherapy for persons with other mental or behavioral disorders, the literature on what psychodynamic therapists refer to as *countertransference* in therapy and therapists for persons with substance use disorders and other substance users is sparse.

There are many reasons for this omission from the larger literature, one of which is that in the early days of psychotherapy and psychotherapy research, persons with these disorders were considered to be essentially untreatable using psychological methods, and these individuals were largely abandoned by psychotherapists. Indeed, in the first, booklet-sized, edition of the *DSM* (American Psychiatric Association, 1952), alcohol- and drug-related diagnoses were a subset of antisocial personality disorder. Antisocial personality disorders were considered at that time—the late 1950s—to be intractable to psychotherapy. This view was one factor leading to the rise in prominence and influence of AA and to the development of the treatment system based on the principles of AA, a system assembled largely by recovered persons themselves, with little formal training in psychiatry, psychology, or psychotherapy (White, 1998).

These factors have led to a chapter that is far less research-based and far more personal experience–based than I would prefer. Nonetheless, I am hopeful that this chapter will serve as an impetus for all who read it to begin the process of reexamining the origins of our negative reactions to our substance-using clients and to take steps to reduce or eliminate those reactions. The people who are our clients deserve nothing less from us.

STIGMA AND SUBSTANCE USE

I'd like to begin by asking you to conduct an experiment in free association (thanks are due to Edith Springer, ACSW, who showed me the power of a similar exercise during a training on harm reduction many years ago). Get a sheet of paper and write in bold letters at the top, centered: ADDICT. Now, letting go of your defenses as much as you can (this exercise is probably best done in private, away from the potentially critical eyes of colleagues or loved ones who might be shocked by some of what you produce), write down every adjective or descriptor that comes to mind when you think about the term *addict* or a person to whom it might be applied. Spend about 10 minutes writing down whatever comes to mind. Once you have your list, count the number of words you have come up with that have a positive connotation for you. What percentage of the words that you thought of would you want to be applied to a close friend or relative? If you are like the audience of counselors working with substance users with whom I first saw Edith Springer conduct a similar exercise, you will likely find that most of the descriptors you came up with are not ones you would like to have applied to someone with whom you are close.

Now, think about the following terms we use to denote persons with substance-related issues: *junkie, acid freak, diseased, dope fiend, liar, manipulator, resistant, criminal, clean–dirty, blasted, burnout, razed, wasted, zombie.* What sorts of images do these words conjure? These words are a common part of our everyday vocabulary with respect to substance users, and we hear and see them regularly in media coverage of celebrities who are substance users. Perhaps more important, we have been exposed to these descriptors and images of substance users from our early days. Is it any wonder that even the most empathetic of us has immediate, automatic negative reactions when we meet a client to whom those terms might be applied? Add to this the fact that, in some settings (e.g., treatment programs serving low-income clients and neighborhoods, municipal jails) where we might be asked to provide services, the clients we meet who have substance use issues are often also suffering from poor health, poor personal hygiene, and poor grooming.

Other popular images of substance users abound. One has only to think of the image of the "Skid Row bum" who uses alcohol excessively or the image of the street "addict" panhandling or lying in a doorway intoxicated on heroin to activate the negative images evoked by the words. That substance use issues are extremely common in our society (by one estimate, for example, nearly 25% of the adult population have or have had significant issues or problems stemming from their use of alcohol at some time in their lives; Babor, 1994). These popular images are perpetuated by the media, which, in an effort to produce an account that will sell newspapers, magazines, or on-air advertising, fail to delve beyond the surface sensationalism in covering substance users.

Presumably, if you are reading this chapter, you are someone who has concern about how to best help people resolve substance-related issues in their lives. You may be a therapist who has been trained to be empathetic, understanding, and accepting of client problems and to view most mental health problems as involuntary products of either intrapsychic conflict or learned attitudes, cognitions, and behaviors. Yet as a product of our society, you have also most likely internalized many of the negative stereotypes that we attach to substance users, especially those who have become dependent on a substance or substances. It is this, perhaps unavoidable, internalization of societal stereotypes and stigma that frequently makes it difficult for even warm, empathetic therapists to work with substance users without experiencing negative reactions to the client or his or her behavior. In this section of the chapter, I provide an overview of what some of those stereotypes are and where they might come from.

The research on stigma and social stereotypes with respect to deviance of all sorts, and mental illness and substance use disorders, is huge, and I make no attempt to review it thoroughly here. Rather, I focus on two aspects of American culture (and, to a lesser degree, other Western cultures with a strong Judeo–Christian basis as well): our societal view of human nature and behavior, and how we make attributions about the causes of the behavior of others. These two perspectives overlap to some degree, but I treat them separately here.

How We View Human Nature and Behavior

Rasinski et al. (2005) noted that two strong sociopolitical perspectives with respect to substance use are operative in American society: Puritanism and libertarianism. Both can trace their origins to the beginning of what became the United States when small groups of persons who were essentially outcasts and exiles (in some cases criminals) from their home countries came to North America in search of a new life. The Puritan view is most associated with stigma and is focused on the idea that to use intoxicants is in some way immoral. This view leads directly to the secondary views that immoral people must be deterred from their immoral behavior, punished for it, and brought back to the right path in life, forcefully if necessary. This perspective has been at the bottom of efforts to control substance use in the United States (we are the only Western nation to have attempted prohibition of alcohol [Musto, 1999] and the only nation to attempt to use law enforcement as the primary tool in combatting use of other substances). Coupled with this cultural belief that substance use is immoral has been an underlying agenda to control ethnic minority groups whose presence stirred fear and concern among the majority White population (Musto, 1999). For example, Musto (1999) pointed to the origins of the decision to include opiates in the Harrison Narcotics Act of 1914 as being due largely to majority White concerns about the increasing presence of immigrants from China and other parts of Asia whose drug of choice was often opium. A similar concern, but with respect to the African American population, led to the designation of cocaine, then an ingredient in a drink popular with African Americans in the South—Coca-Cola—as a dangerous substance. Thus, our drug control laws have their origins not in scientific or medical data about the negative effects of drug use but in often racist attempts to control immigrant ethnic minorities. Were our drug control laws scientifically rational (i.e., based on what we know scientifically about the nature of the harms associated directly with use of particular substances), neither of the two major legal drugs (alcohol and tobacco) would be legal, and at least one (cannabis) of the currently illegal drugs would be legal to obtain and use. Our societal views of substances and substance users are thus intimately bound up with our views of people who are different from us in other ways besides the use of substances and in a strongly negative societal reaction to those different others.

The impact of the Puritan view on our personal perspectives on substance users is profound. If, as the Puritan view suggests, substance users are immoral, then one reasonable approach to assist users away from their immorality is to bring to bear the power of the criminal justice system as a means of control. Thus, beginning in the early 20th century with the 1914 Harrison Narcotics Act and, spurred on by the intemperate (the primary definition of *temperance* is "moderation"; White, 1998) temperance movements of the 19th century, lawmakers began attempting to control substance use through legislation—making both substance use and the possession of substances illegal, thereby adding the stigma of criminality to persons who used banned substances. Thus, as Rasinski et al. (2005) pointed out, substance users are dually stigmatized in our society as both mentally ill and criminal.

Attributions of Behavioral Causes

Attributions of the causes of our own behavior and that of others have been studied for decades (Gilbert, 1998). It has become almost a truism of attribution theory that when making attributions of the causes of our own behavior, we tend to blame circumstances or causes beyond our control, especially when we engage in behavior that is disapproved of by others or that turns out to be harmful to us ("the Devil made me do it!"). In contrast, we tend to focus on internal personality traits and dispositions when explaining similar behavior in other people. Thus, we tend to attribute much more control over one's behavior to others than to ourselves and to believe that "bad" behavior was the other person's voluntary choice, rather than the product of environmental contingencies or influences. In fact, our entire legal system is based on this attributional assumption of personal responsibility and control over one's behavior.

Attributional research suggests that this tendency to attribute behavior in others to an internal, stable personality trait or traits, or to explicit personal choice, is an automatic aspect of how humans perceive others (Gilbert, 1998). When we combine this with the Puritan perspective on substance use outlined earlier, we are left with a view of substance users that makes their substance use (and subsequent problems associated with that use, including dependence on their substance of choice) a personal, voluntary choice over which the individual has full control. A corollary of that view is that individuals who develop problems associated with substance use are also fully able to stop that use immediately and bring those problems to an end any time they choose to do so, and if they fail to do so, they are to be condemned as irresponsible at least, criminal at worst.

This view of substance users and the causes of their substance use is one that pervades American society. It is also one root of the stigma that attaches to problems associated with substance use and to the negative reactions many people (including therapists and medical professionals) have toward substance users. This is illustrated nicely in an article by O'Brien and McLellan (1996) in which they addressed the reluctance of physicians and other medical personnel to treat substance use disorders medically, despite the increasing availability of medications and empirically supported interventions. O'Brien and McLellan pointed out that medical personnel (particularly physicians) often view substance users through the lens of internal attribution I have just outlined. That is, substance users are viewed as intentionally resisting treatment, voluntarily relapsing to substance use following periods of abstinence, and having higher relapse rates and more difficulties maintaining the target substance use status of treatment (abstinence) than persons with other chronic medical conditions. In fact, compared with persons with other chronic medical conditions (e.g., diabetes, asthma, cardiovascular disease), substance users are slightly more responsive to treatment. Yet physicians still are reluctant to treat persons with substance use disorders. This reluctance can be traced, in my view, directly to internal attributions of the behavior of substance-using individuals and the related stigma that derives from the Puritan view of substance use.

There are, of course, other origins to the negative reactions many clinicians have to substance users in clinical practice. For many substance-using clients, change is not easy. Their progress looks more like a sawtooth line with an upward trend than a bullet fired toward a high target. They are also frequently reluctant to tell a therapist the whole story about their substance use, although research has clearly demonstrated that this is due to external factors (e.g., the potential for criminal justice or other sanctions if, for example, a return to substance use after a period of abstinence is reported) and to therapists' tending to be co-opted into becoming agents of others rather than the client (e.g., when therapists agree to collect bodily fluid specimens on behalf of criminal justice agencies or employers).

Substance use issues are also highly comorbid with other serious, and difficult to work with, mental health and personality issues. Since many therapists cringe when a new referral carries the diagnosis of borderline personality disorder, and given the high likelihood of substance use issues with these clients, such clients come to a new therapist with a dual likelihood of eliciting negative reactions just by virtue of the diagnostic labels assigned to them.

Another source of negative reactions to clients also bears discussion here: the tendency (global, I imagine) for therapists to have become therapists because we want to be helpful and to solve problems for our clients. This perspective often makes us prone to view our clients in ways that can evoke negative responses when clients do not change in ways we think they should or when they fail to use the powerful and effective techniques we teach them to bring about those changes. Therapists who are well trained in particular approaches tend to have great faith in the efficacy of those approaches for many clients. Yet it is clear from clinical experience that even empirically supported approaches do not work well for everyone. It is easy (and consistent with attribution theory) for therapists to locate the source of difficulties in therapy or lack of progress toward goals within the client. This view is endemic among traditional therapists who specialize in treating clients with substance use disorders ("He isn't getting better because he is 'in denial';" "She isn't working the program the way I suggested").

A final source of negative reactions to substance users, although perhaps the most rare, is personal experience with family members or close friends who experienced problems related to the use of alcohol or drugs at some time during their lives. Particularly if those problems occurred in the context of a conflictual relationship among members of the therapist's immediate family, these experiences of conflict, uncertainty, and often anxiety and anger may generalize to the therapist's clients in later years, evoking negative reactions based on the therapist's unique developmental experiences with substance users. Surprisingly, these reactions can often occur in therapists with this background who have specifically chosen to work with substance users as a way of attempting to alleviate or avoid the same suffering in others that they experienced themselves. Nonetheless, memories of the negative experiences of living in such a conflict-ridden family may be difficult to ignore and may even be evoked (like stereotypes and attributions) automatically outside the therapist's awareness.

Given that many of our negative reactions to clients have their origins in a combination of strongly held societal beliefs about substance users, our beliefs about our own efficacy in treating substance use issues, and our tendency to attribute "bad" (e.g., lack of therapeutic progress) outcomes to internal aspects of the client that occur automatically, it seems to me that a primary tool to combat negative reactions is to increase our own self-awareness of the content of common negative reactions therapists have, to be vigilant for those reactions in ourselves, and to develop specific strategies for challenging those thoughts as soon as they occur, lest they become barriers to working effectively with a substance-using client. In the next section, I examine some common negative reactions to substance-using clients.

Common Negative Reactions of Therapists to Substance-Using Clients

As noted earlier, the research on therapist countertransference or negative reactions to substance-using clients is quite sparse; I was able to locate only two studies. Najavits et al. (1995) studied the reactions of experienced therapists to substance-using clients, and J. F. Kelly and Westerhoff (2010) examined the impact of how a client was labeled on therapist views of the client. I briefly review each of these studies before becoming more clinical and anecdotal in describing other common negative reactions I have encountered, both in my own experience and in conversations with colleagues, students, and supervisees.

In their study of therapists' emotional reactions to substance-using clients, Najavits et al. (1995) administered a questionnaire (Rating of Emotional Attitudes Toward Clients by Therapists; REACT) to 52 therapists with an average of nearly 13 years of general clinical experience, nearly 8 of which, on average, were working with substance-using clients. Therapists were asked to focus on reactions to real clients with whom they were working as part of a larger study of the treatment of substance use issues. Data from the REACT factored into four factors:

1. therapist in conflict with self (accounting for 28.9% of the variance in responses),
2. therapist focused on own needs (10.7% of the variance),
3. positive connection to the client (7.2% of the variance), and
4. therapist conflict with the client (5% of the variance).

Factor 1 loaded positively on items related to personal doubts about the therapist's ability to help the client, frustration that more progress was not being made, and feeling stressed or worried about the client. Factor 1 items that loaded negatively were therapist feelings of optimism and effectiveness. Factor 2 consisted of items reflecting feelings of exhaustion, anger, boredom, or burnout when working with the client. Factor 3, which, interestingly, was only moderately correlated with ratings of therapeutic alliance, focused on feelings of liking, appreciation, and empathy and tolerance for the client. Finally, Factor 4 reflected feelings of being manipulated by the client, feeling cautious in the client's presence, power struggles, and feelings of helplessness with the client.

Findings overall suggested that these highly experienced therapists endorsed relatively few negative reactions to clients. Nonetheless, ratings of negative feelings, predominantly feelings of boredom, frustration, burnout, helplessness, and disappointment, were found and tended to increase over time. The authors concluded that the level of experience these therapists had may have buffered them against negative reactions, especially early in working with a particular client. These therapists approached each client optimistically, but that optimism sometimes diminished over time as it became apparent that rapid, extensive change was not occurring.

Of note was a differential finding with respect to whether the therapists identified as psychotherapists or as drug counselors, with psychotherapists reporting higher levels of negative reactions to clients than drug counselors. The authors were unable to explain this difference conclusively on the basis of their results but suggested that drug counselors may either have been less aware of negative reactions than psychotherapists (who are often specifically trained to attend to their own reactions to clients as a part of the therapeutic process) or that other factors contributed to this difference. The authors concluded that negative reactions to substance-using clients are common among therapists, with the degree and extent of those reactions tending to increase over time.

J. F. Kelly and Westerhoff (2010) surveyed 516 therapists who were randomly assigned to read and react to two brief client case scenarios. In one scenario, the client was labeled a "substance abuser" and said to suffer from "substance abuse," whereas in the other, the client was said to suffer from a "substance use disorder." Therapists were asked to complete a reaction questionnaire in which they rated the client and their feelings toward him on a number of items that clustered into three main factors: (a) perpetrator-punishment, (b) social threat, and (c) victim treatment. There were no significant differences found between the two scenarios on Factors 2 and 3. However, therapists who reacted to the substance abuser scenario were significantly more likely to believe that the client should be dealt with punitively and held more personally responsible for his or her condition and any behaviors associated with it. J. F. Kelly and Westerhoff suggested that clients who are labeled as substance abusers are much more likely to evoke beliefs in therapists that they have brought their problems on themselves and that they should be held accountable for them, often in a punitive, confrontational fashion.

Although both of these studies have limitations, they provide some initial insight into the kinds of negative reactions therapists may have to clients with substance use issues. In particular, these clients are more likely than others to be seen as frustrating, resistant, dishonest, and unwilling to change. They tend to evoke feelings of frustration and burnout, as well as worry and concern on the part of therapists about the adequacy of their own approach to the client. They are also, depending in part on the label ascribed, more likely to be seen as personally responsible for the predicaments they find themselves in and to be deserving of some sort of punishment or sanction for their behavior. It is of note that the latter attitudes and beliefs appear to reflect the Puritan view of substance use and users outlined earlier in this chapter. These results also suggest that decades of effort on the part of advocacy organizations such as the National Council on Alcoholism and Drug Dependence and federal research agencies such as the National Institute on Drug Abuse to reframe substance use issues as due to biological or other "disease" factors that are beyond the client's control and to cast substance use disorders as a "brain disease" (Leshner, 1997) have been largely unsuccessful in changing the societal and cultural attitudes that appear to produce the stigma from which negative therapist reactions derive; even among trained mental health professionals, such perspectives have not gained full acceptance.

One of the limitations of the research just described is that the researchers had little theoretical basis for designing the questions they asked. Thus, it is likely that these studies missed more finely nuanced negative reactions that may emerge from personal clinical experience or experience talking with colleagues, supervises, and students. In the next section,

I discuss a number of additional negative reactions that I have encountered in these settings.

In my experience, there are a number of common negative reactions that therapists have to substance-using clients. Many of these stem directly from the broad stigma noted earlier that attaches to substance users because many of the drugs such clients use are illegal, difficult to obtain, and often expensive. These factors, plus the tendency of popular media to focus on negative or illegal aspects of the behavior of some substance users, have led to an extremely common view of substance users as not to be trusted. For example, Rasinski et al. (2005) quoted a director of a methadone clinic in Georgia as saying that when he first took a position in a methadone clinic, he was admonished by an experienced staff member there to "never forget that the clients are all liars, cheats, and thieves" (note: opioid replacement therapies such as methadone maintenance have the strongest research evidence for their effectiveness of any treatments for opioid dependence; Institute of Medicine, 1990).

A second, corollary reaction to those based on a belief in the criminality of substance users (or at very least their putative tendency to be unreliable and untrustworthy) is fear. The reaction of fear to a client in a therapeutic situation is not limited to substance users, but with substance users, it is much more likely to occur because they are perceived in the ways just noted. Users of illegal substances often evoke fear as a result of a coalescence of beliefs (often incorrect) about the behavioral and pharmacological effects of those drugs (many people believe, for example, that opioids produce violent behavior, especially when the user is intoxicated, when in fact opioids do the opposite when the individual is intoxicated—they produce a soporific state in which the person may appear to be asleep). Thus, substance users are presumed to be more prone to angry or violent behaviors than nonusers, and it is believed (following attribution theory) that these tendencies are either ingrained in the user's personality or are a direct effect of intoxication on the drug.

A third negative reaction often seen among therapists is the result of a myth that has evolved about what is necessary for substance users to change their substance use. Components of this myth, which is directly linked to the 12-step philosophies of some self-help groups, hold that there are certain prerequisites clients must meet for change to occur. These include admitting that they have a "problem" with substances, accepting the label of *alcoholic* or *addict,* being completely honest with others at all times, completely abstaining from all psychoactive substances (sometimes even those prescribed for them as part of psychiatric treatment), acceptance of recovery as a lifelong process that requires eternal vigilance on the part of the client (despite the, at best, ambivalent stance of 12-step philosophies about the duration of recovery; the subtitle of the Big Book of Alcoholics Anonymous is "How Millions of People *Recovered* From Alcohol Problems," [emphasis added]), and being willing to admit powerlessness over all substance use.

Therapists (as well as members of the general public) who subscribe to these ideas are often subject to feelings of frustration or anger toward clients who fail to adhere to the behaviors prescribed by the myth as necessary to recovery (or who fail to adhere to treatment assignments and other behaviors the therapist believes necessary for the client to overcome substance-related issues). Ironically, there is no research evidence to support the necessity of any of these prerequisites for clients to change their substance use. In fact, research suggests the contrary—that most people recover from substance use issues without doing any of these things (Granfield & Cloud, 1999).

Fourth are negative reactions akin to those found by Najavits et al. (1995) that relate to feelings of frustration and burnout generated by working with these clients. These reactions often appear to stem from a basic perspective many therapists have toward their work: that they are in the business of being helpers and that helpers should do certain things with those they are attempting to help. Among the behaviors that helpers should do (I should note that the view that follows is not limited to professional helpers but also occurs in the lay public—think about how you interact with your teenage children) is to provide firm direction, advice, and expertise that can provide the client with solutions to the problems for which they are seeking help. As trained professionals, helpers should also know and transmit clearly to clients (often quickly, as well, in this age of managed care limitations on reimbursement for psychological treatments) specific methods and techniques for overcoming their difficulties with substances, and it is the client's responsibility to learn and implement these techniques, almost without question. In this view, the therapist is the "expert" on how to resolve substance use issues, and it is the client's job to listen, learn, and follow instructions in order to get better. Of course, this model is very much consistent with an old-fashioned, traditional model of medical care in which the physician asks questions, runs tests, provides a diagnosis and then a treatment prescription, all to a passive client on whom treatment is enacted but who is not an active participant in that treatment other than to follow the doctor's orders. Needless to say, when working with clients who have substance use issues, this model is often inadequate. Recent work on the stages of change (Prochaska, DiClemente, & Norcross, 1992) and motivational interviewing (Miller & Rollnick, 2002) suggests that this perspective may, in fact, be a significant contributor to many of the negative reactions clients have to therapists (which, in turn, may trigger negative therapist reactions to the client) and that one way to overcome those reactions is for the therapist to change his or her behaviors and expectations of what it means to be an effective therapist. In the next section, I discuss this perspective as one way for therapists to overcome negative reactions they experience with clients with substance use issues.

In this section, I have discussed the research on negative reactions and provided some clinical anecdotal observations about some of the more common negative reactions therapists have toward substance-using clients. In the next, I discuss some possible solutions that can at least serve to diminish these negative reactions and allow therapists to engage substance-using clients more effectively.

THERAPIST, KNOW (AND CHANGE) THYSELF

The central problem in reducing or eliminating negative reactions to substance-using clients is one that was brilliantly stated by that eminent philosopher Pogo Possum: "We have met the enemy, and he is us" (W. Kelly, 1987). Most therapists who have grown up in the society and culture of the United States have incorporated the societal attitudes and views of substance users, whether we consciously subscribe to them or not. Research on racial and ethnic stereotypes (Dovidio, Gaertner, Kawakami, & Hodson, 2002) and their activation suggests that even those of us who have consciously rejected those stereotypes must be vigilant lest their automatic activation from deep memory have an impact on our behavior toward members of groups to which we do not belong. Even behaviors that are based on those stereotypes can occur outside of our awareness. Behaviors that have been termed *micro-aggressions* (Sue et al., 2007) can occur in interactions between members of majority and minority groups without the majority group member being aware that they are committing these behaviors. Nonetheless, the impact on the receiver can be significant. I suggest that a similar phenomenon happens between therapists and their substance-using clients and that stereotypes and incorporated stigma both serve as bases for negative reactions by therapists toward these clients. If I am correct in making the analogy between substance users (who are frequently, at least in publicly funded treatment settings, disproportionately members of ethnic minority groups) and members of ethnic minority groups generally, then one solution to avoiding negative reactions is self-awareness on the part of therapists to the fact that they will more than likely experience these reactions and that they need to be alert to their occurrence to forestall them.

On the basis of this line of reasoning, my first suggestion for therapists is to *pay attention to yourself*—to thoughts, feelings, and visceral reactions to clients. Ellis (2003) suggested that therapists need to perform an exercise in cognitive therapy on themselves when negative experiences with clients arise. Ask oneself questions such as the following:

- What is the evidence that this view of the client is true?
- What alternative perspectives might one take on the client behavior that triggered this view?
- Is the client doing this intentionally, or is what I am seeing an automatic or ingrained response to the world that the client has no control over?
- Is my own behavior toward the client mirroring earlier client experiences (in psychoanalytic terms, creating a transference) that the client is then reacting to with me in ways similar to those in past, but different, situations?
- Is the client's behavior triggering reactions that are based in my own developmental history (psychoanalytically, counter-transference)?

A second way to reduce negative reactions is to follow two of Ellis's (2003) other recommendations:

1. Have confidence in your therapy system and its ability to communicate its effectiveness to your clients, but do not insist that they indubitably have to be useful for this particular client—and certainly not for all clients.
2. By all means, care about helping your clients, but do not demand that because you care that they absolutely must benefit from your caring.

Following these directions is not always easy, but recent developments in understanding how to understand the process of change and work with substance-using clients more effectively provide a useful cognitive guide for how to do so.

The transtheoretical model of change developed by Prochaska, DiClemente, and Norcross (1992), often called the *stages of change model*, provides a helpful framework for enabling therapists to combat unrealistic expectations both about a client's readiness and ability to change and about the likely effectiveness of the expertise the therapist brings to the therapy situation. As Prochaska and colleagues' model (and subsequent research on the model) makes clear, not every client, despite being in a change-focused setting such as psychotherapy, is fully ready to make changes. Rather, as DiClemente and Hughes (1990) demonstrated, the majority of clients in an alcohol treatment program were actually in the precontemplation, contemplation, or preparation stages of change, none of which involve actually changing the presenting problem behavior.

Armed with this knowledge, it becomes easier for a therapist to understand (and thus not take personally or react with frustration or anger to) a client's failure to change early on in therapy (recall Najavits et al.'s, 2005, finding that frustration with clients tended to appear only after several sessions, even when the therapist was very positive about client potential for change at the beginning of therapy). It is also clear, from both clinical experience and Prochaska's own research (Prochaska et al., 1992), that clients slip backward and forward among the stages of change, sometimes for reasons that are not readily apparent to the therapist. Thus, a client who appears ready to change at one session may not be so at a subsequent session. This leads to my second recommendation to therapists working with substance users: Assess and be alert to client readiness to change.

My final points focus on reorienting our view of what the therapy process should look like in practice. Earlier I pointed out that many therapists have a view of psychotherapy that is very much akin to the traditional view of the doctor–client relationship in medicine (although this is changing thanks to work such as that of Miller and Rollnick, discussed later). In this view the physician (therapist) is the expert who does treatment *to* the patient (client), whose role is to be cooperative and compliant with the physician (therapist's) recommendations. "The doctor knows best!"

In the past 30 years, an alternative view of the parameters of an effective therapeutic relationship with substance-using clients has been developed by William Miller and colleagues at the University of New Mexico. This view, encapsulated in the approach known as *motivational interviewing* (MI), suggests a dramatically altered perspective on what makes for an effective therapeutic relationship. Miller and Rollnick (2002) suggested that an effective therapeutic relationship has several characteristics that are different from the traditional model of doctor–client.

1. The relationship is collaborative, not expert to client or therapist driven. Both therapist and client are presumed to bring specific, essential, and critical expertise to the therapy sessions. The client is the world's foremost expert in his or her life, including strengths, weaknesses, what has and has not been helpful in the past, and so on. The therapist is an expert in what has helped other people change similar behaviors. The goal of the therapeutic endeavor is to meld these two forms of expertise together in the service of helping the client solve his or her problems.

2. The client is assumed to be autonomous and in control of every decision about his or her life. This assumption (which can, in fact, be demonstrated to be true—e.g., even coerced clients sometimes drop out of therapy despite what, to the therapist, seem to be significant negative consequences for doing so)

frees up the therapist in several ways. First, it relieves much of the burden of achieving a successful outcome to therapy and distributes much of that burden where it actually lies—to the client. All of the most effective approaches to working with substance use issues require that the client take an active role in implementing techniques and making changes agreed on with the therapist for therapy to be a success. Second, taking this perspective frees the therapist to focus on meeting the client where he or she is and helps to reduce excessive expectations about what a particular client might be able to achieve with respect to change.

Adopting this view also allows therapists to focus on strengths and assets that clients bring with them to the therapy encounter. It is often easy (because of the negative stereotypes we hold about substance users) to forget that being a substance user or substance dependent is a difficult life that may require significant resourcefulness on the client's part to sustain. If we think about what is required to sustain a heroin habit, for example, this becomes apparent. A heroin-dependent individual must obtain heroin daily or begin to go into sometimes painful withdrawal. He or she must awaken each morning, typically in early stages of withdrawal and thus not feeling well, arise, determine where and how to obtain his or her next dose (and how to pay for it), obtain clean syringes, and avoid being arrested in the process. Navigating this life requires skills that can also be put to use in helping that individual reduce or stop using heroin, but the therapist needs to recognize and elicit those skills to be helpful in that regard.

3. Be empathetic. Trying to understand the client's life and struggles from the client's perspective can help therapists reduce the stigmatizing views that often automatically color reactions to particular clients.

4. Avoid confrontational approaches. Miller and colleagues have clearly shown that the "resistance" and "denial" often reported in working with substance users are, in fact, elicited by the therapist by virtue of the style of interaction the therapist may adopt. One way to almost certainly elicit resistance is to engage in confrontation or argument with the client about his or her behavior. In fact, Miller and White (2008) reviewed the literature on confrontational approaches to substance use disorders and found not a single study supporting the use of confrontation over nonconfrontational approaches. If we adopt the view

of denial put forward by Miller (1985) as being a manifestation of psychological reactance in a confrontational relationship, denial and resistance either disappear altogether or are markedly decreased in therapy with substance users.

5. When resistance or denial do appear, roll with them, do not attempt to reduce them directly through reasoned argument or other means. Rather, accept that the client is ambivalent about change and focus on identifying and helping the client resolve that ambivalence.

By adopting these behavioral strategies, therapists can minimize the likelihood the client will demonstrate many of the negative in-session behaviors stereotypically attributed to substance users, thus reducing the likelihood of the therapist's negative reactions.

CASE EXAMPLE

I conclude this chapter with a brief case example of how these principles and suggestions can be put into place and the likely impact of doing so on therapist negative reactions. No case can capture all of the various scenarios that might lead to negative reactions on the part of the therapist (at least not a case that will allow me to meet the length requirements for this chapter). What I present does, however, illustrate how incorporating the suggestions I have made can be helpful to therapists in reducing negative reactions and establishing a better working relationship with clients.

Juan was a 25-year-old, married Latino man with two children currently serving an 18-month probation for misdemeanor possession of marijuana. He was referred for treatment by his probation officer because of repeatedly "dirty" (there's one of the stigmatizing words again) urines that were positive for cannabis. Juan's probation officer indicated in her referral call that Juan was one of her best clients. He held two jobs, paid his court-ordered fines, and reported to his probation officer exactly as scheduled, never missing an appointment. However, the urinalysis results were becoming a point of contention between them, until finally the probation officer confronted Juan and gave him an ultimatum: Stop smoking cannabis or be brought back before the court and possibly sent to jail. Juan protested that he only smoked a joint on weekends to relax and that he was not using daily. Unhappily, he agreed to come to our agency for an initial consultation and possible treatment.

The agency I was directing at the time was a training clinic for doctoral clinical psychologists and social work students who were interested in working with clients having substance use issues. The approach used at the agency was one consistent with the approach outlined earlier based on the stages of change model and motivational interviewing (MI). Nonetheless, students often came to us with the same popular views that I have described in this chapter—that "addicts" are liars, in denial, difficult, unmotivated, and manipulative. Much time was spent in supervision trying to prompt trainees to examine their own preconceptions and beliefs about substance users and to challenge those beliefs against the evidence before them. Trainees were also taught how to do MI and to approach clients with the cognitive set outlined earlier.

Juan appeared for his first session with Rebecca on time but clearly reluctant. Rebecca was a third-year doctoral student who had started working in the program only a few weeks previously. After having undergone our basic training in MI and the stages of change model, she was just now beginning to pick up clients. She herself came from a very conservative religious community that held the belief that substance users were immoral and deserved some form of punishment or retribution for their substance use. Rebecca's home community was one that had traditionally been assumed to have few substance use problems but which anecdotal information and some research was beginning to suggest had a significant but hidden group of community members who were having difficulties related to their substance use. Hence, Rebecca's particular interest in working with substance users—she hoped to bring this expertise and experience back to her community.

At the first session Juan provided the following account of his substance use in response to Rebecca's initial open question, "What brings you here today?" Juan indicated that his life was very stressful, what with working two jobs, trying to give his wife time off on weekends from child-care duties, having to report to his probation officer, and save money to buy a house (one of his dreams). He reported that he would smoke a joint after work on some days (not all) but stated that he mostly smoked on one or both weekend days. He asserted that he needed to relax and cannabis was the fastest, most effective means he had to do so. He reported feeling quite anxious about his probation officer's threat to take him back before the judge if he did not stop submitting urines that tested positive for cannabis. He also reported that he felt quite upset that his probation officer seemed to be telling him that he had to give up cannabis for life. Cannabis smoking was, for Juan, a chief means of coping with the stressors he was experiencing in his life, and besides, he said, "it's not hurting anyone!"

Throughout this account, Rebecca used the reflective listening that is central to MI, and rolled with Juan's resistance to stopping use of cannabis for the rest of his life, as he believed his probation officer had mandated. At the end of the session, she scheduled a subsequent appointment with Juan, and we met for supervision later that day.

In supervision, it became clear to me that Rebecca was quite concerned, and a bit offended, that Juan appeared to be lying to her about the frequency and extent of his cannabis use. She was also worried that Juan was high at times when he was the sole caretaker for his children (e.g., his wife would go out to visit relatives or friends leaving Juan to care for the kids alone). Finally, she indicated discomfort with the fact that Juan was clearly breaking the law, and taking some potentially dangerous risks to obtain cannabis. Yet he did not appear to be motivated to change his cannabis use and had argued strenuously against doing so. Nonetheless, Rebecca was optimistic that she could help Juan, and she reported that she liked him as a person, despite her concerns.

After hearing Rebecca's concerns, I asked her to do several things. First, I asked her if she could put herself in Juan's shoes and begin to think about what his life must be like and how difficult it might be for him to cope. Second, I asked her to think about the external treatment mandate and how much she needed to have Juan comply completely with what he believed he was being told he must do (e.g., stop using cannabis forever). Third, I asked her to reframe the situation with Juan and the probation officer in her own mind and see whether she could come up with a solution that would be acceptable to Juan and would also accomplish the goal of keeping him out of jail, a goal he said was very important to him. Rebecca agreed. She also was open about how uncomfortable Juan's substance use and criminal history made her feel toward him, despite finding him a likable man, and how she had the thought that he must somehow be compelled to stop smoking cannabis, both for his own good and the good of his family. I asked her to think about those reactions between now and our next supervision session, which was scheduled right before Juan's next session.

At our next supervision session, Rebecca laid out a plan for her next session with Juan that was based on the self-reflection she had done over the preceding several days. I suggested that she try her plan out and see what happened. She also reported that after considering some of the questions I put to her, she felt much more comfortable about working with Juan, and her nagging doubts and fears had been put in abeyance.

At our next supervision session, following her second session with Juan, Rebecca gave me an account of how her session with Juan went. We also listened to an audiotape (obtained with Juan's consent) of the session. Rebecca had opened the session by thanking Juan for keeping the appointment and then asking him what his main goals for treatment were. Juan said he had only one goal: to get his probation officer off his back about his cannabis use and thereby be able to complete his probation without returning to jail. Rebecca then asked a key question, "How long do you have to go on probation?" Juan indicated that he had a little over 12 months left. Rebecca then asked whether his probation officer would be taking urine specimens from him after his probation was over (and thus know whether he continued to smoke cannabis). "No," replied Juan, "once I'm done, she can't take any urines." Rebecca then asked, "Have you ever thought about quitting pot just for the next year?" "What do you mean?" asked Juan. "Well," said Rebecca, "if the main danger right now is that you will end up in jail because of a 'dirty' urine, but that danger will be over once you are off probation, have you thought about just quitting for now? When your probation is over, you can always decide to smoke again, if you want."

Rebecca discussed her idea with Juan further during the session, and he agreed to think about it between sessions. In her supervision session with me, Rebecca indicated how positively she felt about the session, despite the fact that Juan had still not adopted quitting smoking cannabis as a goal. I indicated that I thought she had come up with a very useful strategy with Juan and that we would see the results at his next session.

At the next session, Juan came in noticeably more relaxed than at either of his previous sessions. He began by telling Rebecca that he had not been completely honest with her about the frequency and extent of his cannabis use. He now reported that he was smoking three to four joints daily and was becoming concerned with the amount of money he was spending. He also reported that he had thought about Rebecca's suggestion of a 12-month hiatus from cannabis and thought that was the way to go. "But," he asked, "how am I going to relax without smoking?" "Well," Rebecca replied, in true MI fashion, "I have some relaxation exercises and other things I could show you that might help with that. Are you interested?" Juan agreed, and therapy began with both Juan and Rebecca feeling comfortable and a solid working alliance established. Juan was able to stop smoking cannabis and learn alternative stress-reduction methods. Although therapy terminated before the end of Juan's probation, his probation officer reported that he had completed his probation with flying colors. It is unknown whether Juan resumed use of cannabis after his probation ended, but it is clear that he (and his family) benefitted from reframing the goal of therapy with respect to cannabis use, at least for the short term.

In addition to demonstrating how self-assessment, personal reframing of client situations, attempting to put oneself in the client's shoes, and rolling with resistance led to a solid working relationship with Juan and a positive outcome to therapy, this case also illustrates the usefulness of supervision or other consultation in helping a therapist reduce or avoid negative reactions to a client. Despite coming into the therapy with Juan holding many of the negative stereotypes about substance users I have discussed, Rebecca was able to make use of supervision to restructure her own thinking and reactions to Juan in a way that helped produce a positive experience for both her and him.

CONCLUDING THOUGHTS

Substance users have long been considered among the most difficult of clients to work with, and they are certainly among those clients who are most likely to elicit strong negative reactions in therapists. I have discussed some of the roots of those reactions in this chapter, outlined what some of the most common are, and presented some ideas for how therapists might change their thinking and behavior with clients to minimize the likelihood of negative reactions strong enough to make it difficult to work with a particular client.

I want to conclude by urging everyone who reads this chapter to think about your own personal reactions to substance users (perhaps by reviewing and challenging your responses to the exercise I described earlier in the chapter) and to think about how to reduce or cope with them. There are two very pragmatic reasons for doing so. First, it is virtually certain that substance users are a part of your practice. The epidemiologic data on co-occurrence of substance use disorders and other mental disorders clearly show that between 25% and 60% of clients seeking mental health services have co-occurring substance use issues (Regier et al., 1990). You will encounter substance users in your practice.

Second, as health care reform moves forward, it is increasingly likely that psychotherapists will practice much more closely with other health care providers in a more integrated service delivery system. There are highly effective interventions that psychotherapists are uniquely skilled at delivering (e.g., brief interventions, cognitive behavioral treatments) that can serve to identify and help substance users avoid significant health and other consequences of substance use later on. As psychotherapists, we are uniquely prepared by our training to play a key role in this endeavor to minimize the medical harm associated with substance use and misuse. As caring helpers, it behooves us to know how to deliver these interventions and be able to do so in a way that engages those clients rather than pushing them away. Managing our own negative reactions to substance users is a critical aspect of that practice.

REFERENCES

Alcoholics Anonymous World Services. (2001). *The Big Book online*. Retrieved from http://www.aa.org/bigbookonline/en_copyrightinfo.cfm

American Psychiatric Association. (1952). *Diagnostic and statistical manual of mental disorders*. Washington, DC: Author.

Babor, T. F. (1994). Avoiding the horrid and beastly sin of drunkenness: Does dissuasion make a difference? *Journal of Consulting and Clinical Psychology, 62,* 1127–1140. doi:10.1037/0022-006X.62.6.1127

DiClemente, C. C., & Hughes, S. O. (1990). Stages of change profiles in outpatient alcoholism treatment. *Journal of Substance Abuse, 2,* 217–235. doi:10.1016/S0899-3289(05)80057-4

Dovidio, J. F., Gaertner, S. L., Kawakami, K., & Hodson, G. (2002). Why can't we just get along? Interpersonal biases and interracial distrust. *Cultural Diversity and Ethnic Minority Psychology, 8,* 88–102. doi:10.1037/1099-9809.8.2.88

Ellis, A. (2003). How to deal with your most difficult client—you. *Journal of Rational-Emotive & Cognitive-Behavior Therapy, 21,* 203–213. doi:10.1023/A:1025885911410

Gilbert, D. (1998). Ordinary personology. In D. T. Gilbert, S. T. Fiske, & G. Lindzey (Eds.), *The handbook of social psychology* (4th ed., pp. 89–150). Boston, MA: McGraw-Hill.

Granfield, R., & Cloud, W. (1999). *Coming clean: Overcoming addiction without treatment.* New York, NY: New York University Press.

Institute of Medicine. (1990). *Treating drug problems: Vol. 1. A study of evolution, effectiveness, and financing of public and private drug treatment systems.* Washington, DC: National Academies Press.

Kelly, J. F., & Westerhoff, C. M. (2010). Does it matter how we refer to individuals with substance-related disorders? A randomized study of two commonly used terms. *The International Journal of Drug Policy, 21,* 202–207. doi:10.1016/j.drugpo.2009.10.010

Kelly, W. (1987). *Pogo: We have met the enemy and he is us.* New York, NY: Simon & Schuster.

Leshner, A. I. (1997, October 3). Addiction is a brain disease, and it matters. *Science, 278,* 45–47. doi:10.1126/science.278.5335.45

Miller, W. R. (1985). Motivation for treatment: A review with special emphasis on alcoholism. *Psychological Bulletin, 98,* 84–107.

Miller, W. R., & Rollnick, S. (2002). *Motivational interviewing: Preparing people for change.* New York, NY: Guilford Press.

Miller, W. R., & White, W. (2008). Confrontation in addiction treatment. *The Counselor Magazine, 17.* Retrieved from http://www.counselormagazine.com/feature-articles-mainmenu-63/27-treatment-strategies-or-protocols/608-confrontation-in-addiction-treatment

Musto, D. F. (1999). *The American disease: Origins of narcotic control* (3rd ed.). New York, NY: Oxford University Press.

Najavits, L. M., Griffin, M. L., Frank, A., Liese, B. S., Nakayama, E., Daley, D., . . . Onken, L. S. (1995). Therapists' emotional reactions to substance abusers: A new questionnaire and initial findings. *Psychotherapy: Theory, Research, Practice, Training, 32,* 669–677. doi:10.1037/0033-3204.32.4.669

Norcross, J. C., Beutler, L. E., & Levant, R. F. (Eds.). (2005). *Evidence-based practices in mental health: Debate and dialogue on the fundamental questions*. Washington, DC: American Psychological Association. doi:10.1037/11265-000

O'Brien, C. P., & McLellan, A. T. (1996). Myths about the treatment of addiction. *Lancet, 347*, 237–240. doi:10.1016/S0140-6736(96)90409-2

Prochaska, J. O., DiClemente, C. C., & Norcross, J. C. (1992). In search of how people change: Applications to addictive behaviors. *American Psychologist, 47*, 1102–1114. doi:10.1037/0003-066X.47.9.1102

Rasinski, K. A., Woll, P., & Cooke, A. (2005). Stigma and substance use disorders. In P. W. Corrigan (Ed.), *On the stigma of mental illness: Practical strategies for research and social change* (pp. 219–236). Washington, DC: American Psychological Association. doi:10.1037/10887-010

Regier, D. A., Farmer, M. E., Rae, D. S., Locke, B. Z., Keith, S. J., Judd, L. L., & Goodwin, F. K. (1990). Comorbidity of mental disorders with alcohol and other drug abuse. *JAMA, 264*, 2511–2518. doi:10.1001/jama.1990.03450190043026

Schaler, J. A. (1999). *Addiction is a choice*. Chicago, IL: Open Court Publishing.

Sue, D. W., Capodilupo, C. M., Torino, G. C., Bucceri, J. M., Holder, A. M. B., Nadal, K. L., & Esquilin, M. (2007). Racial microaggressions in everyday life: Implications for clinical practice. *American Psychologist, 62*, 271–286. doi:10.1037/0003-066X.62.4.271

White, W. L. (1998). *Slaying the dragon: A history of addictions treatment and recovery in America*. Normal, IL: Chestnut Health Systems.

CONCLUSION AND CLINICAL GUIDELINES

ABRAHAM W. WOLF, MARVIN R. GOLDFRIED,
AND J. CHRISTOPHER MURAN

There are certain clients for whom it takes relatively little effort for us as therapists to feel great compassion. Their suffering is readily apparent, they are motivated to change, a working alliance is readily established, and therapeutic movement, even if slow, is apparent. Our primary task with such clients is to maintain a therapeutic relationship that allows the treatment to proceed. The challenge comes when we are faced with clients who frustrate and annoy us yet with whom we need to be compassionate.

The chapters in this volume were written by experienced clinician–scholars who have candidly described their negative reactions when working with difficult clients. Regardless of theoretical orientation, all therapists share a common ground in their struggles to remain compassionate toward individuals who are in pain and seeking help. Difficult clients get to us as therapists. In spite of a therapist's best efforts to adhere to professional standards and treatment guidelines, therapists inevitably experience fear, anger,

DOI: 10.1037/13940-013
Transforming Negative Reactions to Clients: From Frustration to Compassion, A. W. Wolf, M. R. Goldfried, and J. C. Muran (Editors)

frustration, and boredom while interacting with clients. How a therapist confronts these feelings and regains a posture of compassion frequently transforms the therapist as much as the therapy changes the client. Both novice and expert therapists experience shame and self-recrimination in response to their anger toward clients. Our aim in this book is to make a statement that experiencing these feelings is not a sign of failure but an inevitable part of working with individuals in pain who are seeking help and that therapists can become more therapeutic by meeting these challenges.

All therapists have negative reactions to some clients some of the time. It is a universal aspect of psychotherapy, and the contributors to this volume all advise therapists to monitor negative feelings and to remain aware of how such feelings directly and indirectly can have a corrosive effect on the therapeutic relationship. The contributors also show a sophisticated understanding of the relational context of technique and the technical aspects of relationship building and repair. All psychotherapy techniques occur in the context of the psychotherapy relationship, and there are as well specific techniques for building the psychotherapy relationship. As experienced clinicians, the chapter authors understand the need to remain vigilant to their emotional reactions to clients and how these reactions are perceived by their clients. Indeed, among all health care disciplines, psychotherapy may be unique in the degree to which the person of the therapist affects treatment outcome and the need to regain a compassionate stance when this is eclipsed by anger and frustration.

In this final chapter, we focus on three topics. First, we discuss how different theoretical orientations frame therapist personal responses to clients as signal versus noise. All of the chapter authors agree that the therapist's experience of negative emotions toward clients represents a dialectic of self-acceptance versus the need to transform those feelings, but they differ in regard to how to understand the meaning of these emotions. Second, we describe how experimental work in attribution theory, a branch of social cognition, provides an integrative evidence-based framework for understanding therapists' helping and aggressive responses to their clients. Third and finally, we summarize recommendations for monitoring and managing negative responses to clients.

NEGATIVE EXPERIENCES AS SIGNAL VERSUS NOISE

Early psychoanalytic writings, in particular those identified with standard Freudian theory and practice, admonished psychoanalysts to contain their personal reactions to clients as contaminants to the technical ideals of therapeutic neutrality. Traced to Ferenczi's (1932/1988) early contributions, influences from interpersonal and various object relation theories that emphasized the participation of the therapist changed how analysts viewed their personal responses as a unique source of information about the therapeutic process. Chapter 1, by Muran and Hungr; Chapter 8, by Clarkin and Yeomans; Chapter 9, by Levenson; and Chapter 10, by Magnavita, describe such an approach to treatment, whereby therapists remain attuned to their own negative reactions as signals and data about the client's interpersonal world and fluctuations in the psychotherapy relationship. While striving to remain empathic and nonjudgmental toward the client, therapists actively monitor their personal reactions, not as distractions from the therapeutic process but as integral to understanding the interpersonal dance between the client and others in their lives and, as such, as one way of gaining access to and understanding cyclical patterns of dysfunction in the client's life. Although therapists endeavor to contain their feelings of anger and frustration, it is essential to not dismiss these simply as noxious by-products of working with difficult clients or of their own compromised emotional state but to scrutinize these affective states as data with deeper meanings about how a client affects other individuals in his or her world. Clarkin and Yeoman's clients with borderline personality disorder, Magnavita's narcissistic clients, and Levenson's depressed clients actively create the interpersonal worlds that they passively experience as distressing. The therapist uses their experiences in the here-and-now of the therapy situation as a microcosm of the client's world with the goal of increasing the client's awareness of his or her active role in cyclical maladaptive patterns.

Therapists' use of their own reactions in this manner has significant challenges, the most important of which is to avoid blaming the client and thus making him or her feel objectified. Henry, Schacht, and Strupp (1990) demonstrated the danger of therapists unwittingly disclosing even subtle negative reactions to their clients. These challenges may account for the negative effects that have often been found regarding the use of transference interpretations (e.g., Piper, Azim, Joyce, & McCallum, 1991; Piper et al., 1999). Nevertheless, self-awareness and the judicious use of reactions to a client can enrich the therapist's understanding of the client and repair potential ruptures that may compromise the therapeutic alliance. Safran and Muran (2000) proposed the use of therapeutic metacomunication and affective self-disclosure, defining numerous principles to navigate the challenges of talking about and bringing immediate awareness to bear on the client–therapist interactions as the therapeutic relationship currently unfolds (see, e.g., Chapter 1, this volume). They and their colleagues have produced promising research regarding the effect of a treatment model grounded in metacommunication on clients with personality disorders and those who are treatment resistant (Muran, Safran, Samstag, & Winston, 2005; Safran, Muran, Samstag, & Winston, 2005).

Much like the early psychoanalytic attitudes, Chapter 2, by Levendusky and Rosmarin; Chapter 4, by Gottman and Gottman; Chapter 5, by Heatherington, Friedlander, and Escudero; and Chapter 7, by McMain and Wiebe, view therapists' frustration and anger as noise in the therapeutic relationship to be eliminated. Based on learning and systems theories, these therapeutic approaches emphasize behavior change and problem solving, and the chapter authors describe a therapist's frustration and anger as a function of the resistance of a difficult client. For these authors, the therapy relationship is primarily a means to an end; it is the medium through which the psychotherapy techniques function as agents of change. The therapist's frustration is yet another source of resistance that needs to be eliminated for the successful implementation of techniques and skill acquisition. A survey of more than 400 cognitive behavioral therapists who responded to questions about their experiences of not being able to be clinically successful in implementing empirically supported treatment for panic disorders (Goldfried, Wolf, Szkodny, & McAleavey, 2011) revealed that 28% were frustrated with their clients' progress, and 45% said their clients felt they were not validated. It is not essential that therapists scrutinize their anger to discover deeper meanings about their clients' relationships with significant figures in their lives. What is important is that therapists contain and overcome their own anger and frustration, if for no other reason than they must feel motivated and compassionate to deliver effective treatment.

The person-centered and experiential perspective described by Elliott in Chapter 3 also views therapist negative reactions as a source of noise in the psychotherapy relationship. He argues that Carl Rogers's core conditions of accurate empathy, unconditional positive regard, and genuineness/congruence were formulated to prevent negative reactions toward clients. The optimal strategy when a therapist experiences negative reactions is to contain and set aside his or her own feelings while remaining self-aware. A therapist's experience of persistent negative feelings toward a client is a marker of an alliance difficulty. Here, lack of congruence trumps empathy, unconditionality, and positive regard. Elliott proposes specific techniques, which he describes as a *relational dialogue task*, for disclosing and addressing these reactions.

ATTRIBUTION THEORY

Whether the chapter authors in this volume explain their anger and frustration as signal or noise, they agree that these negative emotions compromise a therapist's ability to be compassionate. Our clients get to us and try our patience: the critical and demanding help-rejecters, the ones who don't do homework and follow through with contracts, the relapsing substance abusers, those who are forever "trying." Also, of course, clients with border-line personality disorder who threaten and attempt suicide, living in—and inviting their therapists to live in—crisis mode. In their Chapter 4 discussion of couples counseling, Gottman and Gottman describe how unhappy couples tend to overestimate how the behavior of others is explained by dispositional factors while minimizing the role of situational factors. This is called the *fundamental attribution error*, and it is a central idea in attribution theory that can be applied to the way therapists similarly explain the actions of their clients, as Rotgers describes in Chapter 11, in regard to substance abusers, and Brown in Chapter 6, in regard to how clients who are members of racial/ ethnic minority groups are made the "Other." We propose that attribution theory provides an integrative evidence-based framework for understanding how therapists' attributions of dispositional factors lead to negative emotions.

In 1958, Fritz Heider published *The Psychology of Interpersonal Relations*, which became the impetus for the development of a new area of interest within psychology: social cognition. In this landmark contribution, Heider specifically dealt with the issue of how individuals interpret the behavior of others, which eventually evolved into what is now known as *attribution theory*, a particularly fruitful area within social cognition. In essence, attribution theory refers to the way that individuals interpret the causes or motives for the behavior of others—and self. For example, one may view the person who forgets to send someone a birthday card as being either selfish or absent-minded, with each different attribution resulting in different emotional reactions toward the person (e.g., dislike, forgiveness). Thus, the focus is not so much on *what* individuals do but rather someone's view of *why* they did it.

Attribution theory, as elaborated by Weiner (1986), has been used to explain interpersonal conflict, whereby an individual would interpret the motive of another person in a given way (e.g., "My partner did not go shop-ping because he is lazy") and then react emotionally in light of the attributed motive (e.g., anger). If the very same action was seen as being due to a dif-ferent cause (e.g., "My partner was not feeling well"), then a very different emotional reaction might ensue. In essence, the key to a negative emotional reaction toward the behavior of another can be a function of not so much the behavior that is being observed but of whether one perceives the actor as being capable of doing something differently.

The way that attributions—or, perhaps most significantly, misattributions— can determine frustration and anger in interpersonal situations has received con-siderable clinical and research attention. In providing a cognitive–behavioral interpretation of anger, Deffenbacher (1999) highlighted the key aspects of attribution of cause that is likely to result in anger. Included among these is the perception that the behavior of another person was unwarranted, unjustified, intentional, preventable, and blameworthy. In essence, the individual making the anger-related attribution of another person's behavior is that this other person "should not" have done what he or she did.

Leifer (1999) offered an understanding of anger from a Buddhist perspective, suggesting that the experience of frustration—which results is anger—is the result of a need not being met. This frustration is

> permeated by subtle but powerful feelings of helplessness of which the angry individual is often unaware or in denial. Feelings of helplessness are always associated with frustrated desire. Indeed, the feelings of helplessness may be defined as the perceived inability to satisfy one's desires. No desire—no feeling of helplessness. (p. 345)

In essence, individuals become frustrated or angry at another when they implicitly blame the other for interfering with the ability to have their needs met.

Research on aggressive behavior in children has used attribution theory as an explanatory construct and has found considerable empirical support for its utility. A meta-analysis of 41 studies in this area concluded that aggressive behavior in children was associated with hostile attribution of intent (Orobio de Castro, Veerman, Koops, Bosch, & Monshouwer, 2002). In an attempt to find a solution to reducing aggressive behavior in children, one analogue study offered some evidence that aggressive children can learn to reduce their interpretation of hostile intent in potentially provocative interpersonal situations (Hudley & Graham, 1993).

Clinicians who work with couples fully know that blame and misinterpretation of motive are often at the root of anger and miscommunication in close relationships (Alicke, 2000; Bradbury & Fincham, 1990; Thompson & Kelley, 1981). This clinical observation does, in fact, have considerable research backing. Indeed, a review of theory and research on attributions in marriage clearly revealed that distressed couples are more likely to attribute the motives of their partners as being irresponsible and blameworthy (Bradbury & Fincham, 1990). In problematic relationships, it is typical to interpret the behavior of one's partner as being due to the fact that he or she is "selfish." Moreover, the attribution of negative intent is often general in nature, so that when the partner acts nicely, it is seen as the exception to the rule.

A meta-analysis of research on help-giving behavior has similarly found attribution of motive to play a key role in determining whether people act in helpful ways (Rudolph, Roesch, Greitemeyer, & Weiner, 2004). In a wide variety of help-giving situations, Rudolph et al. (2004) found that "judgements of responsibility determine the emotional reactions of anger and sympathy, and that these emotional reactions, in turn, directly influence help giving and aggression" (p. 815). In such situations, when an individual interprets the problematic behavior of another as being uncontrollable, the resulting emotion and behavior are sympathy and help giving. On the other hand, when the motive or cause of the problematic behavior is attributed to something controllable (e.g., people are faulted for what they are doing or for what is happening to them), anger and the absence of helping follow.

The role that the inaccurate attribution of motive can play in problematic parenting was studied by Slep and O'Leary (1998), who found that parents' attribution of hostile intent on the part of their children was associated with their coercive and angry parenting. With this in mind, Sanders and colleagues in Australia (Sanders et al., 2004) hypothesized that the reduction of such attributions could help parents reduce the anger that interfered with their parenting behavior. They found that adding a reattribution component to an already-existing parent training program enhanced the effectiveness of the training program, helping parents reduce their attributions of bad intentions and blame in their relationships with their children.

Clinical observation and research findings have revealed that family members who are critical and overcontrolling (i.e., high expressed emotion) to a person in the family who has a psychiatric diagnosis (e.g., schizophrenia, obsessive-compulsive disorder, bipolar disorder) contribute to the client's relapse and deterioration (Chambless, 1998): "Specifically, when relatives hold the client responsible for negative behaviors, believing them to be volitional, rather than illness based, they are more likely to be critical or hostile" (p. 3). With this in mind, family interventions are typically added to the therapy and pharmacological treatment of such clinical problems, and the focus is on helping the family recognize and accept the fact that the identified client is not behaving in a deliberate and willful way.

MOVING FROM FRUSTRATION TO COMPASSION: CLINICAL GUIDELINES

The preceding chapters all offer recommendations on how to manage frustration, anger, and other negative emotions that we as therapists experience while conducting psychotherapy. The authors' comments, in addition to other literature on the management of such negative reactions, converge on three main points. First, we need to remain self-aware of our own moment-to-moment reactions toward our clients. Second, we need to regulate and contain the expression of the frequently powerful emotions we can experience when working with difficult clients. Third and finally, the transformation or anger and frustration into empathy and compassion requires that we reframe how we think about our clients. These tasks do not necessarily occur in a linear progression but are interdependent and function in a mutually influential fashion.

Self-Awareness

All the authors in this volume acknowledge the need for therapists to monitor their emotional responses to clients in treatment. Staying focused for extended periods of time is hard work, and therapist self-care is a prerequisite for practicing psychotherapists. Failure to attend to one's own person will compromise one's effectiveness and possibly lead to burnout. Whether we are monitoring our emotional responses to the therapeutic process as participant observers or implementing behavioral or problem-solving interventions, we need to be aware of how our responses to clients are colored by our emotions, how clients perceive these emotions, and how we attempt to manage those feelings. Clients scrutinize our negative reactions to them as closely as we observe their negative reactions—sometimes even more so. They sense when we like them and when we are frustrated with them. Indeed, many of our clients who have been treated badly in the past have developed ultrasensitive radar for how others respond to them. The challenge for us as participant observers is to simultaneously monitor our clients' actions and emotions, our own affective responses to the client, and how the client responds to us both as professional and person. A number of contributors (see, e.g., Chapter 1, this volume) have invoked mindfulness and the value of mindfulness training with regard to self-awareness and interpersonal sensitivity.

Most of us as therapists are aware of the strong frustration and anger we sometimes experience when working with difficult clients. More frequently, feelings of annoyance or boredom manifest themselves in more subtle ways, such as deviations from the customary boundaries—the frame—we use to manage our sessions. Distractions, not remembering what a client said, frequently looking at clock, and changes in session starting and stopping times are all are signals that we are not present. Even the most genuine attempt to make sense of our experience, to see how it even tangentially relates to the specific dynamics of a specific client, can be challenging. Our disclosure to clients of our emotional responses is discussed in several chapters in this volume. All agree that self-disclosure is "strong medicine" that can facilitate but also damage the therapeutic process. How we as therapists remain aware of our reactions and time their disclosure is part of the art of psychotherapy.

In the same way that our clients can experience intrapersonal and interpersonal problems when they resist awareness of feelings, so can we resist awareness of negative reactions to clients and with similar consequences. One source of resistance is the challenge that a psychotherapist's feelings of frustration and anger to his or her clients pose to professional and ethical ideals. The temptation is to blame the client for these feelings, or the objectify the client with diagnoses, that is, to fall prey to the fundamental attribution error of explaining actions as caused by disposition ("She's a borderline") instead of situational factors ("How I am contributing to her response?"). Work with families and couples is particularly challenging with the temptation to vilify one family member for creating problems and identify sympathetically with the others, as Heatherington, Friedlander, and Escudero describe in Chapter 5. As difficult as these hurdles are to experienced psychotherapists, they can be devastating to novices, who may deny their experience entirely or feel that they will never be able to practice psychotherapy. All therapists, novice and expert, have blind spots and are never beyond the need for supervision and consultation in order to increase self-awareness.

Affect Regulation

As therapists, we are exposed to the powerful affective states with which our clients struggle. Clients who live in crisis mode bring their world to our office. This is especially acute with clients who are self-destructive. Clients communicate what it is like to live with sudden and powerful affective storms, and our therapeutic openness and attempts to be empathic make us vulnerable to vicariously experiencing these states. As Levendusky and Rosamin describe in Chapter 2, even cognitive–behavioral therapists need to tolerate a client's fear during exposure sessions and to not interrupt these procedures to rescue the client from their distress. To be empathic and compassionate requires that we as therapists be open to the pain of others, bear witness to their traumas, and tolerate intense feelings of helplessness that accompany client's depressive episodes. In spite of our best efforts to contain our reactions, clients carefully attend to us as their therapists and how we react to their pain. One of the challenges of managing the therapeutic relationship is how successful we are at containing, tolerating, processing, and expressing our feelings. How we respond in a clinical situation when aroused is central to the creation and resolution of ruptures in the therapeutic alliance.

It is in response to these reactive emotional states that we as therapists are at risk for crossing and even violating ethical and professional boundaries. In Chapter 3, Elliot provides a thoughtful and detailed set of guidelines for disclosing negative therapist reactions to clients. McMain and Wiebe's Chapter 7 discussion of therapist groups is an excellent example of peer support when dealing with difficult and suicidal clients. The need for supervision is critical for therapists who experience difficulty in containing expressions of anxiety and other behaviors that threaten the therapeutic relationship. In their discussion on the management of countertransference, Gelso and Hayes (2007) recognized the need for affect regulation when they discussed the importance of anxiety management. Mindfulness training has also been shown to facilitate affect regulation, as well as empathy (e.g., Robins, Keng, Ekblad, Brantley, & Cozza, 2009). Experienced psychotherapists all have anecdotes about how their spontaneous expressions of anger and frustration were pivotal moments in treatment of certain cases. When reading these accounts, it is important to remember that they occurred in the context of long-term therapeutic relationships that could contain and process the therapist's outbursts. As a rule, it is best for therapists to err on the side of restraint.

Reframing

When we as therapists can remain aware of and tolerate our emotional reactions without automatically acting on those impulses and feelings, we are able to transform our experience of the client into more empathic and compassionate states and responses. In the same way that self-awareness is fundamental to affect regulation, affect regulation is facilitated by reframing emotional responses. As discussed earlier, attribution theory is one example of an approach for understanding the genesis of aggressive and helping responses that is grounded in the basic research findings on social cognition. The clinical application of attribution theory can be an invaluable way for us to reframe our understanding of a client's motivation, as Rotgers demonstrates in Chapter 11 in his discussion of stereotypes of substance abusers. A therapist transforms reactions from frustration to compassion by recognizing that a client's failure to comply with treatment is *not* because he or she is trying to give one a hard time or is ungrateful of our efforts but instead is emotionally distracted by another problem in his or her life.

In a qualitative study of 14 psychotherapists identified by peers as compassionate, Vivino, Thompson, Hill, and Ladany (2009) distinguished between empathy and compassion. *Empathy* is characterized as a way of understanding that facilitates an understanding of the client. For us as therapists to move from anger to empathy, we need to make a client's behavior make sense, for example, by understanding how the client is not a "bad" person but is doing the best he or she can in a particular situation. *Compassion* goes beyond empathy and involves a deeper engagement with the client. It is "a process or state of being that connects to the client's overall suffering or struggle and provides the rationale or the impetus to help the client find relief from his or her suffering" (Vivino et al., 2009, p. 167). Both empathy and compassion enjoin therapists to "get out of themselves," to challenge automatic tendencies to perceive a difficult client—as Brown describes in Chapter 6, the "Other." A compassionate response poses a deeper challenge to us as therapists of not only making a difficult client's behavior more understandable and less blameworthy but also stepping out of our usual modes of understanding to identify with and enter into our client's world, to understand what it is like to live in a world of cyclic dysfunction where self-destruction is the only response to despair. Sometimes it is even too much to attain a compassionate state. At these times, even the attempt to be more compassionate is itself an expression of compassion, indicating the therapist's self-awareness and attempt to regulate their behavior.

The contributors to this volume consistently cite the need to work from a specific theoretical framework and to understand client behavior in terms of that framework. This theoretical reframing allows us to make sense of our clients' and our own reactions in a way that enables us to resume the work of therapy. Even more basic than reframing is the need for starting treatment with basic clinical tasks, such as obtaining a good clinical history as a way of placing a difficult client's behavior in some context. As in the case of affect regulation, therapists are never beyond the need for individual or group supervision to help them theoretically formulate their cases and reframe their responses accordingly.

CONCLUSION

Therapists need to be compassionate toward themselves as much as they need to be compassionate toward their clients. In writing about clinical behavior therapy, Goldfried and Davison (1994) cautioned about blaming the client when therapy was not progressing as hoped for by the therapist:

> When progress in therapy for any given client does not proceed smoothly, we frequently accuse the client of either not being motivated enough or perhaps "not being ready for" behavior therapy. We would like to suggest, however, that the client is never wrong. If one truly accepts the assumption that behavior is lawful . . . then any difficulties occurring during the course of therapy should more appropriately be traced to the therapist's inadequate or incomplete evaluation of the case. (p. 17)

Goldfried and Davison went on to say that therapists are likely to encounter clinical situations in which, because of complicating and unfortunate historical, situational, and/or biological factors, it is important to accept the fact that client change may be limited. Accepting this limitation on the part of the therapist and client lets neither feel he or she has failed.

The importance of learning to have patience as therapists is wonderfully illustrated in the personal reflections offered by Lorna Benjamin (a psychodynamic therapist) and Larry Beutler (an experiential therapist), who independently reported that one of the most important lessons they learned about how to be a good therapist came from their early experiences in watching horse whisperers tame wild horses. Benjamin (2001) learned "to take things slowly and with great patience" (p. 29). She added: "I also learned about the impossibility of controlling another creature. The most you can do is persuade and negotiate your mutual interests as you move with the other. Only under the most desperate conditions would one move against another" (p. 29). Interestingly enough, Beutler (2001) similarly reported having learned the same lesson from observing a horse trainer: "Patience is the key—let things happen that happen. Let people find their own comfort. Allow them to learn through struggle. Don't rescue, support" (p. 215). It is also of particular interest that these observations were made by two clinicians who are also researchers, reflecting a creative blending of art and science.

REFERENCES

Alicke, M. D. (2000). Culpable control and psychology of blame. *Psychological Bulletin, 126,* 556–574. doi:10.1037/0033-2909.126.4.556

Benjamin, L. S. (2001). A developmental history of a believer in history. In M. R. Goldfried (Ed.), *How therapists change: Personal and professional reflections* (pp. 19–36). Washington, DC: American Psychological Association. doi:10.1037/10392-002

Beutler, L. E. (2001). From experiential to eclectic psychotherapist. In M. R. Goldfried (Ed.), *How therapists change: Personal and professional reflections* (pp. 203–219). Washington, DC: American Psychological Association. doi:10.1037/10392-012

Bradbury, T. N., & Fincham, F. D. (1990). Attributions in marriage: Review and critique. *Psychological Bulletin, 107,* 3–33. doi:10.1037/0033-2909.107.1.3

Chambless, D. L. (1998). Family overinvolvement and criticism: An introduction to expressed emotion. *In Session: Psychotherapy in Practice, 4,* 1–5. doi:10.1002/(SICI)1520-6572(199823)4:3<1::AID-SESS1>3.0.CO;2-M

Deffenbacher, J. L. (1999). Cognitive–behavioral conceptualization and treatment of anger. *Journal of Clinical Psychology in Session, 55,* 295–309. doi:10.1002/(SICI)1097-4679(19903)55:3<295::AID-JCLP3>3.0.CO;2-A

Ferenczi, S. (1988). *The clinical diary of Sandor Ferenczi* (M. B. N. Z. Jackson, Trans.). Cambridge, MA: Harvard University Press. (Original work published 1932)

Gelso, C. J., & Hayes, J. A. (2007). *Countertransference and the therapist's inner experience: Perils and possibilities.* Mahwah, NJ: Erlbaum.

Goldfried, M. R., & Davison, G. C. (1994). *Clinical behavior therapy* (expanded ed.). New York, NY: Wiley Interscience.

Goldfried, M. R., Wolf, A. W., Szkodny, L., & McAleavey, A. (2011, August). *Dissemination of findings from clinician to researcher: Clinical experiences in treating for panic disorder, generalized anxiety disorder, and social phobia.* Paper presented at the 119th Annual Convention of the American Psychological Association, Washington DC.

Heider, F. (1958). *The psychology of interpersonal relations*. New York, NY: Wiley. doi:10.1037/10628-000

Henry, W. P., Schacht, T. E., & Strupp, H. H. (1990). Patient and therapist introjects, interpersonal process and differential psychotherapy outcome. *Journal of Consulting and Clinical Psychology, 58*, 768–774. doi:10.1037/0022-006X.58.6.768

Hudley, C., & Graham, S. (1993). An attributional intervention to reduce peer-directed aggression among African-American boys. *Child Development, 64*, 124–138. doi:10.2307/1131441

Leifer, R. (1999). Buddhist conceptualization and treatment of anger. *Journal of Clinical Psychology, 55*, 339–351.

Muran, J. C., Safran, J. D., Samstag, L. W., & Winston, A. (2005). Evaluating an alliance-focused treatment for personality disorders. *Psychotherapy: Theory, Research, Practice, Training, 42*, 532–545. doi:10.1037/0033-3204.42.4.532

Orobio de Castro, B., Veerman, J. W., Koops, W., Bosch, J. D., & Monshouwer, H. J. (2002). Hostile attribution of intent and aggressive behavior: A meta-analysis. *Child Development, 73*, 916–934. doi:10.1111/1467-8624.00447

Piper, W. E., Azim, H. F. A., Joyce, A. S., & McCallum, M. (1991). Transference interpretations, therapeutic alliance, and outcome in short-term individual psychotherapy. *Archives of General Psychiatry, 48*, 946–953. doi:10.1001/archpsyc.1991.01810340078010

Piper, W. E., Ogrodniczuk, J. S., Joyce, A. S., McCallum, M., Rosie, J. S., O'Kelly, J. G., & Steinberg, P. I. (1999). Prediction of dropping out in time-limited, interpretive individual psychotherapy. *Psychotherapy: Theory, Research, Practice, Training, 36*, 114–122. doi:10.1037/h0087787

Robins, C. J., Keng, S.-L., Ekblad, A. G., Brantley, J., & Cozza, C. M. (2009, March). *The effects of mindfulness-based stress reduction on mindfulness and psychological functioning*. Poster presented at the Sensation to Emotion Conference, New York, NY.

Rudolph, U., Roesch, T. G., Greitemeyer, T., & Weiner, B. (2004). A meta-analytic review of help giving and aggression from an attributional perspective: Contributions to a general theory of motivation. *Cognition & Emotion, 18*, 815–848. doi:10.1080/02699930341000248

Safran, J. D., & Muran, J. C. (2000). *Negotiating the therapeutic alliance: A relational treatment guide*. New York, NY: Guilford Press.

Safran, J. D., Muran, J. C., Samstag, L. W., & Winston, A. (2005). Evaluating an alliance-focused intervention for potential treatment failures. *Psychotherapy: Theory, Research, Practice, Training, 42*, 512–531. doi:10.1037/0033-3204.42.4.512

Sanders, M. R., Pidgeon, A. M., Gravestock, F., Connors, M., Brown, S., & Young, R. (2004). Does parental attributional retraining and anger management enhance the effects of the Triple P—Positive Parenting Program with parents as risk of child maltreatment? *Behavior Therapy, 35,* 513–535. doi:10.1016/S0005-7894(04)80030-3

Slep, A. M. S., & O'Leary, S. G. (1998). The effects of maternal attribution on parenting: An experimental analysis. *Journal of Family Psychology, 12,* 234–243. doi:10.1037/0893-3200.12.2.234

Thompson, S. C., & Kelley, H. H. (1981). Judgments of responsibility for activities in close relationships. *Journal of Personality and Social Psychology, 41,* 469–477. doi:10.1037/0022-3514.41.3.469

Vivino, B. L., Thompson, B. J., Hill, C. E., & Ladany, N. (2009). Compassion in psychotherapy: The perspective of therapists nominated as compassionate. *Psychotherapy Research, 19,* 157–171. doi:10.1080/10503300802430681

Weiner, B. (1986). *An attributional theory of motivation and emotion.* New York, NY: Springer-Verlag.

INDEX

Countertransference, *continued*
  interactive, 198
  with narcissistic spectrum disorders,
      235–239
  and personality disorders, 233–235
  recognition of, 133–134
  with specific populations, syndromes,
      or symptoms, 203–204
  with substance-using clients,
      247–248, 253–255
  in time-limited dynamic psycho-
      therapy, 200
  tracking of, 229–233
  in training, 207–208
  in transference-focused psycho-
      therapy, 177–178
  and treatment course, 9–10
  in unified framework, 227–229
Countertransference Questionnaire,
    234
Couples therapy, 232. *See also* Gottman
    method couples therapy
Couples transference, 232
Covertly narcissistic family, 232–233
Covert withdrawal, 81
Coyne, J. C., 201, 202
CRBs (clinically relevant behaviors),
    55–56
Criminality, 256
Criminal justice system, 245, 250–251
Cultural competence, 139–157
  bias with, 145–149
  in case example, 150–156
  definition of, 140–141
  hate and self-hate with, 145–149
  and intersectionality of identities,
      143–145
  paradigms for, 141–143
  prejudice with, 145–149
  training for, 149–150
Cultural diversity, 124–125, 144–145
Culture
  and narcissism, 223, 224
  and substance use, 250–251
Cummings, E. M., 201–202
Cyclical maladaptive pattern (CMP)
  in case illustration, 212–213
  in formulation and intervention,
      199–201
  in training, 208

D'Andrea, M., 144
Daniels, J., 144
Davis, P. T., 201–202
Davison, G. C., 279
DBT. *See* Dialectical behavior therapy
Defense mechanisms
  in narcissistic clients, 230–231
  of therapist, 14
  in time-limited dynamic psycho-
      therapy, 197–198
Deffenbacher, J. L., 273–274
Demands, 231–232
Denial, 261–262
Dependence, substance, 247
Depp, Johnny, 100
Depression, 61–66, 194. *See also*
      Chronic depression
Desperately Seeking Susan (film), 223
Deutsch, C. J., 7
*Diagnostic and Statistical Manual of Men-
      tal Disorders (DSM)*, 224, 246
Dialectical behavior therapy (DBT),
      163–173
  for borderline personality disorder,
      161–162
  in case illustration, 171–173
  role of teams in, 166–167
  theoretical foundations for, 163–165
  therapist strategies in, 167–171
Dialogue, 79–81, 100
Diathesis–stress model, 48
DiClemente, C. C., 259
Difference, 148, 149
Difficult clients
  in couples therapy case examples,
      103–111
  in Gottman method couples therapy,
      101–103
  negative reactions to, 269–270
  therapeutic alliance with, 23–25
Dilemma, shared, 34
Dillard, J. P., 202
Direct depth approach, 29
Direct surface approach, 29
Direct systems, 125, 131–132
Disclosure markers, 76, 77
Disembodied techniques, 201
Disengagement, emotional, 94–96
Disowned bias, 146
Dissociation, 26

Distress
    client lack of, 72
    in cognitive behavior therapy, 53
    marital, 121
Disturbance, contact, 72
Diversity, 124–125, 144–145. *See also*
        Cultural competence
Domain levels, 229–233
Donaldson-Pressman, S., 232
Don Juan DeMarco (film), 100
Dovidio, J. F., 147
Dreams, 100
*DSM (Diagnostic and Statistical Manual
    of Mental Disorders)*, 224, 246
Dunaway, Faye, 100
Dyad, object relations, 178
Dyadic systems, 195
Dynamic focus, 199
Dysfunctional relationships
    characteristics of, 93–96
    in family systems, 232–233
    in Gottman method couples therapy,
        93–96
    patterns of interaction in, 197–198
Dysregulation, of emotion, 164

Ear, clinical, 40
Early phase of treatment
    alliance difficulties in, 79
    anger toward client in, 237–238
    initial session, 239–242
Effectiveness, 57–58
Efficacy, 57–58
EFT. *See* Emotion-focused therapy
Ekman, P., 206
Elliott, R., 79, 80
Ellis, A., 258–259
Ellis, H., 223
Emergent phenomenon, 229
Emery, G., 203
Emotion. *See also* Affect
    and compassion, 238
    dysregulation of, 164
    primary adaptive, 73
    reframing of, 278–279
    in relational schemas, 25
    secondary reactive, 73–74
    in time-limited dynamic psycho-
        therapy, 199
    turning away vs. turning toward, 98

Emotional disengagement, 94–96
Emotional security hypothesis, 201–202
Emotional tolerance, 236
Emotion-focused therapy (EFT)
    in case illustration, 84–87
    congruence dilemma in, 75–76
    therapeutic relationship in, 71
    training in, 83
Empathy
    absence of, 72
    for BPD clients, 169
    in couples therapy, 102
    definition of, 278
    in five-factor theory, 13
    in humanistic–experiential therapy,
        69
    with narcissism, 225
    and narcissistic personality, 230
    for substance-using clients, 261
    in TLDP training, 208–209
    and vicarious introspection, 120
Enactments, 135
Engagement, 118–120
Enthusiastic turning toward, 98
Entitlement, 233
Environmental factors, 48, 169
Escalation of negativity, 94
Ethnic minorities, 258
Etic paradigms, 142–143, 149
Etiological theory, 52–53, 164–165
Evidence-based approaches
    and actual experiences encountered,
        59
    in cognitive behavior therapy, 46
    and practice-based evidence, 59–60
    with substance-using clients, 247
Existential dilemmas, 27
Expectations
    for BPD clients, 169, 176
    for change, 252, 259–260
    of others' reactions, 200
Experience(s)
    group encounter, 82–83
    immediate details of, 34–35
    lack of, 120–122
    negative, 7
    new, 198
    and technique, 59–60
Experiential–affective approaches,
        196–197

Pope, K. S., 6–8, 146
Portman, Natalie, 223
Positive sentiment override, 95, 98–99
Positivity, 94
Power issues, 81
Practice-based evidence, 59–60
Prejudice, 145–149
Pressman, R. M., 232
Price, M. G., 95
Primary adaptive emotion, 73
Process coding, 40–41
Process factors, 53
Prochaska, J. O., 259, 260
Professionalism, 4
Proficiency, 59–60
Psychoanalytic perspective, 270–271
Psychodynamic approaches, 53
The Psychology of Interpersonal Relations
    (F. Heider), 273
Psychotherapy process, 60
Psychotic clients, 75
Puritanism, 249–251
Purpose, shared, 100–101

Racially "mixed" individuals, 145
Racism, 250
Radical behaviorism, 12
"Raisin experience," 206
Rasinski, K. A., 249–250, 256
Rating of Emotional Attitudes Toward
    Clients by Therapists (REACT),
    253–254
Rational dialogue task, 79–81
Reaction intensity, 9
Readiness
    for change, 259–260
    of therapist, 76, 77
Recognition, 27–28, 229–233
Referrals, mandated, 127–128
Reframing, 278–279
Regard, negative, 72
Regulation, of affect, 277–278
Relatedness, 36
Relational, attachment-based experi-
    ential perspective, depression in,
    201–209
Relational context
    in cognitive behavior therapy,
        46–47, 51–58

in person-centered therapy, 72–74
    training for recognition of, 38
Relational level, 134
Relational matrix, 28–30, 33
Relational perspective, 11
Relational schemas, 25–26
Relational techniques, 71
*Relational Therapy for Personality
    Disorders* (J. J. Magnavita), 232
Relational–triadic level, 229
Relationship dialogue, 82
Relationships. *See also* Therapeutic
    relationship
    research on, 91–92
    in Sound Relationship House theory,
        96–102
    in time-limited dynamic psycho-
        therapy, 197–198
    in transference-focused psycho-
        therapy, 180
Repair attempts, 95
Resentment, 93
Resistance
    in family therapy, 118–120
    of self-awareness, 276–277
    by substance-using clients, 261–262
Response, orienting, 164–165
Responsiveness, 36
The Restoration of the Self (H. Kohut),
    221
Restrictions, 129–130
Rice, L. N., 71
Robinson, E. A., 95
Rogers, C. R., 70, 72, 74, 272
Rollnick, S., 52, 260
Ronningstam, E. F., 223
Root, Maria, 145
Rossberg, J. I., 203–204, 233–234
Rudolph, U., 274–275
Rupert, P. A., 7
Rush, J. A., 203
Russ, E., 226

Safe environment, 206
Safran, J. D., 40, 80, 206, 271
Sanders, M. R., 275
Sanislow, C. A. III, 12–13
Schacht, T. E., 271
Schemas, 25–26, 131–132

Schwartz, J. M., 229
Schwartz, R. C., 203
Secondary reactive emotion, 73–74
Segrin, C. G., 202
Self(-ves)
    acts of self toward, 200
    fixation on, 222–223
    in master–slave dialectic, 27
    multiple, 25–26
    others' actions toward, 200
    overvaluation of, 225
Self-awareness
    in cognitive behavior therapy, 55–56
    and compassion, 276–277
    in dialectical behavior therapy, 165
    with family therapy, 134–135
    in-session focusing for, 78–79
    in person-centered and experiential
        psychotherapy, 72–79
    with substance-using clients,
        258–262
    in training, 32, 205–207, 238–239
Self-care, 12
Self-concept, 202
Self-consciousness, 81
Self-destructive clients, 277–278
Self-disclosure
    in dialectical behavior therapy,
        167–168, 170–171
    in humanistic–experiential therapy,
        11
    markers of, 76, 77
    metacommunication with, 271
    and negative reactions, 10–12
    of personal limits, 170
    and phase of therapy, 236–238
    unintended, 271
    withholding vs., 74–76
Self-esteem, 223, 225–226
Self-exploration, 39
Self-hate, 145–149
Self-insight, 13
Self-integration, 13
Self-knowledge, 179
Self–other balance, 225
Self-reflectiveness
    in dialectical behavior therapy, 167
    with family therapy, 132–134
    with narcissism, 225

Self-states, 25–26
Sensitivity training, 32, 33
Sentiment override, 95, 98–99
Shame, 148, 230
Shapiro, D. A., 79–80
Shared dilemma, 34
Shared fondness, 98
Shared meaning, 100–101
Shared purpose, 100–101
Shaw, B. F., 203
Shea, S. C., 222
Shedler, J., 226
Sherman, M. D., 7
Shuster, B., 202
Signals, 270–272
Skills
    behavioral indexes of, 202
    with conceptualization, 13
    with dialectical behavior therapy,
        165
    for therapeutic alliance, 32–38
Skinner, B. F., 12
Slep, A. M. S., 275
Social locations, 145
Social services, 127
Social skills, 202
Social support, 150
Sociocultural–familial level, 229, 233
Sociopolitical perspectives, 249–250
Sound Relationship House theory
    conceptualization of relationship in,
        101–103
    foundations of, 93
    for Gottman method couples therapy,
        96–101
Special treatment, 233
Splitting, 185
Springer, Edith, 248
Stages of change model, 259
Stark, M. J., 8
States of arousal, 9
Stereotypes
    about substance users, 248–249
    activation of, 258
    in cultural competence, 145–146
Stigmatization, 248–258
    and behavioral attributions, 251–253
    common negative reactions to,
        253–258

ABOUT THE EDITORS

Abraham W. Wolf, PhD, is a professor of psychology and psychiatry at the School of Medicine, Case Western Reserve University, and the former director of Psychotherapy Training at MetroHealth Medical Center. Dr. Wolf is a fellow and past president of Division 29 (Psychotherapy) of the American Psychological Association. He is the author of numerous articles on psychotherapy and health psychology. He is a consulting editor for *Psychotherapy*, *Professional Psychology*, *Psychotherapy Research*, and the *Journal of Sex & Marital Therapy*.

Marvin R. Goldfried, PhD, is a distinguished professor of psychology at Stony Brook University. He is the recipient of numerous awards from various psychological associations, a past president of the Society for Psychotherapy Research and the Society of Clinical Psychology, and the current president of Division 29 (Psychotherapy) of the American Psychological Association. He is the founder of the journal *In Session* and the author of numerous articles and books. Dr. Goldfried is a cofounder of the Society for the Exploration of Psychotherapy Integration, and the founder of AFFIRM: Psychologists Affirming Their Lesbian, Gay, Bisexual, and Transgender Family.

J. Christopher Muran, PhD, is the associate dean and a professor at the Derner Institute for Advanced Psychological Studies, Adelphi University, and the director of the Psychotherapy Research Program, Beth Israel Medical Center. Supported in part by the National Institute of Mental Health, his research has resulted in numerous publications, including such books as *The Therapeutic Alliance in Brief Psychotherapy*, *Negotiating the Therapeutic Alliance: A Relational Treatment Guide*, *Self-Relations in the Psychotherapy Process*, *Dialogues on Difference: Studies of Diversity in the Therapeutic Relationship*, *The Therapeutic Alliance: An Evidence-Based Guide to Practice*, and *Bringing Psychotherapy Research to Life: Understanding Change Through the Work of Leading Clinical Researchers*. He is a fellow of the American Psychological Association and the managing editor of *Psychotherapy Research*.